W9-CFJ-654

Windows Vista for Seniors

Studio Visual Steps

Windows Vista
for Seniors

For everyone who wants to learn to use the computer at a later age

www.visualsteps.com

This book has been written using the Visual Steps™ method.
Edited by Ria Beentjes, Chris Holingsworth, Marleen Vermeij and Alex Wit

© 2007 Visual Steps B.V.
Cover design by Studio Willemien Haagsma bNO

Third printing: October 2007
ISBN 978 90 5905 274 1

Resources used: Some of the computer terms and definitions seen here in this book have been taken from descriptions found online at the Windows Help and Support website.
(http://windowshelp.microsoft.com/Windows/en-US/default.mspx)
Additional technical resources include:
The Microsoft TechNet forums
(http://forums.microsoft.com/technet/default.aspx?forumgroupid=204&siteid=17),
The Windows Vista Community website (http://www.microsoft.com/windowsvista/community/default.mspx),
The Windows Vista Developer Center website (http://msdn2.microsoft.com/en-us/windowsvista/aa904962.aspx) and Tips&Tricks (http://www.windowsvistatnt.com/).

Do you have questions or suggestions?
E-mail: info@visualsteps.com

Would you like more information?
www.visualsteps.com

Website for this book:
www.visualsteps.com/vista
Here you can register your book.

Register your book
We will keep you aware of any important changes that are necessary to you as a user of the book. You can also take advantage of our periodic newsletter informing you of our product releases, company news, tips & tricks, special offers, free guides, etc.

Table of Contents

Foreword 13
Register Your Book 13
Visual Steps Newsletter 13
Introduction to Visual Steps™ 14
What You'll Need 15
How This Book Is Organized 17
The Screen Shots 17
How to Use This Book 18
Test Your Knowledge 19
For Teachers 19

1. Starting Windows Vista   21
    1.1 Desktop Computer or Laptop 22
    1.2 Turning on Your Desktop Computer or Laptop ... 23
    1.3 Starting *Windows Vista* 24
    1.4 Mouse or Touchpad 26
    1.5 How to Hold the Mouse 27
    1.6 Moving the Mouse 28
    1.7 What Can You Do with the Mouse? 31
    1.8 Pointing 32
    1.9 The Mouse Buttons 33
    1.10 Clicking 33
    1.11 The *Desktop* 40
    1.12 Pointing to an Object 41
    1.13 The *Start Menu* 42
    1.14 Opening the Program *Calculator* 44
    1.15 The Menu Bar 47
    1.16 Calculating by Clicking 49
    1.17 Minimizing a Window 50
    1.18 Starting Another Program 51
    1.19 Maximizing and Minimizing 52
    1.20 Making a Window Reappear on the *Desktop* 54
    1.21 Closing a Program 55
    1.22 Restoring a Maximized Window to Its Former Size 56
    1.23 Turning off Your Computer 57
    1.24 Shutting Down Your Computer 60
1.25 Exercises 62
1.26 Background Information 63
1.27 Tips 68

2. More Use of the Mouse in Windows Vista   **69**

2.1 Getting Ready   70
2.2 The Next Three Mouse Actions   70
2.3 Dragging   71
2.4 Dragging with a Scroll Bar   73
2.5 Using the Scroll Wheel of a Mouse   75
2.6 Enlarging and Reducing a Window   76
2.7 Back to the Beginning   78
2.8 Using *Windows Help and Support*   79
2.9 Double-Clicking   83
2.10 The Many Faces of a Window   86
2.11 Changing the View   87
2.12 Right-Clicking   90
2.13 Exercises   94
2.14 Background Information   96
2.15 Tips   99

3. Keyboard Skills   **109**

3.1 Opening *WordPad*   110
3.2 The Keyboard   111
3.3 Repeat Keys   112
3.4 A Typing Error?   113
3.5 Capital Letters   114
3.6 Words on the Next Line   115
3.7 Beginning a New Paragraph   115
3.8 Colon or @?   116
3.9 The Cursor Keys   117
3.10 The Beginning and End of the Text   118
3.11 Correcting Mistakes   120
3.12 Removing Empty Lines   121
3.13 Moving Quickly through Text   121
3.14 Starting a New Document   122
3.15 Accents and Other Special Punctuation   124
3.16 Typing Apostrophes   125
3.17 Closing *WordPad*   126
3.18 Exercises   127
3.19 Background Information   129
3.20 Tips   132

4. Writing a Letter   133

4.1 Starting a Letter 134
4.2 A Larger Font 134
4.3 Today's Date 135
4.4 Undoing 136
4.5 Typing a Letter 137
4.6 Saving a Document 138
4.7 Closing *WordPad* 140
4.8 Opening a Document 140
4.9 Printing the Letter 142
4.10 Save Changes? 146
4.11 Exercises 149
4.12 Background Information 150
4.13 Tips 155

5. Word Processing   157

5.1 The Cursor and the Mouse 158
5.2 Selecting a Word 159
5.3 Undoing a Selection 160
5.4 Deleting a Word 160
5.5 Dragging a Word 161
5.6 Typing Over a Word 163
5.7 Selecting a Paragraph 163
5.8 Dragging a Paragraph 164
5.9 Mini Word Processing 165
5.10 Splitting and Pasting Paragraphs 167
5.11 Copying, Cutting and Pasting 169
5.12 Exercises 174
5.13 Background Information 178
5.14 Tips 179

6. Folders and Files   183

6.1 Opening Your *Personal Folder* 184
6.2 Changing the Display of the Folder Window 185
6.3 Understanding the Different Parts of a Folder Window ... 187
6.4 The Folder *Documents* 188
6.5 File and Folder Icons 189
6.6 Making a New Folder 190
6.7 Saving in a Folder 191
6.8 Copying Files 195
6.9 Moving a File 199
6.10 Dragging and Dropping Files 201
6.11 Selecting Multiple Files 202
6.12 Changing the File Name 204

6.13 Deleting Files 206
6.14 The *Recycle Bin* 208
6.15 Copying to a USB Stick 210
6.16 Safely Removing a USB Stick 214
6.17 Exercises 216
6.18 Background Information 219
6.19 Tips 222

7. Text Layout   227
7.1 Text Layout 228
7.2 Text Layout in *WordPad* 229
7.3 Selecting Text 230
7.4 Underlining Words 230
7.5 Boldface 231
7.6 Italics 232
7.7 Colored Letters 232
7.8 Other Types of Layout Effects 233
7.9 Undoing Effects 234
7.10 The Font 235
7.11 The Font Size 238
7.12 Determining Layout in Advance 240
7.13 Exercises 241
7.14 Background Information 244
7.15 Tips 248

8. Surfing the Internet   249
8.1 Some Information First: The Modem 250
8.2 Is Your Modem Ready? 251
8.3 Starting *Internet Explorer* 251
8.4 Contacting Your Internet Service Provider .. 254
8.5 Typing an Address 255
8.6 Wrong Address 257
8.7 Refreshing a Page 259
8.8 Forward and Backward 260
8.9 Clicking to Browse 263
8.10 Using the Scroll Bars 265
8.11 Printing a Web Page 266
8.12 Saving a Web Address 267
8.13 The Home Button 269
8.14 Opening a Favorite 269
8.15 Disconnecting from the Internet 271

8.16 Exercises 273
8.17 Background Information 275
8.18 Tips 279

9. E-mail, Your Electronic Mailbox — 287

9.1 Opening *Windows Mail* 288
9.2 The E-mail Address 290
9.3 Sending an E-mail 291
9.4 The *Outbox* 293
9.5 Sending and Receiving 293
9.6 Reading a Message 296
9.7 Including an Attachment 298
9.8 Opening and Saving an Attachment 303
9.9 Saving an Attachment 305
9.10 Exercises 306
9.11 Background Information 308
9.12 Tips 312

10. How to Make Working with Your Computer More Pleasant — 317

10.1 The *Control Panel* 318
10.2 Customizing the Mouse 319
10.3 The Pointer Speed 320
10.4 The Mouse Pointer Visibility 323
10.5 The Size of the Mouse Pointer 324
10.6 A Black Mouse Pointer 325
10.7 The Double-Click Speed 326
10.8 Left-Handed Users 327
10.9 Has the Mouse Been Customized? 329
10.10 Tips for Using a Mouse 330
10.11 Customizing the Keyboard 332
10.12 Your Keystroke 333
10.13 Customizing the Display 335
10.14 Changing the Size of the Text and Icons 336
10.15 A Different Background 339
10.16 The Screen Saver 343
10.17 Tips for the Display 346
10.18 Customizing *Windows Sidebar* 347
10.19 Customizing the Sound 352
10.20 Music as a Test 354
10.21 How Do I Insert a CD in the CD or DVD Drive? ... 354
10.22 Sound Knobs on Your Computer 357
10.23 Customizing Sound Signals 359
10.24 Tips for the Sound 361

10.25 Adjusting the *Power Plan* 362
10.26 Test Your Knowledge 365
10.27 More about *Windows Vista* 369
10.28 Background Information 371

Appendices

A. Clicking, Dragging and Double-Clicking in Solitaire   375
B. How Do I Do That Again? 383
C. Changing Your Keyboard Settings 393
D. Index 395

Foreword

We wrote this book in order to introduce seniors to the computer. We will show you the basics of the operating system *Windows Vista*, step by step. Use this book right next to your computer as you work through each chapter at your own pace. You will be amazed how easy it is to learn this way. When you have finished this book, you will know how to start programs, how to write a letter, how to surf the Internet and how to send an e-mail. This book makes use of the Visual Steps™ method specifically developed for adult learners by Addo Stuur. You do not need any prior computer experience to use this book.

We hope you will enjoy reading this book!

The Studio Visual Steps authors

P.S.
When you have completed this book, you will know how to send an e-mail. Your comments and suggestions are most welcome.
Our e-mail address is: mail@visualsteps.com

Register Your Book

You can register your book. We will keep you aware of any important changes that are necessary to you as a user of the book. You can also take advantage of:
Our periodic newsletter informing you of our product releases, company news, tips & tricks, special offers, etc.
You can find information on how to register your book in
Chapter 8: *Surfing the Internet*.

Visual Steps Newsletter

The free Visual Steps Newsletter will inform you of our product releases, free tips & tricks, special offers, free guides, etc.
It is sent to you periodically by e-mail. Please rest assured that we will not use your e-mail address for any purpose other than sending you the information you have requested and we will not share this address with any third-party. Each newsletter contains a clickable link to unsubscribe from our newsletter.

Introduction to Visual Steps™

The Visual Steps manuals and handbooks offer the best instruction available for anyone new to computers. Nowhere else in the world will you find better support while getting to know the computer, the Internet, *Windows* and other computer programs.

Visual Steps manuals are special because of their:

- **Content**
  The adult learners needs, desires, know-how and skills have been taken into account.
- **Structure**
  Get started right away. No lengthy explanations. The chapters are organized in such a way that you can skip a chapter or redo a chapter without worry. Easy step by step instructions and practice exercises to reinforce what you have learned.
- **Illustrations**
  Every single step is accompanied by a screenshot. These illustrations will guide you in finding the right buttons or menus, and will quickly show you if you are still on the right track.
- **Format**
  A sizable format and pleasantly large letters enhance readability.

In short, I believe these manuals will be excellent guides.

Dr. H. van der Meij

Faculty of Applied Education, Department of Instruction Technology, University of Twente, the Netherlands

What You'll Need

In order to work through this book, you will need a number of things on your computer.

The primary requirement for working with this book is having the US version of

- *Windows Vista Home Premium*

or

- *Windows Vista Ultimate*

or

- *Windows Vista Home Basic*

on your computer.

You can check this yourself by turning on your computer and looking at the welcome screen.

If you have *Windows Vista* on your computer, you will then also already have the following things on your computer.

In *Windows Vista*, the group *Accessories* will have been installed with the following programs:

- *WordPad*
- *Paint*
- *Calculator*

You should also see the group *Games*, in which you will find the program:

- *Solitaire*

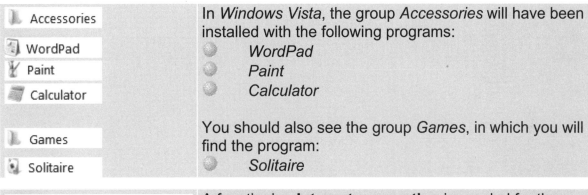

A functioning **Internet connection** is needed for the two chapters about the Internet.
For the settings for your Internet connection, please see the software and information supplied by your Internet Service Provider.
(Chapters 8 and 9)

In order to work with the Internet, you must have the following two programs installed on your computer:

- *Windows Internet Explorer 7*
- *Windows Mail*

These programs are included in *Windows Vista*.
(Chapters 8 and 9)

You also need:

A computer mouse. If you are working on a laptop with touchpad, you may want to purchase an external mouse in order to more easily follow the steps in this book.

The following things are useful. But it is not a problem if you do not have them. Simply skip over the relevant pages.

An empty USB memory stick for saving files. (Chapter 6)

A printer is recommended for some of the exercises. If you do not have a printer, do not worry. Simply skip thes e exercises. (Chapter 4)

A music CD. (Chapter 10)

How This Book Is Organized

This book is set up in such a way that you do not necessarily have to work through it from the beginning to the end.

The Basics

- Be sure to read and work carefully through Chapters 1 and 2 first. These discuss the basics in *Windows Vista*.
- Then you can continue with Chapters 3, 4 and 5. These chapters introduce the keyboard and the mouse, as well as basic word processing. These are skills that every computer user must master. The objective of these chapters is being able to write a letter.

Once you have mastered the basics, you can choose from the following topics:

Optional Subjects

- **Folders and files**
  You can choose to work with folders and files in Chapter 6. This chapter can be worked through separately.
- **Text layout**
  Or you can choose to layout text in Chapter 7.
- **Internet**
  If you want to learn how to use the Internet, read Chapters 8 and 9. For this you will need a functioning Internet connection.
- **Customizing computer settings**
  In Chapter 10, you can learn how to customize your computer settings to suit your individual needs or desires.

The Screen Shots

The pictures in this book were made on a computer running *Windows Vista Ultimate*. To enhance the readability of the book we have adjusted certain settings on the computers we used for creating the book so that the icons will appear larger in the book than how they will look on your computer screen. This makes no difference however in performing the requested actions or doing the exercises.
In the last chapter of this book you will find information about adjusting settings on your own computer. You will then be able to determine for yourself what you want *Windows Vista* to look like on your computer.

How To Use This Book

This book was written using the Visual Steps™ method. It is important that you work through the book **step by step.** If you carefully follow all of the steps, you should not encounter any surprises.

There are various icons used in this Visual Steps™ book. This is what they mean:

Actions
These icons indicate that something must be done:

⊖	The miniature mouse indicates that you must do something with the mouse.
⌨	The mini-keyboard means that you must type something using the keyboard.
☞	The little hand indicates that you must do something else, such as putting a CD-ROM into the computer.

In addition to these actions, in some spots in the book **extra assistance** is provided so that you can successfully work through each chapter.

Help
Extra assistance is indicated by the following icons:

⇨	The arrow gives a warning.
✕	The bandage offers assistance if something goes wrong.
✓	The check mark is used with the exercises. These exercises directly reinforce what you have learned in the chapter you just read.
👣1	Have you forgotten how to perform an action? Use the number beside the footsteps to look it up in the back of the book in the section *How Do I Do That Again?*

This book also contains general information and tips about computers and *Windows Vista*. This information is given in separate boxes.

Extra Information
These boxes are marked with the following icons:

The small book indicates that extra background information is available for you to read at any time. You do not actually need this information to work through a chapter or to do the exercises.

The light bulb indicates an extra tip that can be useful when using *Windows Vista*.

Test Your Knowledge

Have you finished reading this book? Test your knowledge then with the test *Windows Vista*. Visit the website: **www.ccforseniors.com**

This multiple-choice test will show you how good your knowledge of Windows *Vista* is. If you pass the test, you will receive your **free Computer Certificate** by e-mail.

For Teachers

This book is designed as a self-study guide. It is also well suited for use in a group or a classroom setting. For this purpose, we offer a free teacher's manual containing information about how to prepare for the course (including didactic teaching methods) and testing materials. You can download this teacher's manual (PDF file) from the website which accompanies this book: **www.visualsteps.com/vista**

1. Starting Windows Vista

The computer you are sitting in front of is also called a *PC*. This is an abbreviation for *Personal Computer*. In the past twenty-five years, the PC has conquered the world, marching from the office to the home.

Nowadays nearly everyone has heard of *Windows*. But it was not all that long ago 1993 in fact - that *Windows* was used on PCs for the first time. Since then, *Windows* has evolved in step with the PC.

But what exactly is *Windows?* It is a program used to manage your computer's software and hardware resources. Before *Windows*, computers were operated by typing various complicated commands. With *Windows* you use your mouse to operate your computer. You can perform many different tasks by pointing and clicking the objects on your screen with your mouse.

As you work through this chapter, you will understand why this operating system is called *Windows*. You will see that nearly everything that happens is displayed in "window panes" on your screen.

In this chapter, you will learn how to:

- turn on your computer and start *Windows Vista*
- point and click with the mouse
- enter commands
- open and close programs
- minimize and maximize a window
- use the taskbar
- turn off your computer

⇨ Please note:

This book assumes that you are working with a computer mouse. If you are working on a laptop with touchpad, you may want to purchase an external mouse in order to more easily follow the steps in this book.

1.1 Desktop Computer or Laptop

Computers come in different sizes and shapes. Desktop computers are designed for use at a desk or table. Desktop computers consist of separate components.

This is a desktop computer:

Monitor:

Computer case or housing:

Keyboard:

Mouse:

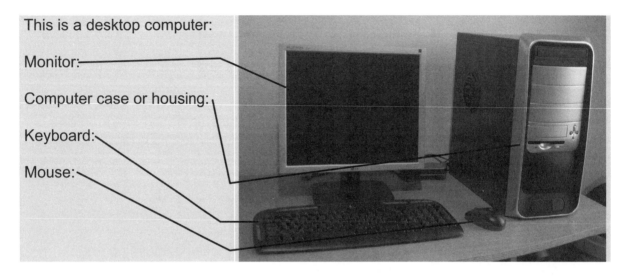

Laptop computers are lightweight portable PCs. They are often called *notebook computers* because of their small size. Laptops can operate on batteries, so you can take them anywhere. The screen folds down onto the keyboard when not in use. Laptops combine all computer components in a single case.

This is a laptop computer:

Screen:

Keyboard:

Touch pad:

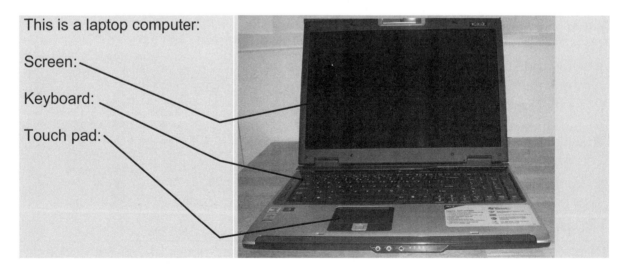

Operating *Windows Vista* on either type of computer is the same. It does not matter whether you use a desktop or a laptop.

In order to use your computer, you first need to turn it on. You will learn how to do this in the next section.

1.2 Turning on Your Desktop Computer or Laptop

First, make sure your computer is plugged into an electrical outlet. You turn on your computer by pressing the power button found on the case. Turn on your monitor by pressing its power button. You will see this symbol: 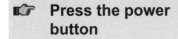 on or near this button.
If you are using a computer for the first time it may take a little while to locate these power buttons.

Here you see how to turn on your computer.

If you are using a desktop computer, the power button is often located on the front of the case:

☞ **Press the power button**

With many computers, the monitor will also be automatically started. With other computers, you must do this yourself.
If you do not see anything happening on your monitor after a short wait then your monitor most likely has not yet been turned on.

☞ **Press the power button**

Your computer is now turned on.

 HELP! I can not find the power button.

If you are unable to locate the power button, consult your computer's instruction manual or ask the person who sold it to you where the power button is located.

On a laptop, the power button is most likely found on the keyboard. You can easily identify this button by this symbol: .

☞ **Press the power button**

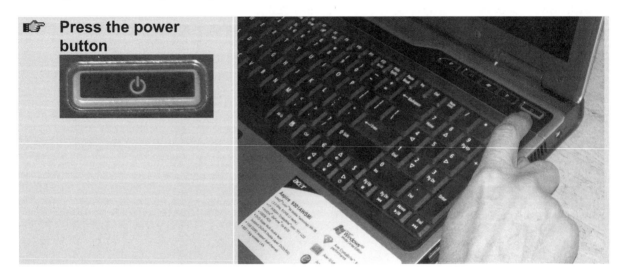

The laptop is now turned on. The screen does not need to be turned on separately.

HELP! I can not find the power button.

If you are unable to locate the power button, consult your laptop's instruction manual or ask the person who sold it to you where the power button is located.

1.3 Starting Windows Vista

Windows Vista is automatically started when you turn on your computer.

After a short time, you will see a screen that looks like this:

This screen is called the *Welcome Screen*.

Please note:

The screenshots used throughout this book may differ significantly from what you see on your computer screen. The appearance of your *Desktop* in *Windows Vista* can be customized in many ways. Perhaps someone who recently used your computer added a new desktop background for example. Computer manufacturers can also influence the appearance of your desktop. This will not interfere however with any of the tasks you need to do. You can continue reading.

In the figure below you see two small pictures called *icons* in the center of your screen. There may be more icons on your own screen. Or just one. The icons themselves may look different than the ones you see here. Even the names found under the icons on your screen may be different.

Somewhere on the screen you see an arrow.

This arrow is called the *pointer.*

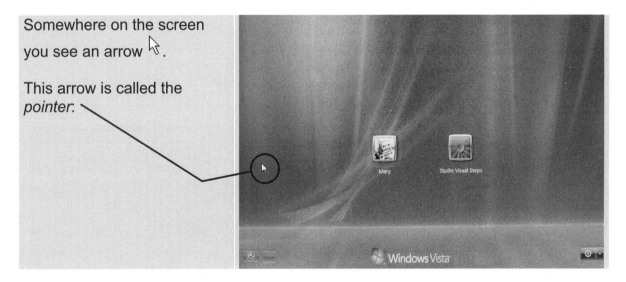

You direct the movement of the pointer on your computer screen by gently moving your mouse. In this chapter you will learn more how to do this.

1.4 Mouse or Touchpad

The pointer can be used as if it were your fingertip. You use it to "point" to things on the screen such as the icons in the figure above. You can move the pointer in any direction on your computer screen. You can "click" the items to perform various actions. This is done with a computer mouse:

Your desktop computer will usually be supplied with a computer mouse:

There are many types of designs and options available in computer mice.

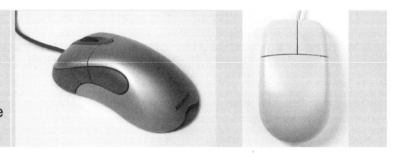

If you are working with a laptop, you can choose whether to operate it with a computer mouse or use the built in touchpad. The touchpad is a sensitive square which reacts when you move your fingertip across it.

Here you see the touchpad for this laptop:

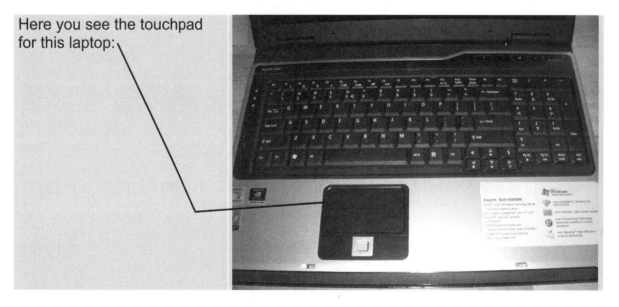

If you are using a laptop for the first time it is good idea to become familiar with a computer mouse. You will then be able to work on a desktop computer later on.

 Please note:

In this book you will learn how to use a computer mouse.
If you do not yet have a mouse you can purchase one at your local computer store.

Tip

Take your laptop with you when you go to buy a computer mouse at the computer store. The sales representative can then show you how to connect your new mouse to your laptop. Then when you get home you can get started right away.

Here you see a laptop with a computer mouse attached:

 Tip

Later on, if you want to learn more about using the touchpad to operate your laptop, read the Tip **Working with a touchpad** on page 103.

1.5 How to Hold the Mouse

The mouse sits on your desk or table. The mouse is designed to fit comfortably in the palm of your hand. Here is how to hold the mouse:

Place your mouse beside your keyboard on a clean, smooth surface, such as a mousepad.

Hold the mouse gently with your index finger resting on the left button and your thumb resting on the side.

The mousepad is a surface for enhancing the movement of a computer mouse. It is not absolutely necessary. You can use your mouse on a smooth, clean surface such as the table or desk where your computer is located.

 Tip

What's the best way to hold the mouse?

Not like this:

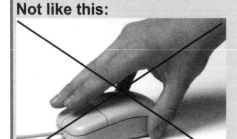

But like this:

Don't grasp it between two fingers with the other fingers in the air.
Don't lift your wrist from the tabletop.
Don't squeeze or grip your mouse tightly.

Place your mouse at elbow level.
Hold the mouse gently with your index finger resting on the left button.
Your thumb is resting on the side.
Hold the flat part of your hand lightly on top of the mouse. Let your wrist rest on the tabletop.
Your upper arms should fall relaxed at your sides.
Keep the front of the mouse aimed away from you.

It is important to teach yourself the proper way to hold the mouse from the very beginning. You will only have sufficient control of the mouse and be able to move it precisely if you keep it in the palm of your hand.

1.6 Moving the Mouse

You operate the computer almost entirely by using the mouse. The first few times that you use the mouse, it will seem awkward and unfamiliar. Just remember that everyone else had to start from the beginning, too. It is a matter of practicing. The more you use the mouse, the more proficient you will become.
To move the mouse, you slide it slowly on your desk surface or mousepad in any direction. As you move the mouse, the pointer on your screen moves in the same direction. Try it:

Somewhere on the screen you will see the pointer :

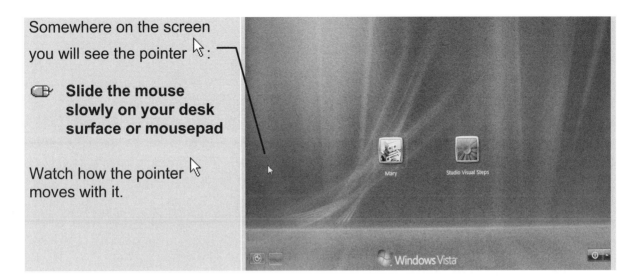

☞ **Slide the mouse slowly on your desk surface or mousepad**

Watch how the pointer moves with it.

If you run out of room when you move your mouse on your desk surface or mousepad, just pick it up, bring it back closer to you and gently set it down again. Remember: hold the flat part of your hand lightly on top of the mouse. If you grip the mouse too tightly you may inadvertently press one of the buttons. You will learn how to use these buttons later. For now try to move the mouse again:

Somewhere on the screen you can see the pointer :

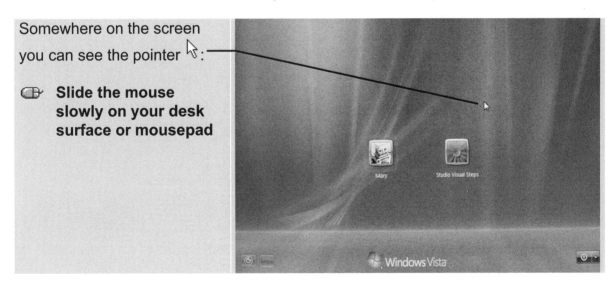

☞ **Slide the mouse slowly on your desk surface or mousepad**

When you move the mouse with your hand, the pointer on your screen will move in the same direction.

⇨ **Please note:**

Move the mouse by pivoting your arm at your elbow. Avoid pivoting the mouse with your wrist. This is to guard against possible injury such as *RSI*, repetitive strain injury.

Slide the mouse slowly to the left on your desk surface or mousepad

The pointer on your screen moves in the same direction.

 **Slide the mouse slowly to the right on your desk surface or mousepad**

When you move the mouse in different directions, the pointer on your screen follows the same movements.

 **Slide the mouse slowly away from you on your desk surface or mousepad**

 **Slide the mouse slowly towards you on your desk surface or mousepad**

The pointer on your screen moves in the same direction.

➡ Please note:

If you run out of room when you move your mouse on your desk surface or mousepad, just pick it up, bring it back closer to you and gently set it down again.

Slide the mouse slowly in a circle on your desk surface or mousepad

 Slide the mouse slowly in a triangle on your desk surface or mousepad

The pointer on your screen will move in the same direction.

It is a good idea to repeat these exercises a few times until you feel you have sufficient control over your mouse. Then you can continue with the next section.

⇨ Please note:

If you run out of room when you move your mouse on your desk surface or mousepad, just pick it up, bring it back closer to you and gently set it down again.

1.7 What Can You Do with the Mouse?

You can use your mouse to interact with objects on your computer screen.
Most mouse actions combine pointing with pressing one of the mouse buttons.
Pointing to an object on the screen means that you move your mouse until the pointer touches that object. Then you can use one of the mouse buttons.
There are four basic ways to use your mouse buttons:

- click (single-click)
- double-click
- right-click
- drag

With these mouse actions you can move objects, select them, open them, edit them, even throw them away. You instruct your computer to perform different tasks by using these mouse actions.
In this chapter you will learn how to point and click with your mouse.

1.8 Pointing

The first thing you need to know is how to point to things with the pointer on the screen. Pointing to an object on the screen means moving your mouse until the pointer touches or hovers above the object. In the previous section you learned how to move the pointer around your computer screen. In the figure below, you see two small pictures, *icons*, in the center of the screen. On your own computer screen you might see more of these icons, or perhaps just one. For the following exercises this does not matter.

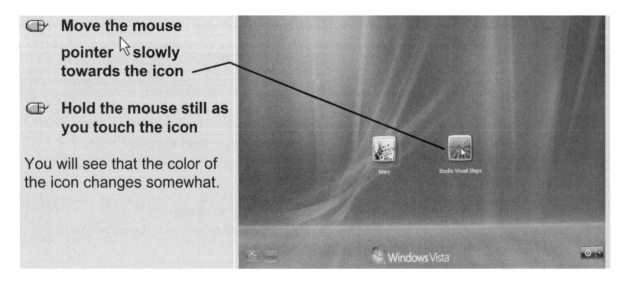

Move the mouse pointer slowly towards the icon

Hold the mouse still as you touch the icon

You will see that the color of the icon changes somewhat.

The mouse pointer is resting now on top of the icon.
Were you unable to do this the first time? Try again.

Remember: hold the mouse gently with your index finger resting on the left button. Your thumb is resting on the side. Hold the flat part of your hand lightly on top of the mouse. Let your wrist rest on the tabletop.

When the pointer touches the icon you can perform your first mouse action. You will need a mouse button to do this. In the next section, you will read about which mouse button to use for this task.

1.9 The Mouse Buttons

Computer mice are available in a wide variety of types and colors. And yet they are all similar: every mouse has at least two buttons.

The most important button is the **left mouse button**:

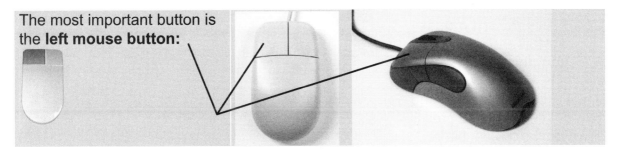

Mouse buttons can be pressed and released. This is called "clicking". You can hear a clicking sound when you press one of these mouse buttons.

1.10 Clicking

Clicking is the mouse action that you will use the most. First read how you go about clicking. You do not have to do any clicking yet. Clicking is done like this:

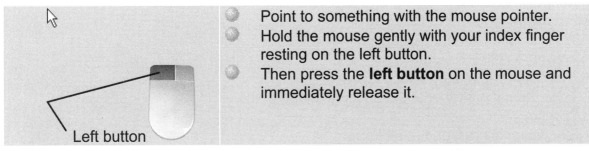

Left button

- Point to something with the mouse pointer.
- Hold the mouse gently with your index finger resting on the left button.
- Then press the **left button** on the mouse and immediately release it.

Now try this yourself:

☞ **Point to an icon**

☞ **Hold the mouse still**

The pointer ⬚ appears to be touching the icon.

You will see that the color of the icon changes somewhat.

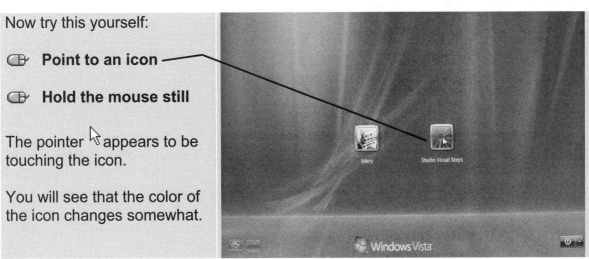

Mary   Studio Visual Steps

Windows Vista

Now *click* the icon using the left mouse button:

Hold the mouse gently with your index finger resting on the left button. **Press the left mouse button and immediately release it** You will hear a short clicking sound the instant you press down on the mouse button.	

The screen will change when you click the icon.

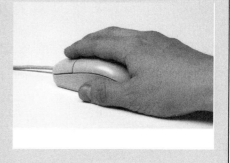 **HELP! When I pressed down on the button, the pointer moved.**

This usually means that you have moved the mouse after pointing and before clicking.

Remember:

- Hold the mouse gently with your index finger resting on the left button.
- Your thumb is resting on the side.
- Hold the flat part of your hand lightly on top of the mouse.
- Let your wrist rest on the tabletop.

Then you will not need to look at your hand when you click.

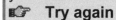 **Try again**

The precise window that appears on your screen will depend on your particular computer. You may see the window shown in the figure below:

If you see this window, you can skip the following steps.

Proceed further on page 37.

Or you may see this window:

If you see this window, you will need a password in order to continue.

The password is typed in the white area of the box where you see the word

password

To type the password, it is necessary to use the keyboard of your computer.

Of course you will need to know what the password is beforehand.
If you do not know the password, ask the owner of the computer that you are using what it is.

⌨ Type the password

As you type you will see small black circles appear in the white area of the box.
This is normal.
In this way, no one can see what you have typed. This keeps your password hidden from others.

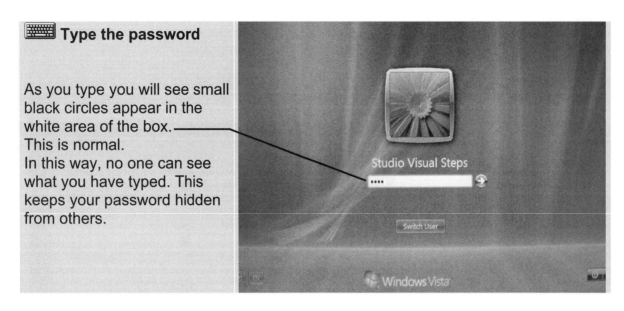

When you have finished typing the password, you can continue.

🖰 **Point to**

🖰 **Hold the mouse still**

Now you can click .

🖰 **Press the left mouse button and immediately release it**

Do not give up if it does not work on the first try and you find yourself moving your mouse accidentally when trying to click. You just need to practice a bit more.

Remember: hold the mouse gently with your index finger resting on the left button. Your thumb is resting on the side. Hold the flat part of your hand lightly on top of the mouse. Let your wrist rest on the tabletop. Then you will not need to look at your hand when you click.
Try it again.

Now you see this window:

 HELP! I see a different window.

If you see a different window than the one shown above, it may look like the one shown in this figure:

The picture that you see here is your *Desktop* background. You can personalize your computer with a different background. Remember that *Windows Vista* allows you to adjust many settings to suit your own taste. Perhaps someone else has already made a change to your *Desktop* background. You can proceed further on page 40 with the section:
The Desktop.

This figure shows a rectangular box or frame that is filled with text and pictures.

This rectangular box is called a *window*.

This particular window is known as the *Welcome Center* of *Windows Vista.*

You do not need to use the *Welcome Center* at this time. You may close this window now:

There is a special button available to close a window:

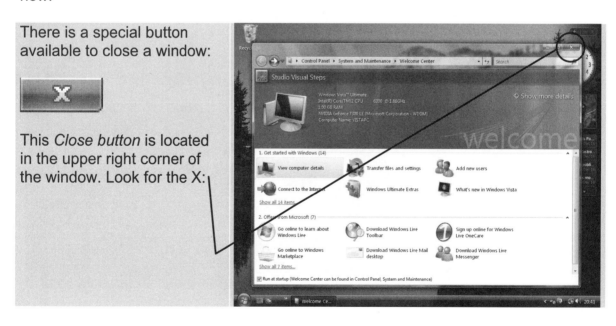

This *Close button* is located in the upper right corner of the window. Look for the X:

You can see the *Close button* more easier in this close-up view of the upper right corner of the *Welcome Center*.

There are three buttons next to one another.
You need to use the red button on the far right which contains the letter X

 Point to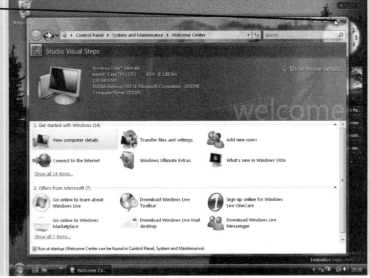

The pointer is resting on top of the letter X:

The button glows a brighter red and a small box appears with this information: Close

You can click now:

Press the left mouse button and immediately release it

When you click the close button, you *close* the *Welcome Center*. That means that the window has disappeared.

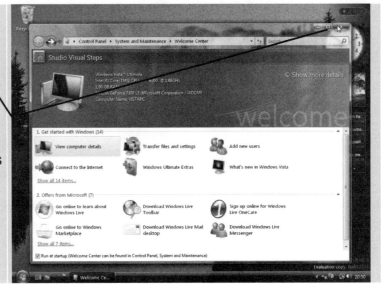

HELP! When I pressed the button, the pointer moved.

This usually means that you have moved the mouse after pointing and before clicking.

Remember:

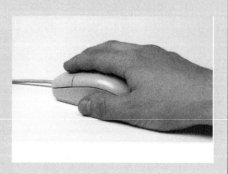

- Hold the mouse gently with your index finger resting on the left button.
- Your thumb is resting on the side.
- Hold the flat part of your hand lightly on top of the mouse.
- Let your wrist rest on the tabletop.

Then you will not need to look at your hand when you click.

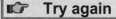 **Try again**

1.11 The Desktop

After you have closed the *Welcome Center* window, you see the screen shown in the figure below.

This screen is called the *Desktop.*

Now take a look at what can be found on your *Desktop*:

This screenshot shows a picture of a landscape. This picture may be different than the one that appears on your *Desktop*.

Remember that *Windows Vista* allows you to adjust many settings to suit your own taste. Perhaps someone else has already done this for you.

Later in the book you will learn how to make these sort of changes yourself.

There is a long horizontal bar at the bottom of your *Desktop.*
This bar is called the *Taskbar.*

On the far left side of the *Taskbar* you see this button

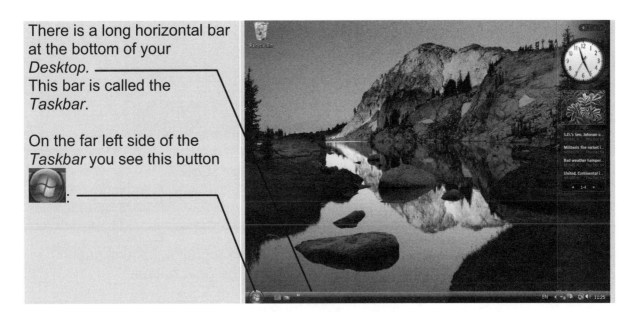

The *Desktop* is the main screen area that you see after you turn on your computer and log on to *Windows.* Like the top of an actual desk, it serves as a surface for your work. When you open programs or folders, they appear on the *Desktop.* Later in this book you will read more about the different kinds of programs and folders.

1.12 Pointing to an Object

When you point to something, a small box often appears that describes the item.
Try it:

☞ **Move the mouse pointer to the button**

☞ **Hold the mouse still**

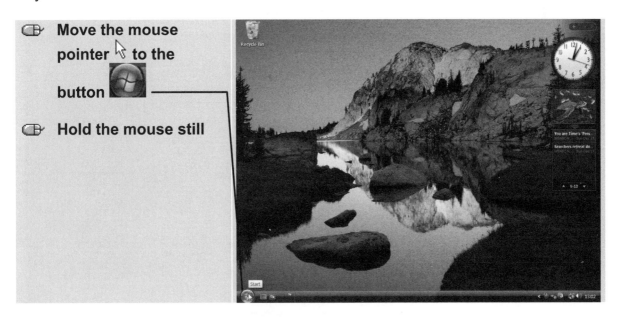

You see that a little box
appears close to this icon
.

You can see this more easily
in this close-up view:

Pointing to an object often reveals a descriptive message about it.

1.13 The Start Menu

The *Start menu* is the main gateway to your computer's programs, folders, and
settings. To open the *Start menu* you will need to click the *Start* button:

Point to

Press the left mouse
button and
immediately release it

You will hear once more a
short clicking sound the
instant you press down on the
mouse button.

After your click on   a
large box appears:

This box is called the *Start
menu*.
It's called a menu because it
provides a list of choices, just
as a restaurant menu does.

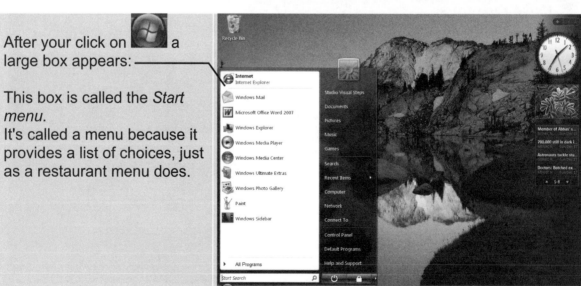

The *Start menu* on your *Desktop* may appear smaller.
Later in this book you will learn how to adjust the size of this box.

This figure shows a close-up of the *Start menu*:

The large left pane shows a short list of programs on your computer: ──────────

Your computer manufacturer can customize this list, so its exact appearance will vary from computer to computer.

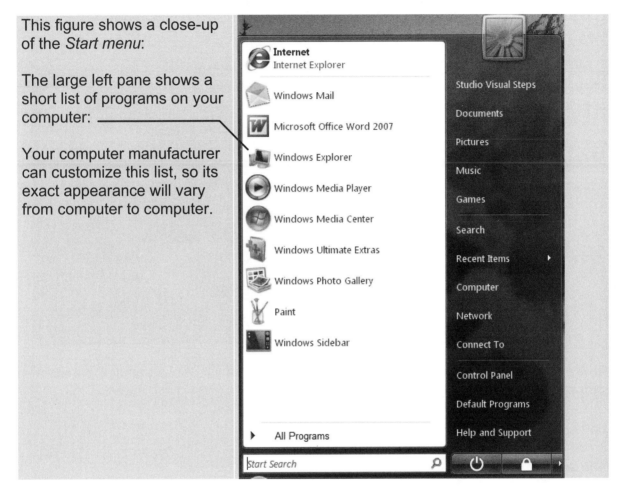

Almost everything you do on your computer requires using a program. A *program* is a set of instructions that a computer uses to perform a specific task.
For example, if you want to calculate a number, you use the program *Calculator*.

You are going to start the program *Calculator*. This program is not found in the short list of programs. You can find this program in ▶   All Programs .

1.14 Opening the Program Calculator

You are going to start the program *Calculator*. The *Start menu* is already opened. Down near the bottom you see ▶ All Programs :

🖱️ **Point to** ▶ All Programs

You can click now:

🖱️ **Press the left mouse button and immediately release it**

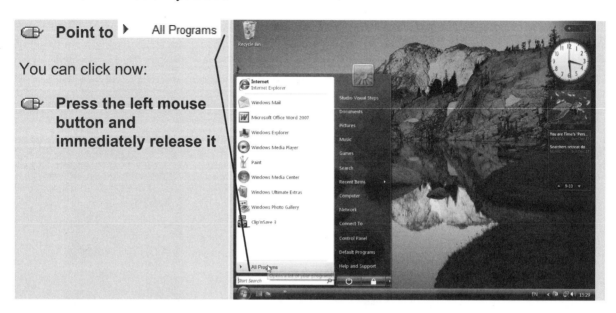

Now another menu appears in the same box. You see a list of programs and a list of folders.

You can easily recognize a folder by this icon
So what is inside the folders? More programs.
You are going to open the folder called *Accessories*:

🖱️ **Point to**
   Accessories

It automatically turns blue.

🖱️ **Press the left mouse button and immediately release it**

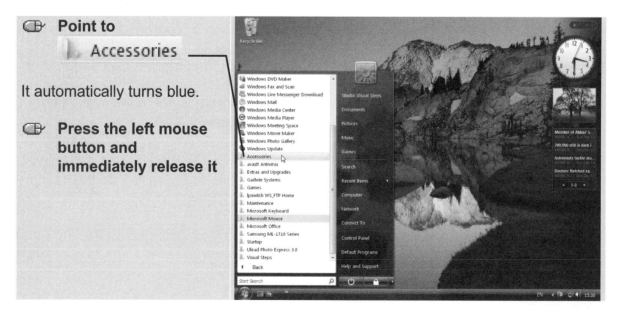

HELP! I opened the wrong folder.

Can you still see the menu, but the wrong folder has been opened?

☞ **Point to** Accessories

☞ **Press the left mouse button and immediately release it**

The programs that are stored in the folder

Accessories appear.

You will see the program *Calculator*:

☞ **Point to**
Calculator

It automatically turns blue.

☞ **Press the left mouse button and immediately release it**

Shortly thereafter, this calculator appears:

Now, look down at your *Taskbar*. Notice that a small button has appeared:

The *Taskbar button* shows an icon and the name of the program.

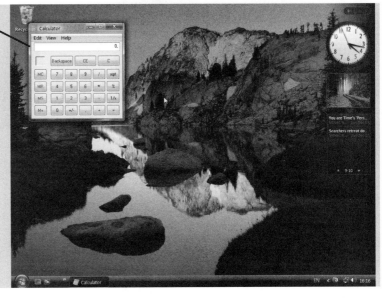

HELP! The wrong program appears.

Did you accidentally open the wrong program?

☞ **Point to** [**X**] **at the top right corner of the wrong program**
☞ **Press the left mouse button and immediately release it**

The program will close.

☞ **Now go back through the steps above to open the *Calculator***

You have instructed your computer to open the program *Calculator*.

This figure shows the window of the *Calculator* program.

At the top of the window, you see the *Title bar* with a program icon, the name of the program and three buttons on the right: ——————

All of the programs in *Windows Vista* use a window such as this and they all work in virtually the same way. This makes them easy to use.

1.15 The Menu Bar

Most programs contain dozens or even hundreds of commands (actions) that you use to work the program. Many of these commands are organized under menus. Like a restaurant menu, a program menu shows you a list of choices. To keep the screen uncluttered, menus are hidden until you click their titles in the *Menu bar*, located just underneath the *Title bar*.

This is the *Menu bar*.

☞ **Point to** Help

The word Help changes to the button Help :

You can click this type of button.

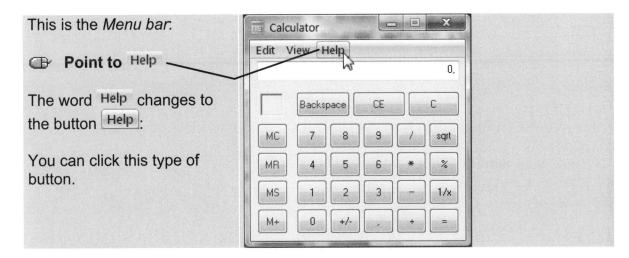

⇨ **Please note:**

From this point on in this book you will see this mouse icon ☞ and the word "**Click**" when you are asked to click an item. For example: the instruction
☞ **Click** Help
is the same as
☞ **Point to** Help
☞ **Press the left mouse button and immediately release it**

☞ **Click** Help

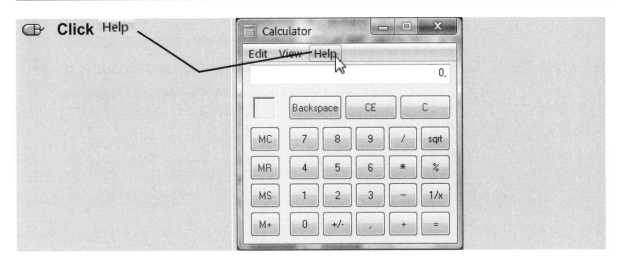

Now a menu appears:

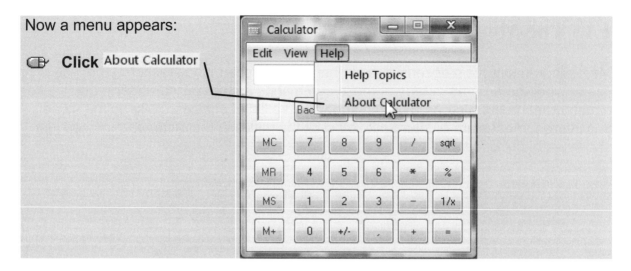

CB **Click** About Calculator

A second window appears. It floats above the *Calculator* window:

The second window contains information about the program:

At the bottom you see a button that says **OK**. That means: Okay, I understand.

CB **Click** [OK]

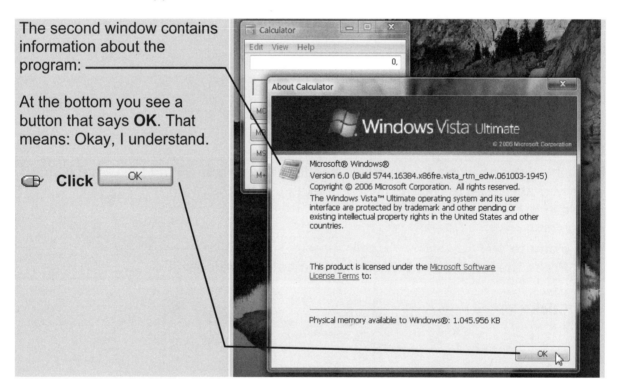

Now the second window is closed.

1.16 Calculate by Clicking

The *Calculator* works just like a real calculator. You can press the buttons by clicking them with the mouse:

 **Please note:**

The instruction ⊂⮞ **Click ...** is the same as:
⊂⮞ **Point to ...**
⊂⮞ **Press the left mouse button and immediately release it**

⊂⮞ **Click** `8`

⊂⮞ **Click** `+`

⊂⮞ **Click** `5`

⊂⮞ **Click** `=`

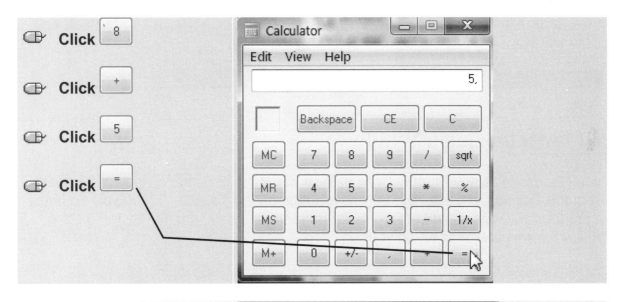

The outcome is displayed in the white section:

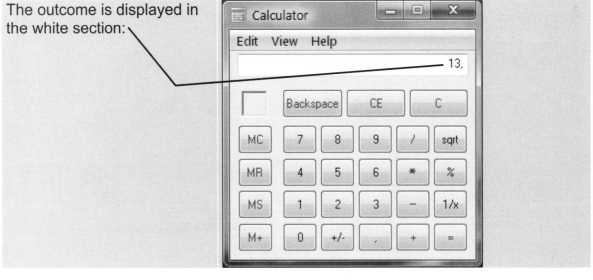

Tip

| **Is it difficult to click on the right spot?** |
| This usually means that you have moved the mouse after pointing and before clicking. |

Remember:
- Hold the mouse gently with your index finger resting on the left button.
- Your thumb is resting on the side.
- Hold the flat part of your hand lightly on top of the mouse.
- Let your wrist rest on the tabletop.

Then you won't need to look at your hand when you click.

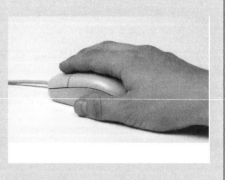

☞ **Try again**

1.17 Minimizing a Window

You can minimize any window. *Minimizing* a window means the window disappears from the *Desktop* and is visible only as a button on the *Taskbar*. When you minimize a program window, you do not close the program; instead, you merely reduce the space the window takes up on your desktop.

To minimize a window, use the *Minimize button* 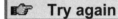 at the top right.

☞ **Click** ▭

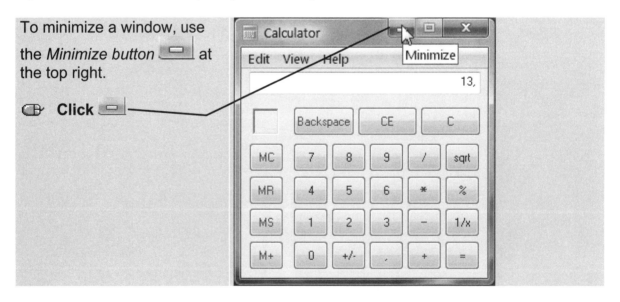

The window is minimized and disappears from the *Desktop*:

Next to  you still see the *Calculator* button on the *Taskbar*.

Remember: you did not actually close the program *Calculator*; you simply reduced the space it takes up on your *Desktop*.

1.18 Starting Another Program

In *Windows Vista* you can have more than one program opened at a time.
Take a look:

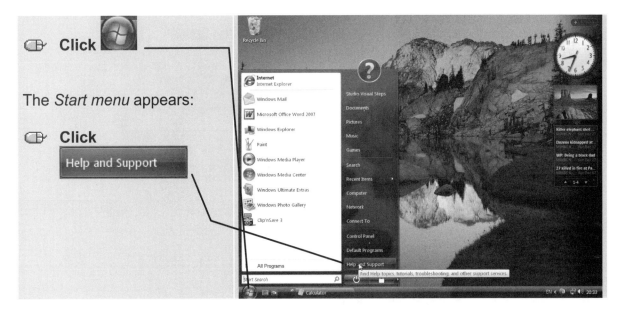

☞ **Click**

The *Start menu* appears:

☞ **Click** Help and Support

Now you see the window for *Windows Help and Support*:

In this figure you see that the window takes up about one half of the surface of the *Desktop*.
This may be different on your own *Desktop*.

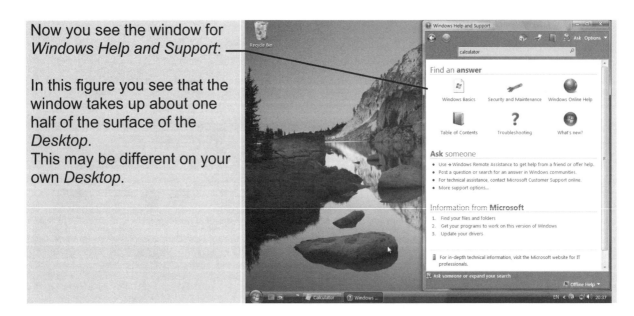

You did not receive a manual with *Windows Vista*. All of the information you need is contained in this digital Help system. We will discuss this in more detail later.

1.19 Maximizing and Minimizing

The *Windows Help and Support* window can fill the entire screen. Expanding a window to its largest allowable size is called maximizing.

There is a button for maximizing the window.

It is in the middle of the three buttons in the upper right corner of the *Windows Help and Support* window:

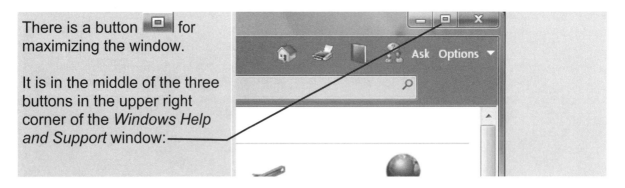

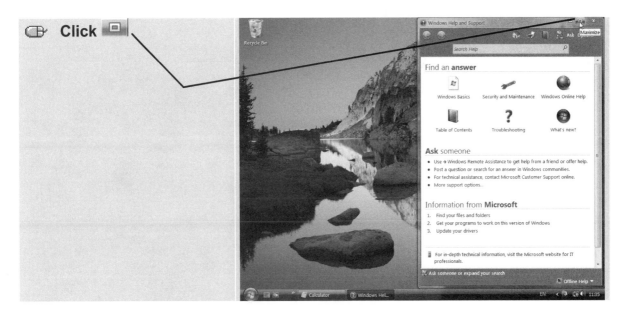

The window changes size. The window now fills the entire screen.

The *Windows Help and Support* window can also be reduced (minimized).

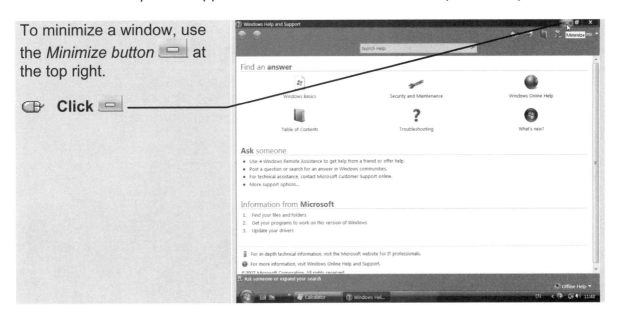

The window will be minimized.
Now you have opened two programs: the *Calculator* and *Windows Help and Support*. Both windows are now minimized. The programs are not closed, you simply reduced the space they take up on your desktop.

If you look down to the
Taskbar you will see the
buttons of the two programs:

Remember: the bar next to ![icon] is called the **Taskbar**. For every program that you
open a button is created on the *Taskbar* corresponding to that item.

1.20 Making a Window Reappear on the Desktop

To make a minimized window reappear on the *Desktop*, just click its button on the
Taskbar. The window appears exactly as it was before you minimized it.
Try it:

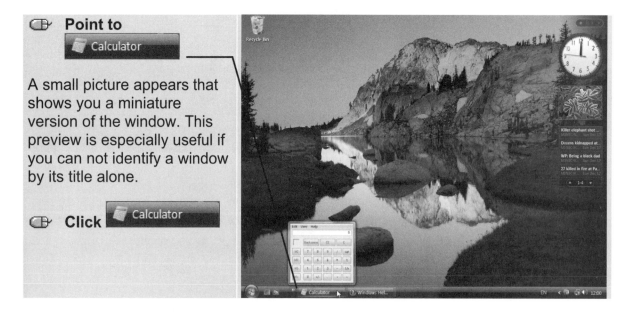

☞ **Point to**
   Calculator

A small picture appears that
shows you a miniature
version of the window. This
preview is especially useful if
you can not identify a window
by its title alone.

☞ **Click** Calculator

The window for the *Calculator* appears on the *Desktop*:

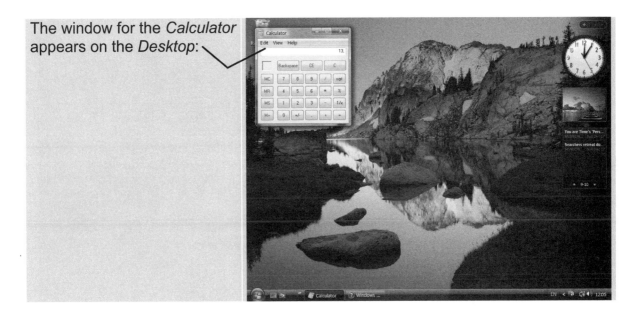

1.21 Closing a Program

A window can also be definitively **closed**. If you close the *Calculator* window, you close the program.

You can close a window by using this window button

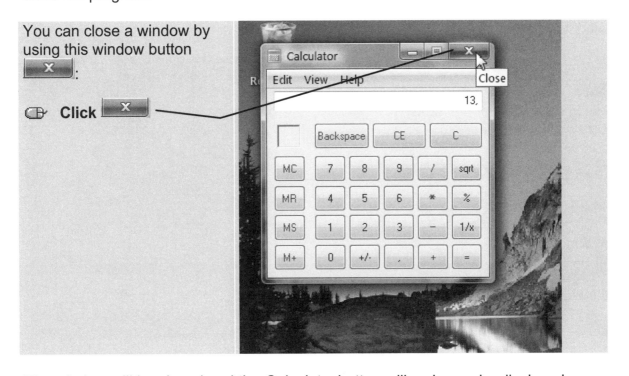

The window will be closed and the *Calculator* button will no longer be displayed on the *Taskbar*. The program is now closed.

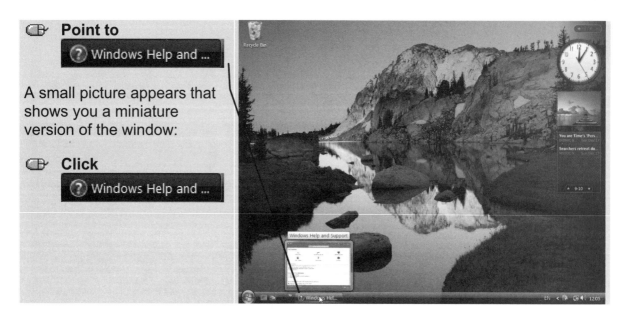

Point to
☞ ⑦ Windows Help and ...

A small picture appears that shows you a miniature version of the window:

Click
☞ ⑦ Windows Help and ...

The window *Windows Help and Support* will appear.

1.22 Restoring a Maximized Window to Its Former Size

The window *Windows Help and Support* was maximized. To return a maximized window to its former size, you can use its *Restore button*.

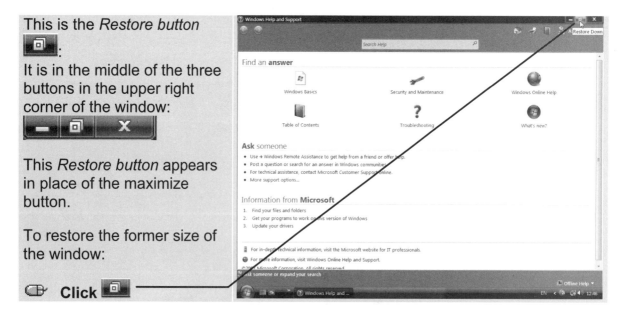

This is the *Restore button*.

It is in the middle of the three buttons in the upper right corner of the window:

This *Restore button* appears in place of the maximize button.

To restore the former size of the window:

☞ **Click** 🗗

The window is now restored to its former size.

Now you can close this window:

☞ **Click**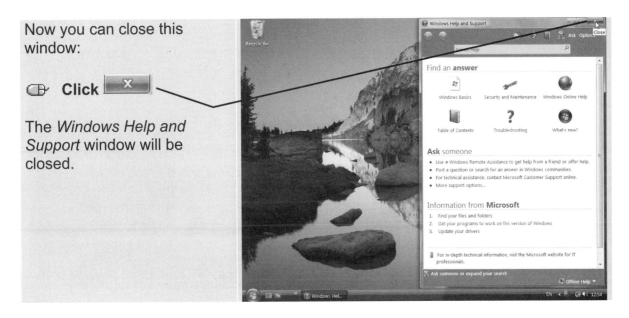

The *Windows Help and Support* window will be closed.

Windows Help and Support is now closed and its corresponding button on the *Taskbar* has disappeared.

1.23 Turning off Your Computer

When you are done using your computer, it is important to turn it off properly. Not only to save energy, but also to ensure that your work is saved.
Point to the *Start button*:

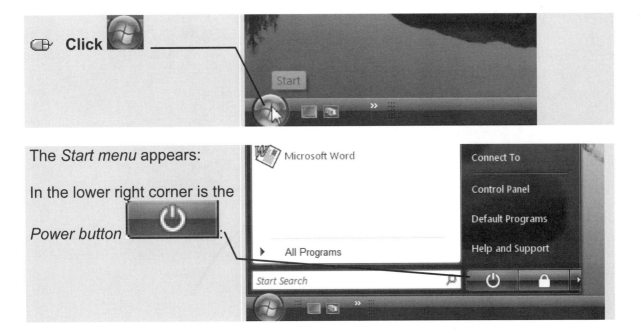

☞ **Click**

The *Start menu* appears:

In the lower right corner is the

Power button:

When you click this button ![button], your computer goes to sleep. That means that *Windows Vista* automatically saves your work, turns off the display, and any noise from the computer's fan stops. The whole process takes only a few seconds. Try it:

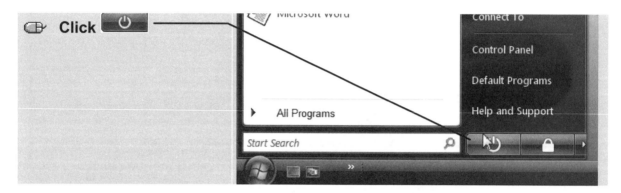

Your computer screen will turn black immediately. Your computer is now "asleep". Usually, a light on the outside of your computer case blinks or turns yellow to indicate that the computer is sleeping. The next time you turn on your computer, the screen will look exactly as it did when you put your computer to sleep.

While your computer is sleeping, it uses a very small amount of power to maintain your work in its memory. If you are using a laptop, you do not have to worry: The battery will not be drained. After the computer has been sleeping for several hours, or if the battery is running low, your work is saved to the hard disk, and then your computer turns off completely, drawing no power.

To wake your computer:

☞ **Press the power button**

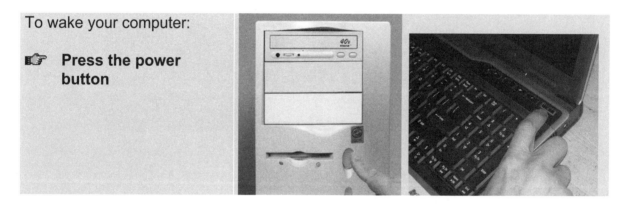

Because you do not have to wait for *Windows* to start, your computer wakes within seconds and you can resume work almost immediately.

Sometimes, a password is required before you can begin working. In this case, you need to type the password in the white area shown in the figure below:

⌨ **Type the password**

🖱 **Click**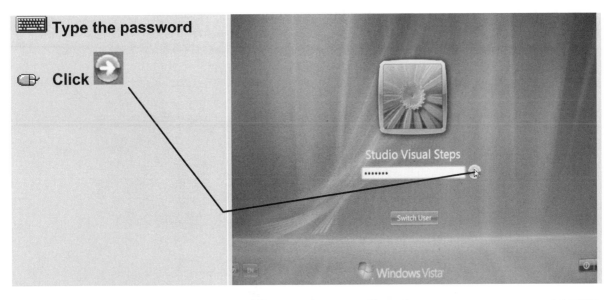

Then your *Desktop* will reappear:

If you had any programs open, you will see their windows now, or if the windows were minimized their corresponding buttons on the *Taskbar*.

1.24 Shutting Down Your Computer

Even though putting your computer to sleep is the fastest way to turn it off, and the best option for resuming work quickly, there are certain times when you should shut down instead. Perhaps you want to move your computer to another location, and you need to unplug it. Or when you want to add a new hardware device such as a printer or scanner. You will need to shut down the computer before connecting the new device. In these situations you use the option *Shut Down*.
Point to the *Start button*:

Click

The *Start menu* appears:

Click

A white box appears to the right with a list of options:

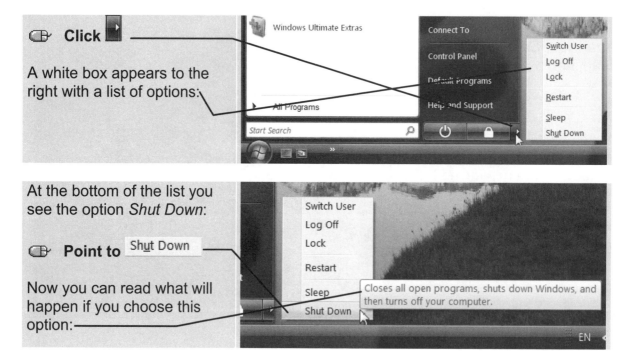

At the bottom of the list you see the option *Shut Down*:

Point to Sh<u>u</u>t Down

Now you can read what will happen if you choose this option:

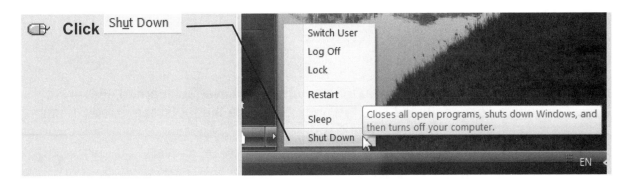

Windows Vista is now closed and the computer is shut down.

 Tip

Do you see the *Start menu* and you prefer leaving your computer on? If you click on an empty place on the *Desktop*, the *Start menu* and the box with the *Shut Down* option disappear. You can then proceed further.

⇨ **Please note:**

If for safety reasons you want to remove the plug of your computer from the electrical outlet, you must always choose the option ***Shut Down***.

Because does not save your work, be sure you save your work before shutting down.

In this chapter you have learned how to turn your computer on, how to turn it off and how to shut it down. You have practiced using the mouse and you know how to open and close a program.

The following exercises will help you master what you have just learned.

1.25 Exercises

The following exercises will help you master what you have just learned. Have you forgotten how to do something? Use the number beside the footsteps to look it up in the appendix *How Do I Do That Again?*

Exercise: Opening and Closing

✓ Turn on your computer.

✓ Open the *Calculator*. $\ell\ell^5$

✓ Minimize the *Calculator* window. $\ell\ell^1$

✓ Open *Windows Help and Support*. $\ell\ell^6$

✓ Maximize the *Windows Help and Support* window. $\ell\ell^2$

✓ Minimize the *Windows Help and Support* window. $\ell\ell^1$

✓ Open the *Calculator* window from the *Taskbar*. $\ell\ell^7$

✓ Close the *Calculator*. $\ell\ell^4$

✓ Open the *Windows Help and Support* window from the *Taskbar*. $\ell\ell^8$

✓ Close the *Windows Help and Support*. $\ell\ell^4$

✓ Turn off your computer (sleep or shut down). $\ell\ell^9$

When you have practiced enough, you can read the background information and tips on the next page. If you would rather keep working with your computer, you can go on to Chapter 2. The background information and tips can be read another time.

1.26 Background Information

Dictionary	
Desktop	The *Desktop* is the main screen area that you see after you turn on your computer and log on to *Windows Vista*. When you open programs or folders, they appear on the *Desktop*.
Icon	A small picture that represents a folder, program, or object.
Menu, Menu bar	Most programs contain dozens or even hundreds of commands (actions) that you use to work the program. Many of these commands are organized under menus. Menus are hidden until you click their titles in the menu bar, located just underneath the title bar.
Mouse actions	Most mouse actions combine pointing with pressing one of the mouse buttons. There are four basic ways to use your mouse buttons: clicking, double-clicking, right-clicking, and dragging.
Power button	The *Power button* turns off your computer:
Program	A set of instructions that a computer uses to perform a specific task, such as word processing or calculating.
Start button	Button that opens the *Start menu.*
Start menu	The *Start menu* is the main gateway to your computer's programs, folders, and settings. It is called a menu because it provides a list of choices, just as a restaurant menu does.
Taskbar	The *Taskbar* is the long horizontal bar at the bottom of your screen. The *Taskbar* is usually visible.
Taskbar button	A button representing an open folder or program. These buttons appear on the *Taskbar*.
Title bar	The horizontal bar at the top of a window that contains the name of the window.
Welcome Screen	The *Welcome Screen* is the screen that you use to log on to *Windows*. It displays all of the accounts on the computer.

- Continue reading on the next page -

Window	A rectangular box or frame on a computer screen in which programs and content appear.
Window buttons	Buttons that are used to manipulate the window:
Windows Sidebar	Long, vertical bar that is displayed on the side of your *Desktop*. Contains mini-programs called *gadgets*.
Windows Vista	Operating system: the computer program that manages all other computer programs on your computer. The operating system stores files, allows you to use programs, and coordinates the use of computer hardware (mouse, keyboard).

Source: Windows Help and Support

What are the various parts of Windows Vista Desktop called?
The *Desktop* is the main screen area that you see after you turn on your computer and log on to *Windows*. Like the top of an actual desk, it serves as a surface for your work. When you open programs or folders, they appear on the *Desktop*.

Icon:
A small picture that represents a file, folder, program, or other object. For example the *Recycle Bin* icon.

Window:
A rectangular box or frame on a computer screen in which programs and content appear.

Windows Sidebar:
contains mini-programs called *gadgets*, which offer information at a glance and provide easy access to frequently used tools.

Start menu:
The *Start menu* is the main gateway to your computer's programs, folders, and settings. And as "Start" implies, it is often the place that you will go to to start or open things.

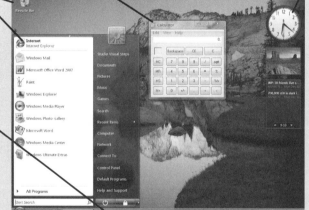

Taskbar:
The long horizontal bar at the bottom of your screen. It contains the *Start button* and shows which programs or documents are opened.

Start button: Opens the *Start menu.*

Taskbar button: Whenever you open a program, *Windows* creates a button on the *Taskbar* corresponding to that item. The button shows the name of the program.

What's in the Start menu?

The *Start menu* is the main gateway to your computer's programs, folders, and settings. It is called a *menu* because it provides a list of choices, just as a restaurant menu does. And as "Start" implies, it is often the place that you will go to to start or open things. To open the *Start menu*, click the *Start button* found in the lower-left corner of your screen. Or, press the *Windows* logo key on your keyboard. The *Start menu* appears:

The large left pane shows a short list of programs on your computer:
Your computer manufacturer can customize this list, so its exact appearance will vary. You might notice that over time, the lists of programs in your *Start menu* change. The *Start menu* detects which programs you use the most, and it places them in the left pane for quick access.

In the lower left corner is the search box which allows you to look for all kind of things on your computer by typing in search terms.

The right pane provides access to commonly used folders, files, settings, and features.
It is also where you go to log off from *Windows* or turn off your computer.

What are the various parts of a window called?

All of the programs in *Windows Vista* are displayed in a window. Most windows have the same basic parts:

Title bar:
Displays the name of the program.

Menu bar:
Contains items that you can click to make choices in a program.

Menu:
a list of commands (choices)

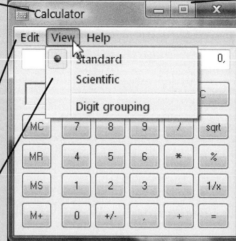

Window buttons:
These are used to manipulate the window. When you click:

⬜ *Minimize button*: the window disappears from the desktop and is visible only as a button on the *Taskbar*.

⬜ *Maximize button*: the window fills the entire screen (not available in *Calculator*).

⬜ *Restore button*: a maximized window returns to its former size (this button appears in place of the *Maximize button*).

☒ *Close button*: closes program or document window and removes its corresponding button from the *Taskbar*.

Borders and corners:
You can drag these with your mouse pointer to change the size of the window. (See next chapter.)

The Power button

You will see the *Power button*  after you have clicked the *Start button:*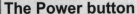

The *Power button* normally looks like this:
When you click this button, your computer goes to sleep.
Because *Windows* saves your work, there is no need to close your programs and files before putting your computer to sleep.
To wake your computer, press the power button on your computer case.

The Power button (sleep)

The *Power button* can change its appearance. Under some circumstances, the button looks like this:
When you click the button in this form, your computer shuts down. Shutting down closes all open programs, along with *Windows* itself, and then turns off your display and computer completely. Because shutting down does not save your work, you must save your files before shutting down.
The *Power button* shuts down your computer under the following circumstances:

The Power button (shut down)

- The *Sleep* option is not available on your computer hardware.
- The *Power button* is set to "always shut down the computer". The *Power button* setting can be changed.

There is one other form that the *Power button* can take. If you have set your computer to receive updates automatically, and the updates are ready to be installed, the button appears with a shield on it:
When you click the button in this form, *Windows* installs the updates and then shuts down your computer when installation is complete.
Updates are additions to software that can prevent or fix problems and enhance the security of a computer.

The Power button (install updates and shut down)

1.27 Tips

 HELP! I see something else all of a sudden.

Has another image suddenly appeared on your screen?
A moving illustration such as this, perhaps:

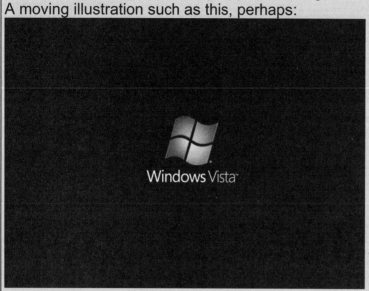

This means that your computer's **screen saver** has been activated. The screen saver prevents your screen from "burn-in". Burn-in can happen when the same, motionless image is on your screen for a long period of time while you are not using the computer. You can change the settings for the screen saver in *Windows Vista* to suit your taste. For example, you can set the number of minutes that the image has to remain motionless before the screen saver is activated. You can also turn the screen saver off. You can read about this later in this book.

☞ **You can remove the screen saver from your screen by pressing a key on the keyboard or by slightly moving the mouse**

 Tip

Circle

Has your mouse pointer ⌖ changed into a spinning circle ◯ ?
This means your computer is busy doing something.

☞ **Just wait patiently until your computer is done and the circle has disappeared**

2. More Use of the Mouse in Windows Vista

The mouse has become an essential part of the computer. But it is actually a relatively new addition. The mouse did not become a standard part of the PC until *Windows* was introduced.

Before then, only computers made by *Apple* had a mouse, and it had only one button. It quickly became evident that operating a PC had to be made easier so that more people could use it.

This is why the software became increasingly *graphic*: pictures and buttons replaced complicated commands. *Windows Vista* is an excellent example of this.

The most important commands can be carried out by using the mouse. Various aspects of *Windows Vista* were developed to make it easier to use – there are various kinds of buttons in many sizes on the screen: buttons to press, on and off buttons, buttons that turn and scroll bars. The mouse has also been given more and more functions.

In this chapter, you will learn how to utilize these functions. Maybe someday in the future the mouse will become less important, if computers can "listen" and accept verbal commands. Until then, however, the mouse has center stage in *Windows Vista*.

In this chapter, you will learn how to:

- drag with the mouse
- drag a scroll bar
- use a scroll wheel
- change the size of a window
- use the *Windows Help and Support*
- double-click with the mouse
- right-click with the mouse

2.1 Getting Ready

Before you begin:

☞   Turn the computer (and the monitor) on

☞   Open the *Calculator* 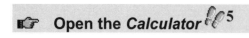5

The *Calculator* window is
opened:

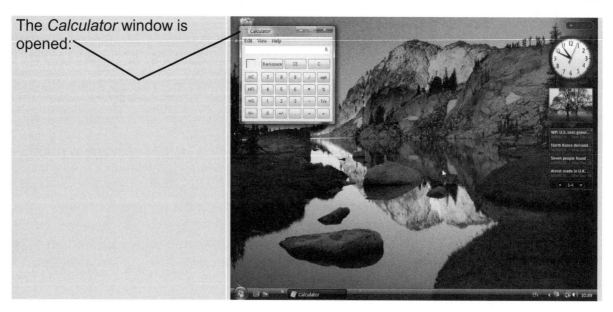

2.2 The Next Three Mouse Actions

In the previous chapter, you learned that there are four basic ways to use your
mouse buttons:

- click (single-click)
- drag
- double-click
- right-click

You have practiced how to click (single-click with the left mouse button) in the
previous chapter. In this chapter, you will learn how to perform the other three mouse
actions.

2.3 Dragging

Dragging is used to move windows and icons around on your *Desktop*.
Dragging is done like this:

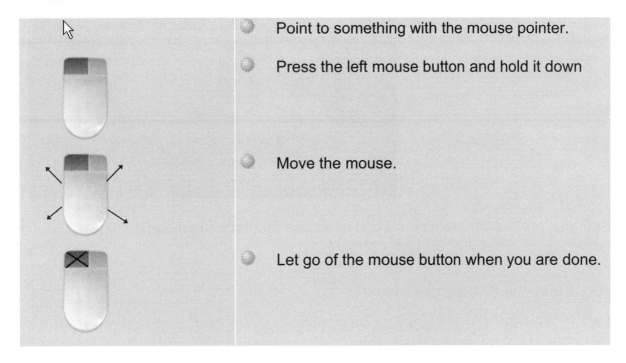

◎	Point to something with the mouse pointer.
◎	Press the left mouse button and hold it down
◎	Move the mouse.
◎	Let go of the mouse button when you are done.

For example, you can move the *Calculator* window to another location on the *Desktop* by dragging its title bar. The title bar is the horizontal bar at the top of a window which contains the name of the window. Try it:

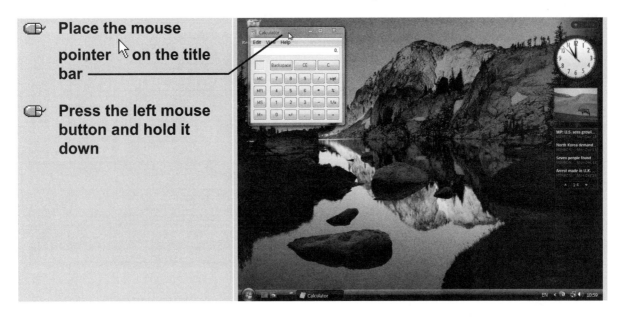

☞ **Place the mouse pointer ⍞ on the title bar**

☞ **Press the left mouse button and hold it down**

While holding down the left mouse button, slide the mouse over the tabletop

The *Calculator* window slides with the mouse pointer.

 Release the mouse button

At the end of this chapter you will find exercises for practicing dragging. Now you can close the *Calculator* window.

☞ **Close the *Calculator* window** 🦶⁴

💡 **Tip**

Dragging in Solitaire
A good way to practice dragging, is by playing the popular card game *Solitaire* on the computer. It is the perfect, handy way to learn to use the mouse.

This *Solitaire* program comes with *Windows Vista* and it has probably already been installed on your computer.

In Appendix A at the back of this book you can read how to start this program and play the game.

2.4 Dragging with a Scroll Bar

There are many situations in *Windows* where you must *drag* something. You can practice dragging different objects while using the *Help and Support* window.

☞   **Open *Windows Help and Support*** 👣6

This figure shows the *Windows Help and Support* window:

☞   **Click** Windows Basics

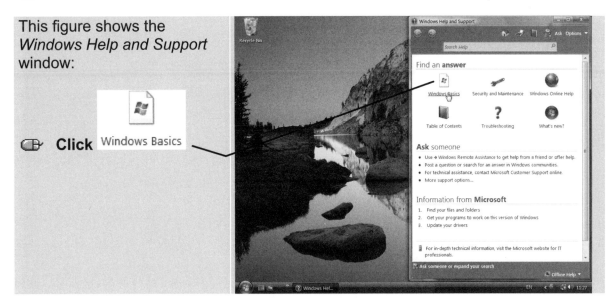

When a document, (web)page, or picture exceeds the size of its window, *scroll bars* appear. The scroll bar allows you to see the content that is currently out of view. This happens in the *Help and Support* window. Part of the content is not fully visible. Take a look:

In the right-hand side of the window, you see a vertical bar:

This bar is called a *scroll bar*.

☞   **Place the mouse pointer 🕵 on the scroll bar**

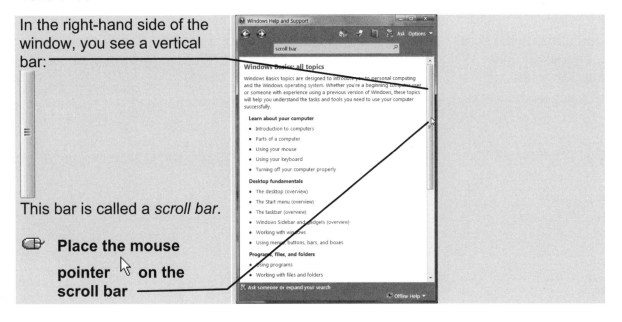

Press the left mouse button and hold it down

The scroll bar turns blue.

Keep pressing the left mouse button, and drag (slide) the mouse pointer down

The scroll bar will also move down:

Release the mouse button

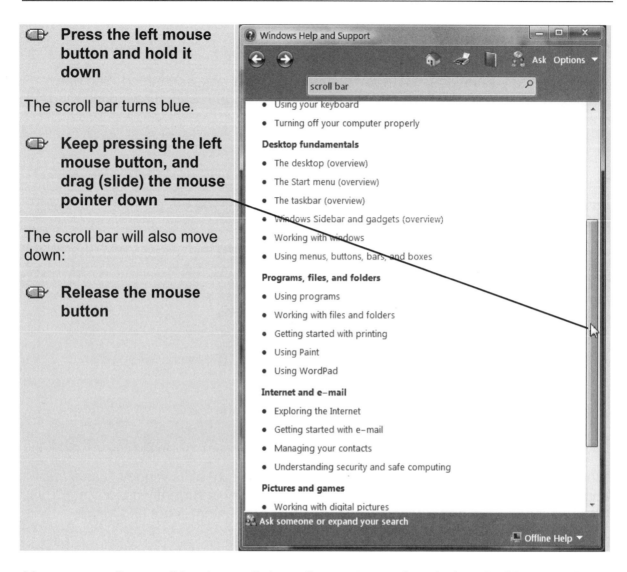

You can use the scroll bar to scroll down the contents of a window, in this case, the topics listed under *Windows Basics: all topics*. These scroll up so that you can read through to the last lines in the list.

2.5 Using the Scroll Wheel of a Mouse

Many mice nowadays include a scroll wheel between the buttons. If you see a scroll bar and your mouse has a scroll wheel, you can use this wheel to scroll through documents and web pages.

The scroll wheel between the
left and right mouse button:

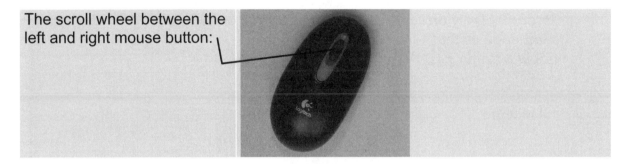

You can roll the wheel gently using your index finger.
Do not press the wheel! On some mice, the scroll wheel can be pressed to act as a third button. This is not necessary here.
Try using the scroll wheel now:

☞ **Click somewhere in the page, for example in the white area (not on any text)**

Now you can scroll:

☞ **Roll the wheel gently using your index finger**

To scroll down:

☞ **Roll the wheel gently backward (toward you)**

To scroll up:

☞ **Roll the wheel gently forward (away from you)**

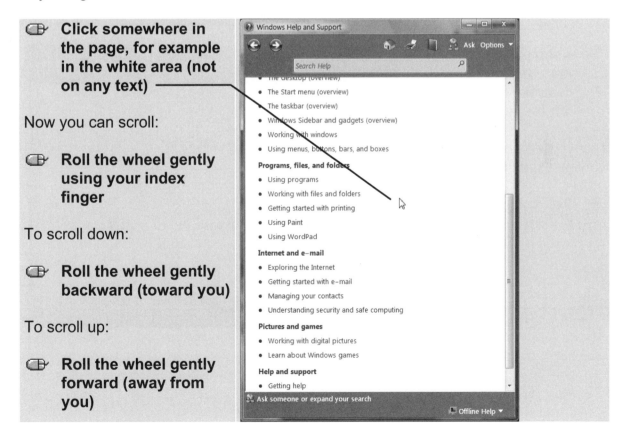

You see the page moving up and down and the scroll bar along with it.

2.6 Enlarging and Reducing a Window

When a window is not maximized, you can change its size by dragging the edges of the window's frame with the mouse. Try it:

Place the mouse pointer precisely on the left edge of the window's frame

The mouse pointer changes into a double arrow ⟺:

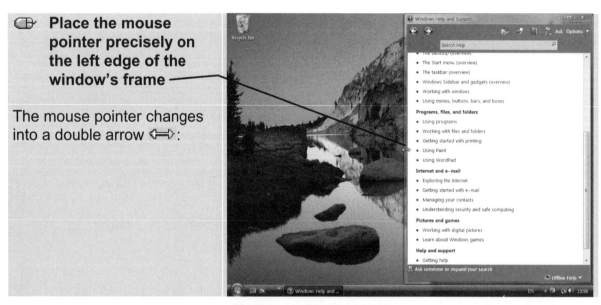

Keep pressing the left mouse button and drag the mouse to the left

You will see the size of the window expand.

Release the mouse button

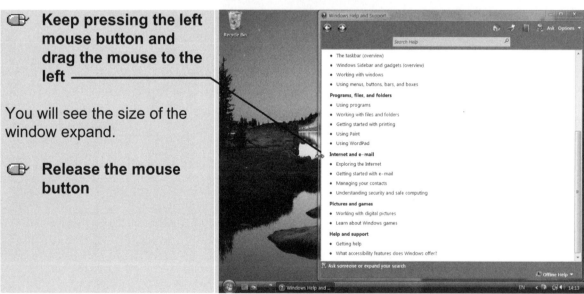

By dragging with the mouse, you can also change the height of a window.
Remember: this is only possible when the window is not maximized.

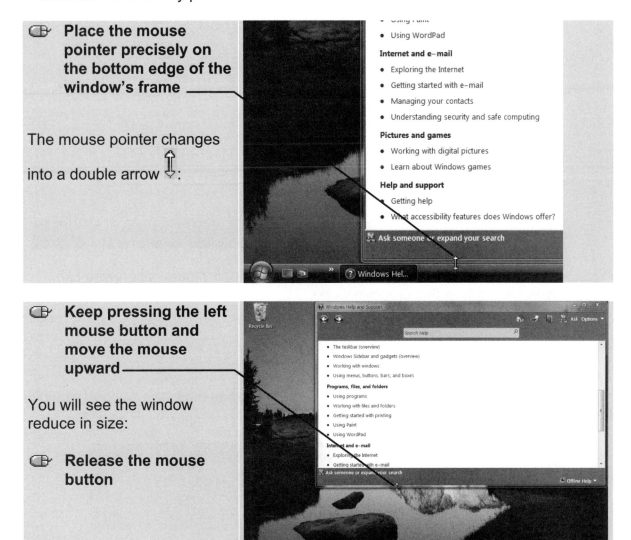

☞ **Place the mouse pointer precisely on the bottom edge of the window's frame**

The mouse pointer changes into a double arrow ⇕:

☞ **Keep pressing the left mouse button and move the mouse upward**

You will see the window reduce in size:

☞ **Release the mouse button**

For the next few steps, it is handy to maximize the window so that it fills the screen:

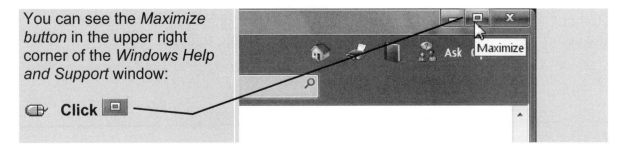

You can see the *Maximize button* in the upper right corner of the *Windows Help and Support* window:

☞ **Click** ▢

Now the window is maximized and fills the entire *Desktop*:

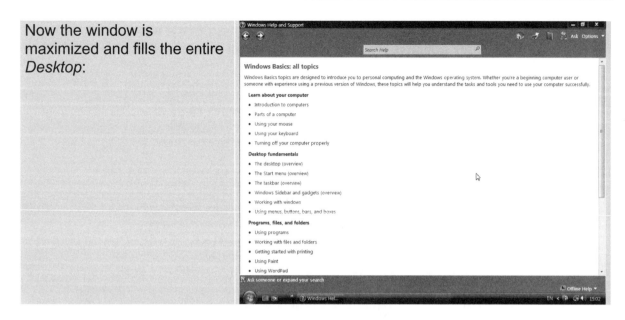

Because you already have the *Windows Help and Support* window open, you can take a closer look at how this program works.

2.7 Back to the Beginning

It is easy to go back to the previous screen of the *Windows Help and Support* window by using the back and forward buttons.

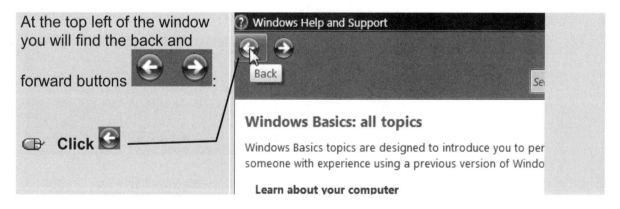

Remember: When you point to something, a small box often appears that describes the item. This is very handy when you are not sure where to click.

You are now back at the beginning of the *Windows Help and Support* program:

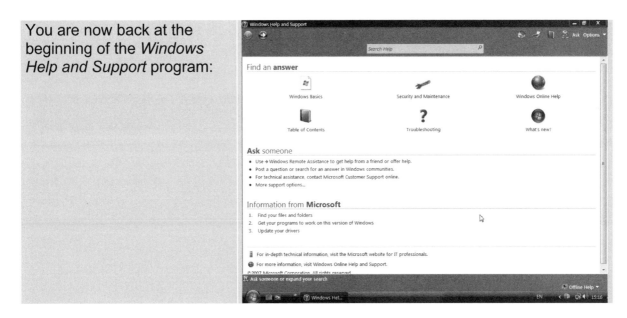

You will see *Windows Vista* has many windows with these back and forward buttons . You will learn more about these later in the book.

2.8 Using Windows Help and Support

Windows Help and Support is an extensive digital manual for *Windows Vista*.

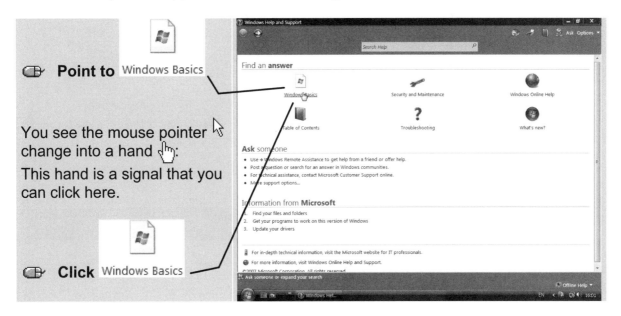

Point to Windows Basics

You see the mouse pointer change into a hand:
This hand is a signal that you can click here.

Click Windows Basics

Windows Basics topics are designed to introduce you to personal computing and the *Windows* operating system. By clicking the topics, you can find the information you need.

Let's take a look:

Click • Using your mouse

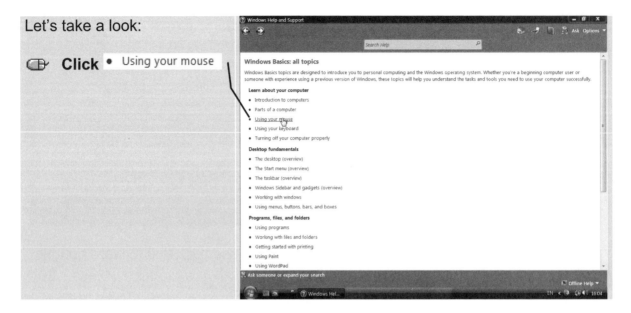

The relevant information is now displayed:

You can read the entire article by using the scroll bar or your scroll wheel.
You can also click a topic on the right side of the page:

Click
• Pointing, clicking, and dragging

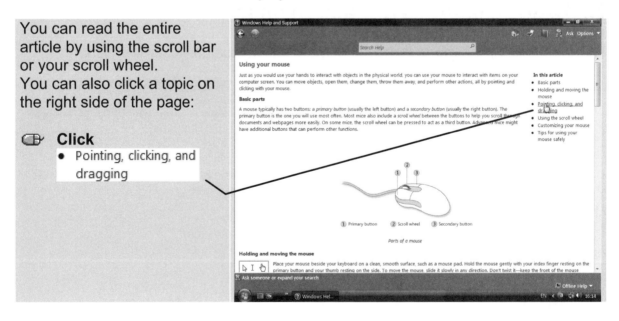

Now information about
pointing, clicking and
dragging appears:

Notice that some of the words
in the text are colored green.
These words can be clicked.

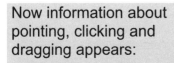 **Click** desktop.

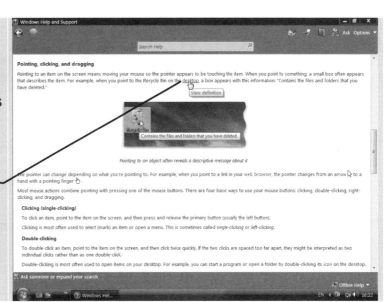

A box with a description
about the word appears:

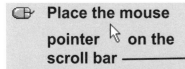 **Click anywhere
outside of this box**

The box will disappear.

appears to be touching the item. When you point to something, a small b
he desktop, a box appears with this information: "Contains the files and fc

> The work area on a computer screen that simulates the top of an
> actual desk. You can arrange icons on the desktop, such as the
> Recycle Bin and shortcuts to programs, files, folders, and various
> types of documents, just as you would arrange real objects on
> top of a desk.

nd folders that you have deleted.

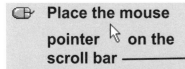 **Place the mouse
pointer ⬚ on the
scroll bar**

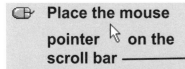 **Press the left mouse
button and drag the
scroll bar to the top of
the page**

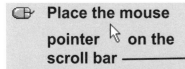 **Release the mouse
button**

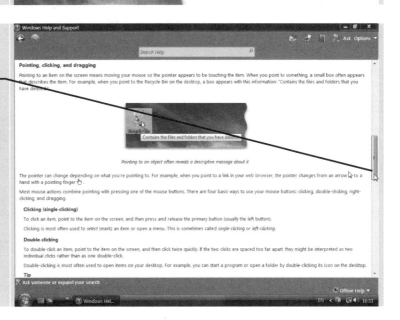

You now see the top of the page again:

To return to the previous page:

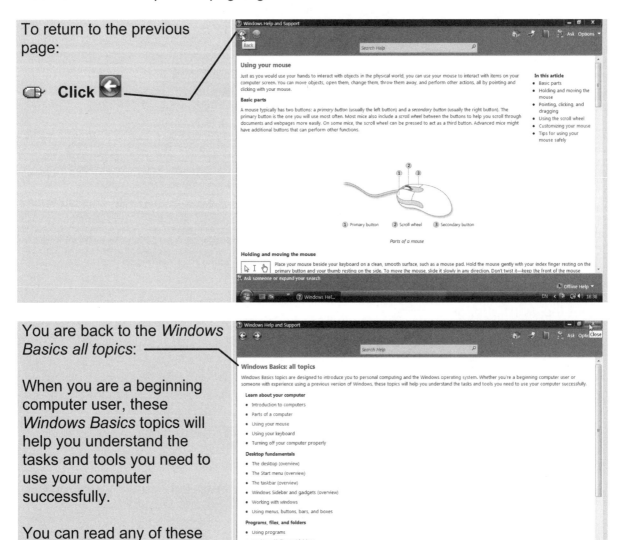

⊞ **Click** ⬅

You are back to the *Windows Basics all topics*:

When you are a beginning computer user, these *Windows Basics* topics will help you understand the tasks and tools you need to use your computer successfully.

You can read any of these topics later at your own leisure.

Now you can close the *Windows Help and Support* window.

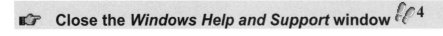
☞ **Close the *Windows Help and Support* window** 🦶⁴

Now once again you see the *Desktop* for *Windows Vista:*

 Tip

The previous size of the *Help and Support* window
Windows Vista "remembers" the size that you gave to the *Windows Help and Support* window. When you start the *Windows Help and Support* program, the window will automatically be maximized.

However, if you click on the restore button , the window will appear in the size that you gave it the last time you used it.

2.9 Double-Clicking

Until now, you have clicked only once on a word, a command or a button. However, in *Windows Vista* you sometimes need to *double-click* on things, such as this icon at the upper left of your *Desktop*:

Recycle Bin

Double-clicking is most often used to open items on your desktop. For example, you can start a program or open a folder by double-clicking its icon on the desktop.
This is how to double-click:

- Point to something with the mouse pointer.

- Press the left mouse button **twice in rapid succession**.

A program can be quickly started with an icon. Try to double-click an icon.

Point to the icon

Double-click

Recycle Bin

Now you see this window:

⇨ **Please note:**

When double-clicking, it is important that you **do not move the mouse** between the two clicks. When you do, *Windows* interprets this as two single clicks on two different spots. You might need to try a few times before double-clicking works for you.

HELP! Double-clicking will not work.

Try the following trick:

 **Click once on the icon**

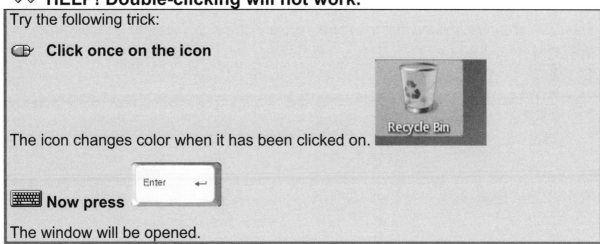

The icon changes color when it has been clicked on.

Now press Enter ⏎

The window will be opened.

☞ **Close the *Recycle Bin* window** ✏4

Now try again:

☞ **Double-click the *Recycle Bin* icon again**

You see this window again:

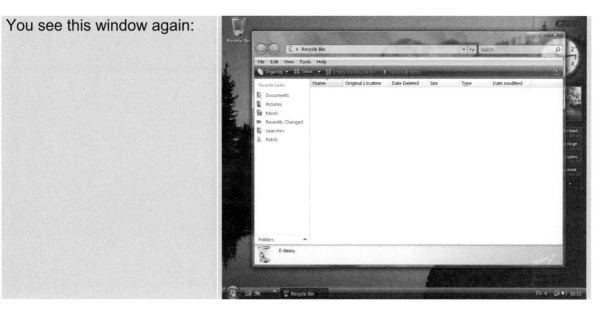

2.10 The Many Faces of a Window

You have probably noticed that the screenshots in this book sometimes differ from what you see on your screen. This is in part due to the fact that *Windows Vista* can be customized. Now you will open a window where this is very evident:

Click Folders

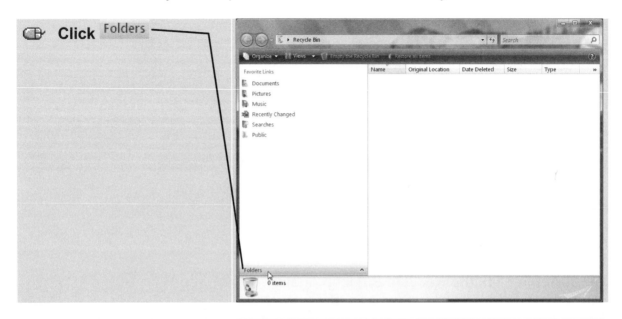

From the list under the title *Folders* choose *Computer:*

Click Computer

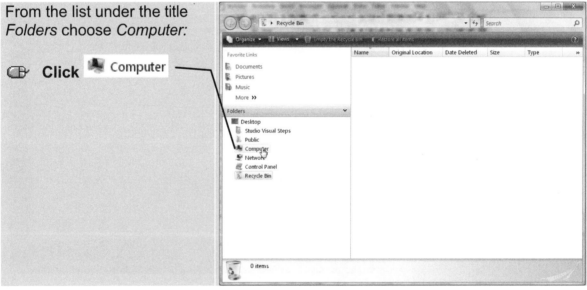

In the right pane of the window you see the various parts of your computer:

The window that your see on your own computer will probably differ from the one pictured here.

You may have other types of hardware devices.

The manner in which the items are displayed may also be different.

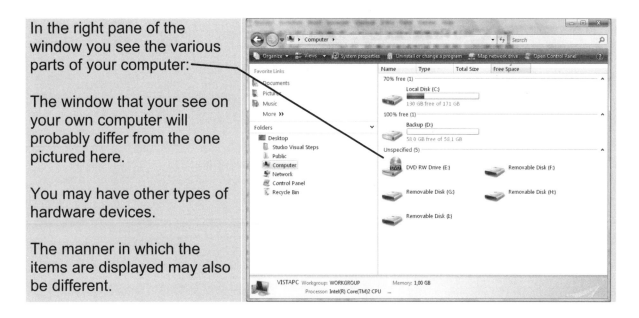

2.11 Changing the View

You can change the appearance of your files and folders in the window.

In the menu bar you see a split button . Clicking the main part of the button performs a command, whereas clicking the arrow opens a menu with more options.

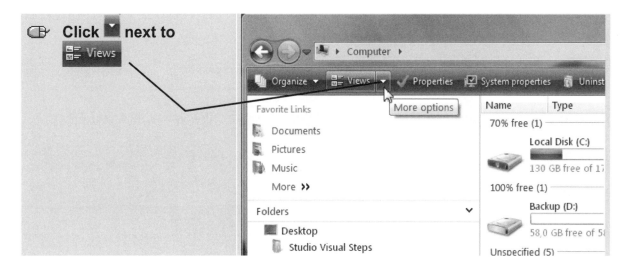

A menu appears with several options:

☞ **Click** List

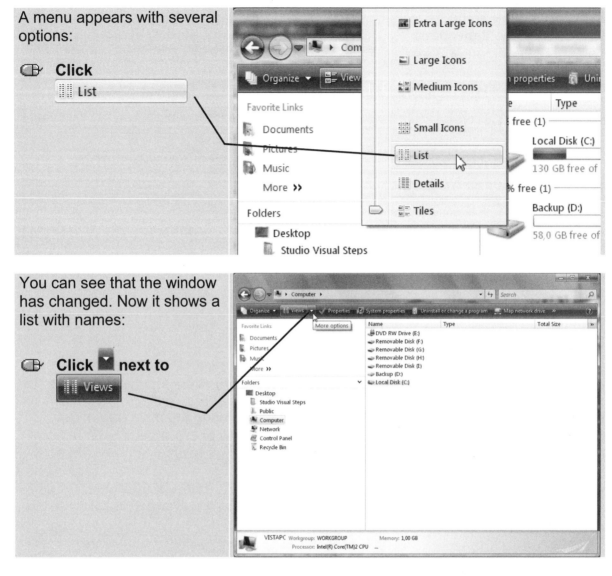

You can see that the window has changed. Now it shows a list with names:

☞ **Click** ▼ next to Views

Instead of clicking, you can also drag the slider ⮑ toward the value that you want:

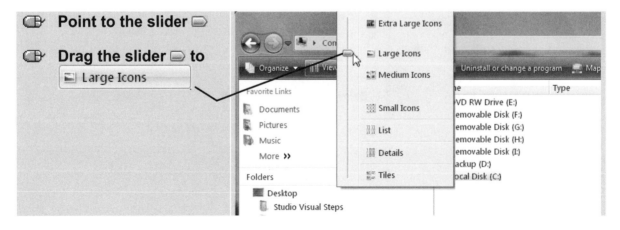

☞ **Point to the slider** ⮑

☞ **Drag the slider** ⮑ **to** Large Icons

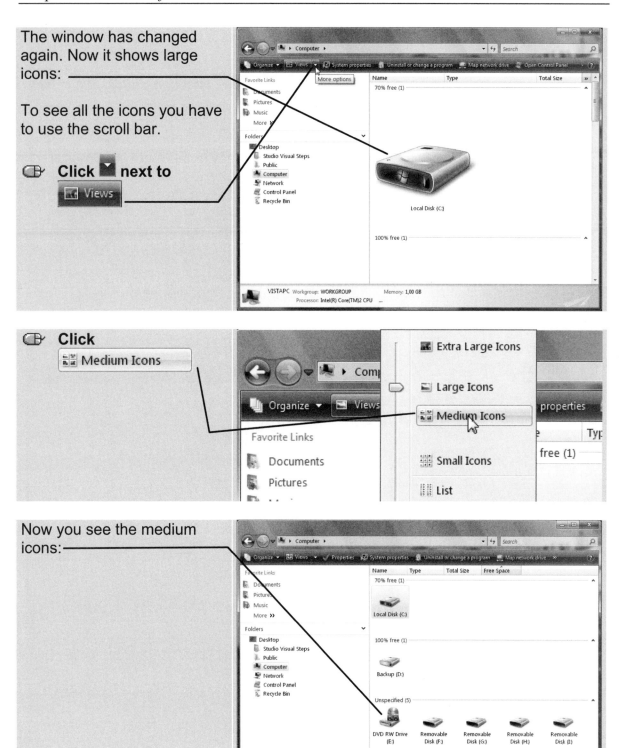

The window has changed again. Now it shows large icons:

To see all the icons you have to use the scroll bar.

Click ▼ next to ⊞ Views

Click ⊞ Medium Icons

Now you see the medium icons:

Nearly every *Windows Vista* window has a button ⊞ Views ▼ with which its appearance can be changed. You can use this to choose the appearance that you like best.

2.12 Right-Clicking

The last topic we will discuss in this chapter is the mouse action: *right-clicking.* After all, there is a reason why the mouse has two buttons.
Right-clicking is done like this:

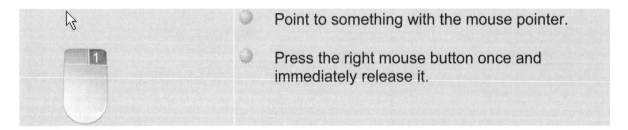

| | Point to something with the mouse pointer. |
| | Press the right mouse button once and immediately release it. |

This is the same action as the regular click, but with the right mouse button.
However, the right mouse button has an entirely different function, as you will see:

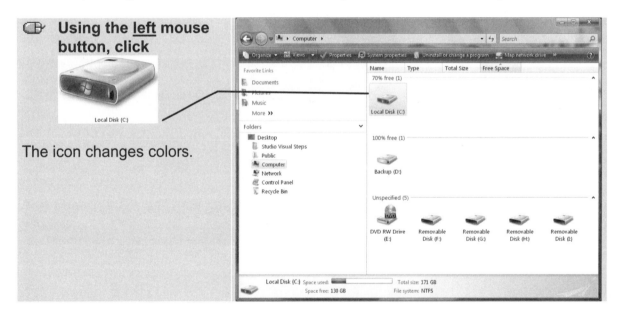

Using the left mouse button, click

The icon changes colors.

Now use the right mouse button, click

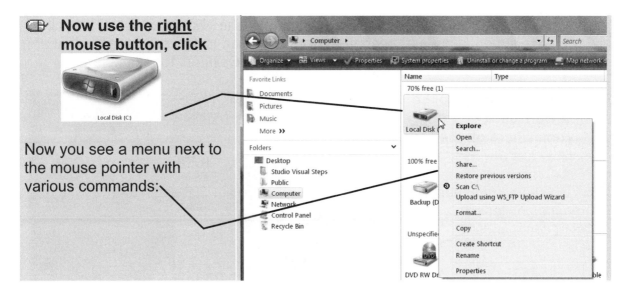

Now you see a menu next to the mouse pointer with various commands:

This is how to make this menu disappear:

Using the left mouse button, click an empty space somewhere on the screen

You see that the menu has disappeared:

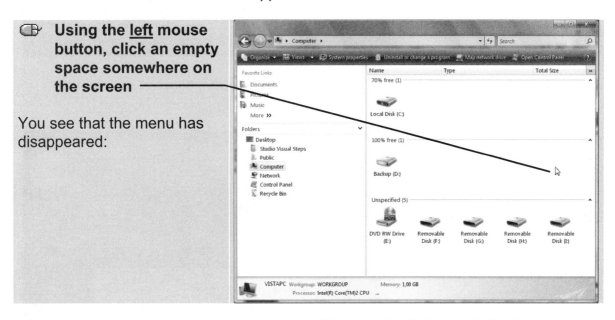

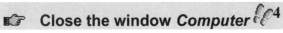 **Close the window** *Computer*

You can right-click icons, folders and many other items in *Windows Vista*. This will always make a menu appear. These menus can be used to enter commands that are related to the item you clicked. You can right-click the *Desktop*, for example:

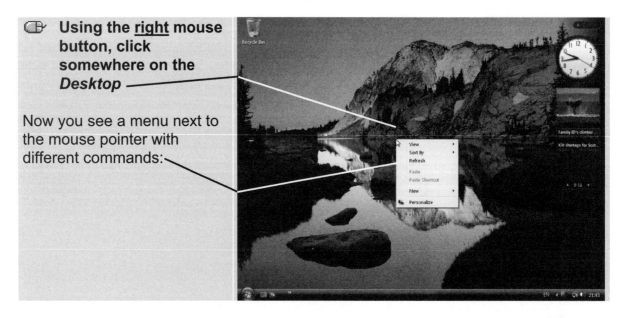

Using the right mouse button, click somewhere on the Desktop ———

Now you see a menu next to the mouse pointer with different commands:

If you want to select a command from a menu of this type, you must use the left mouse button.

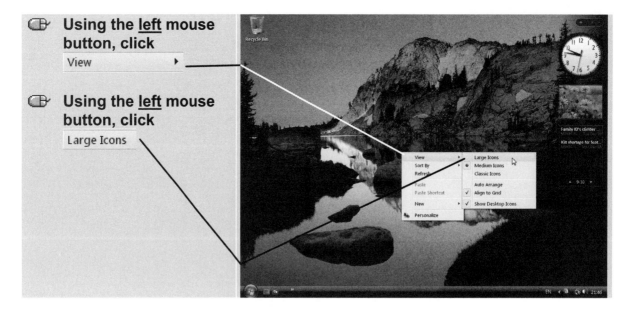

Using the left mouse button, click
View ▶

Using the left mouse button, click
Large Icons

Notice that the icon of the *Recycle Bin* is now enlarged:

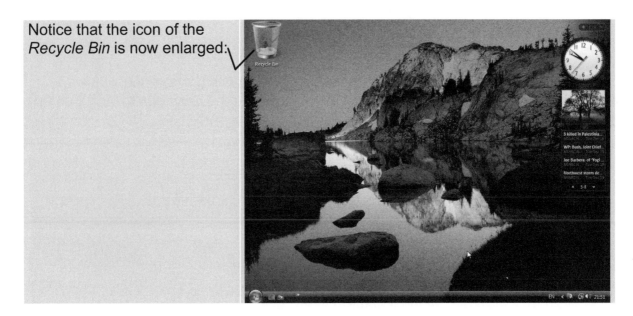

Right-clicking an item usually displays a *menu*: a list of things you can do with the item.

We have introduced you to all four mouse actions. You have also seen various parts of *Windows Vista*. You can practice what you have learned with the following exercises.

2.13 Exercises

The following exercises will help you master what you have just learned. Have you forgotten how to do something? Use the number beside the footsteps to look it up in the appendix *How Do I Do That Again?*

Exercise: Dragging a Window

✔ Open the *Calculator*. 𝓁𝓁⁵

✔ Drag the *Calculator* window to the middle. 𝓁𝓁¹¹

✔ Drag the *Calculator* window to the bottom right. 𝓁𝓁¹¹

✔ Drag the *Calculator* window to the top left. 𝓁𝓁¹¹

✔ Close the *Calculator* window. 𝓁𝓁⁴

Exercise: Clicking, Double-Clicking and Dragging

✔ Open the *Recycle Bin*. 𝓁𝓁¹⁰

✔ Drag the *Recycle Bin* window to the top left of the screen. 𝓁𝓁¹¹

✔ Close the *Recycle Bin* window. 𝓁𝓁⁴

✔ Open the *Windows Help and Support* window. 𝓁𝓁⁶

✔ Maximize the size of the *Windows Help and Support* window. 𝓁𝓁²

✔ Restore the size of the *Windows Help and Support* window to its the previous size. 𝓁𝓁³

✔ Close the *Windows Help and Support* window. 𝓁𝓁⁴

Exercise: Left- and Right-Clicking

✔ Using the **right** mouse button, click somewhere on the *Desktop*.

✔ Using the **left** mouse button, click View ▸ .

✔ Using the **left** mouse button, click Medium Icons .

✔ Using the **right** mouse button, click the icon Recycle Bin .

✔ Using the **left** mouse button, click Open .

✔ Close the *Recycle Bin* window. 👣4

Exercise: Using Windows Help and Support

✔ Open the *Windows Help and Support* window. 👣6

✔ Open Windows Basics . 👣21

✔ Select the topic • Introduction to computers and read the information. Do not forget to use the scroll bar.

✔ Go back to the previous page by clicking ⬅.

✔ Select the topic • Parts of a computer and read the information. Do not forget to use the scroll bar.

✔ Go back to the previous page by clicking ⬅.

✔ Select the topic • Using your mouse and read the information. Do not forget to use the scroll bar.

✔ Close the *Windows Help and Support* window. 👣4

2.14 Background Information

Dictionary

Back and forward buttons	Buttons you use to go back or forward to a (web)page or screen you have already looked at.
Click	Press and release the primary mouse button (usually the left button). Clicking is most often used to select (mark) an item or open a menu. This is sometimes called single-clicking or left-clicking.
Double-click	Press and release the left mouse button twice in rapid succession. The mouse action that is most often used to open items on your *Desktop*. For example, you can start a program or open a folder by double-clicking its icon on the *Desktop*.
Drag	To move an item on the screen by selecting the item and then pressing and holding down the left mouse button while sliding or moving the mouse. For example, you can move a window to another location on the *Desktop* by dragging its title bar.
Right-click	Press and release the right mouse button. Right-clicking an item usually displays a list of things you can do with the item. For example, when you right-click the *Recycle Bin* on your desktop, *Windows* displays a menu allowing you to open it, empty it, delete it, or see its properties. If you are not sure what to do with something, right-click it.
Scroll bar	When a document, web page, or picture exceeds the size of its window, scroll bars appear to allow you to see the information that is currently out of view. Drag a scroll box up, down, left, or right to scroll the window in that direction.
Scroll wheel	Small wheel between the two buttons of a mouse. If your mouse has a scroll wheel, you can use it to scroll through documents and web pages. To scroll down, roll the wheel backward (toward you); scroll up: roll the wheel forward (away from you).
Slider	A slider lets you adjust a setting along a range of values. A slider can be dragged.

Windows Help and Support	The built-in help system for *Windows*. It's a place to get quick answers to common questions, suggestions for troubleshooting, and instructions for how to do things. To open it: click the *Start button* and then click *Help and Support*.

Source: Windows Help and Support

The parts of the computer

The large cabinet that holds the computer itself is called the computer case or housing:

The case holds the computer's memory and the processor chip that makes everything work.
This computer case also holds the CD drive and/or DVD drive.

Computer case

Every computer has a monitor. The quality of the screen is much better than that of a regular television. Letters and graphic elements are therefore extremely sharp and easy to read.
The size of the computer screen is expressed in *inches*. The minimum size of a computer screen these days is 17 inches. Larger screens measuring 19 or 21 inches are becoming more popular.

Other hardware elements are the keyboard, the mouse, the speakers and the printer.

TFT monitor

A portable computer or *laptop* is a complete system. The case, the keyboard, the mouse, and the display are integrated into a single unit.

The flat display is flipped up when the laptop is being used.

Laptop

How does a traditional mouse work?
The standard mouse is actually relatively simple in
terms of technology. Turn the mouse over.
You can see a little ball that rolls as the mouse is
moved over the tabletop.

If you take the ball out, you can see three little wheels
inside that register the movements of the ball and
transmit these to the computer.
When the mouse slides, the ball rolls and the wheels
on the inside move.

A variation on this mouse uses an infrared light (LED)
or laser light instead of a ball.

2.15 Tips

 Tip

Proper mouse placement
Sometimes the mouse will be too far from you on the tabletop or located at the edge of the mousepad.

In that case it is difficult to work with the mouse. It is almost as if the mouse is trying to get away! This is how you put the mouse back in the right place on the tabletop:

☞ **First move the mouse pointer to the middle of the screen**

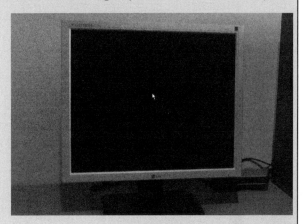

☞ **Now pick up the mouse**

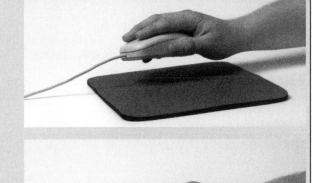

☞ **Put the mouse in the right place**

Tip

Are you left-handed?
Then use the mouse with your left hand. You can switch the settings for the mouse buttons to make your mouse more suitable for left-handed users.

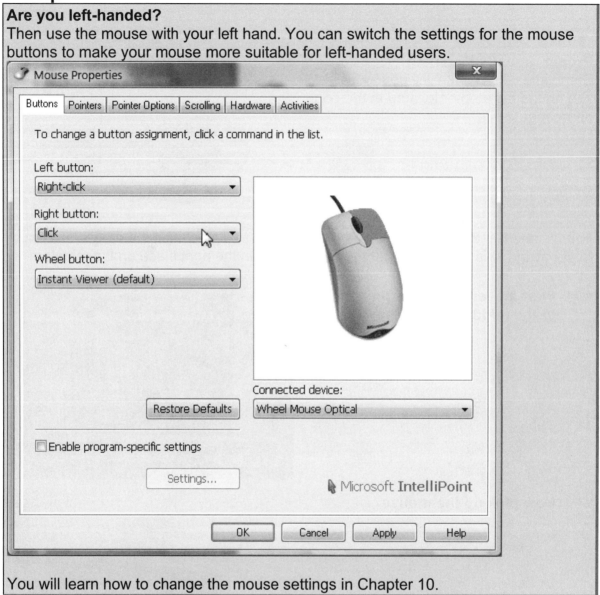

You will learn how to change the mouse settings in Chapter 10.

Tip

Windows Vista Demos: Desktop basics

Windows Vista Demos are narrated video demonstrations, designed to introduce you to personal computing. Watch as tasks are performed on screen. This is how you start the demo *Desktop basics*:

☞ **Click**

In the *Start menu*:

☞ **Click** `Help and Support`

At the top of the window:

⌨ **Type:** demo

☞ **Click** 🔍

In the search results:

☞ **Click** `7.   Demo: Desktop basics`

In the next window:

☞ **Click** `→ Watch the demo`

The program *Windows Media Player* opens and the demo starts playing:

☞ **Watch the demo**

To close *Windows Media Player*:

☞ **Click** X

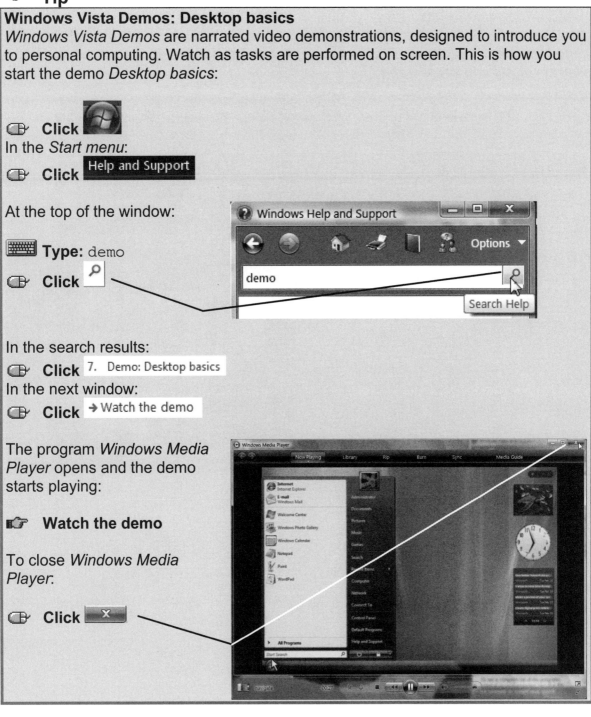

Tip

Using Windows Flip 3D
With *Windows Flip 3D* (available in *Windows Vista Home Premium* and *Windows Vista Ultimate)* you can quickly preview all of your open windows without having to click the *Taskbar buttons*.

To open *Flip 3D*:

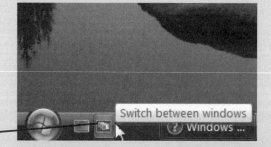

⌨ **Press** 🔲 **and** ⭾ Tab

or:

🖱 **Click** 🔲

Flip 3D displays your open windows in a stack. At the top of the stack, you'll see one open window.

To display a window:

🖱 **Click a window in the stack**

To close *Flip 3D*:

🖱 **Click outside the stack**

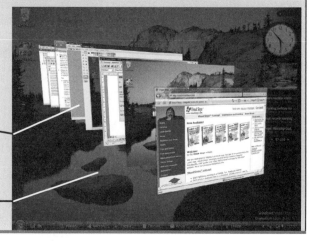

Tip

Working with a touchpad
Owners of a laptop can either use a computer mouse or the touchpad in order to move the pointer on the screen, and to click and drag.

A touchpad is used to move the pointer, using motions of the user's finger. It's a substitute for a computer mouse.

Touchpad:———

The buttons below or above the pad serve as standard mouse buttons: click (single-click with left mouse button) and right-click (using right mouse button).
On this laptop these buttons are below the touchpad:

Depending on the model of touchpad, you may also click by tapping your finger on the touchpad.

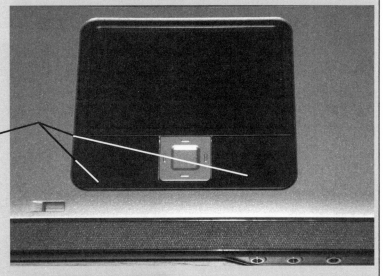

This model has also a special button for dragging the scroll bar of a window:

- Continue reading on the next page -

Some touchpads also have "hotspots": locations on the touchpad that indicate user intentions other than pointing. For example, on certain touchpads, moving your finger along the right edge of the touch pad will control the scrollbar in a vertical direction for the window that is presently *active*. Moving the finger on the bottom of the touchpad often scrolls in horizontal direction.

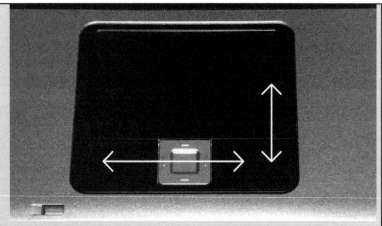

Some touchpads can emulate multiple mouse buttons by either tapping in a special corner of the pad, or by tapping with two or more fingers.

☞ **Read your instruction manual to learn what types of features are available for your specific laptop's touchpad.**

As soon as you have read the information, you can try it:

Moving the pointer

☞ **Put your finger on the right side of the touchpad**

☞ **Slide your finger slowly to the left**

The pointer ⇖ on the screen moves with it.

☞ **Slide your finger slowly in different directions**

The pointer ⇖ on the screen moves with it.

- Continue reading on the next page -

☞ **Put your finger on the touchpad**

☞ **Slide your finger slowly over the touchpad**

☞ **Point to**

Is the touchpad too small and your finger touches the edge? Lift your finger, reposition it and continue.

Is the pointer on the *Start button?* Now you can click the *Start button* by tapping once on the touchpad or by using the special button below, above or beside the touchpad.

☞ **Lift your finger and tap once**

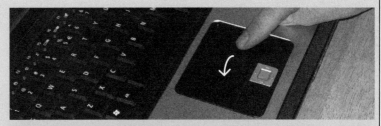

It has to be a quick tap.

or

☞ **Lift your finger and press the left button**

The *Start menu* will appear.

☞ **Point to** All Programs
☞ **Lift your finger and tap once**
or
☞ **Lift your finger and press the left button**

Go on:

☞ **Point to** Accessories
☞ **Lift your finger and tap once**
or
☞ **Lift your finger and press the left button**

Go on:

☞ **Point to** 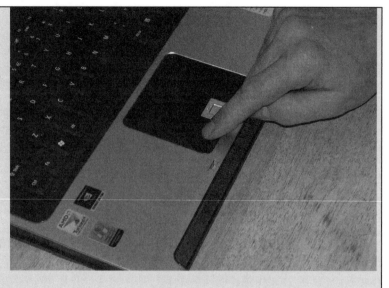 Calculator
☞ **Lift your finger and tap once**
or
☞ **Lift your finger and press the left button**

Now the *Calculator* window appears. To close it:
☞ **Point to** X
☞ **Lift your finger and tap once**
or
☞ **Lift your finger and press the left button**

Double-clicking
To practice double-clicking with the touchpad:

☞ **Point to** 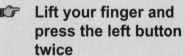 Recycle Bin

☞ **Lift your finger and tap twice**

or
☞ **Lift your finger and press the left button twice**

The *Recycle Bin* window appears.

☞ **Close the *Recycle Bin* window**

Scrolling
To practice scrolling with the touchpad:

☞ **Open *Windows Help and support***

There is a scroll bar in this window.

☞ **Point to the arrow ▾ below the scroll bar**

☞ **Tap once to move the scroll bar down**

☞ **Repeat this action**

or

☞ **Point to the middle of the window**

☞ **Slide your finger over the right scroll area of the touchpad**

or

☞ **Point to the middle of the window**

☞ **Press the scroll button**

You may have another button on your laptop.

☞ **Close the *Windows Help and support* window**

Right-clicking

To practice right-clicking:

☞ **Point to an empty area of the *Desktop***

☞ **Lift your finger and press the right button**

A menu appears. To close this menu:

☞ **Point beside the menu**

☞ **Lift your finger and tap once**

or

☞ **Lift your finger and press the left button**

Now you know the basics of using the touchpad of your laptop. Just like learning to work with the mouse takes time and patience so does learning to use the touchpad. With practice you will soon feel comfortable and have good control over your finger movements.

3. Keyboard Skills

Word processing is the application that made the *Personal Computer* (PC) so popular. It is also the most widely-used application. The typewriter era is long gone, thanks in part to how easy computers have made it to write and produce texts.

As a computer user, it is useful to have good keyboard and word processing skills. These skills are not only needed for writing letters or e-mail messages, for example, but also for various other things. A certain degree of keyboard skill is also necessary, because not everything can be done with the mouse.

Windows Vista has a simple word-processing program that you can use to practice typing. The program is called *WordPad* and was installed on your computer together with *Windows Vista*.

In this chapter, you will learn how to:

- open *WordPad*
- type using the keyboard
- correct a typing error
- type capital letters
- begin a new paragraph
- type various special characters
- move the cursor
- start a new document
- close *WordPad*

3.1 Opening WordPad

WordPad is a basic word-processing program that you can use to create and edit documents. You can open it by using the *Start* button:

The *WordPad* program is located in the folder named *Accessories*:

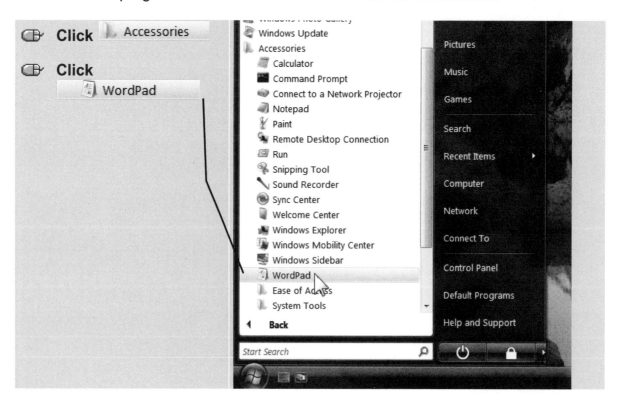

Now you see the empty
WordPad screen:

The text you type will appear
in the big white box. This box
is like a blank sheet of paper.

At the top left, you will see a
short blinking vertical line.
This is called the **cursor**:

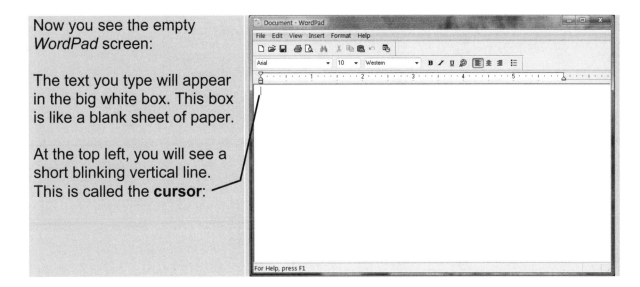

3.2 The Keyboard

A computer keyboard has over one hundred keys. That is much more than the old-
fashioned typewriter. When you look at the keyboard, you will see keys for letters and
numbers, as well as various other keys. You will learn how to use these keys in this
book.

The position of the letters and
punctuation marks is still the
same as on a typewriter:

At the bottom you see a large
key. This is called the space
bar:

The space bar is used to type
spaces (white space)
between words.

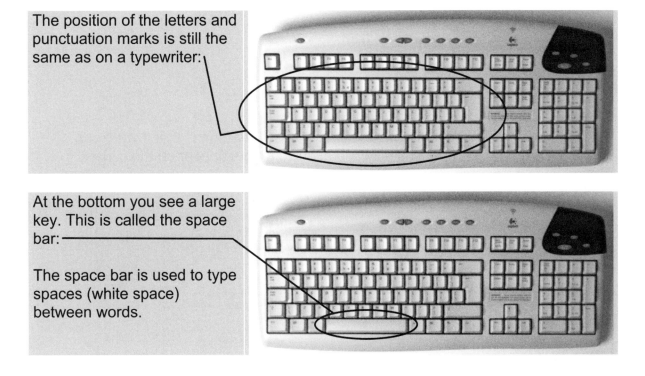

The keyboard of a laptop is almost the same:

Sometimes there are fewer keys on the right-hand side of the keyboard. This does not matter as these keys will not be used while working with this book.

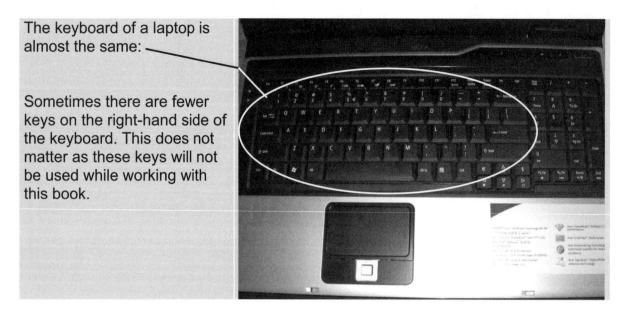

Now you can start typing. The letters will appear where the cursor is:

Type:
this is a first
line

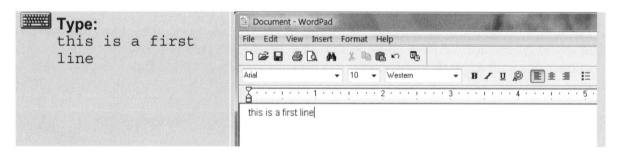

3.3 Repeat Keys

The keys on a computer keyboard are repeat keys. This means that if you keep pressing a key, you will automatically see multiple letters appear on the screen. Try it:

Press the key for the

letter "o" **and keep pressing it**

You see more and more o's appear:

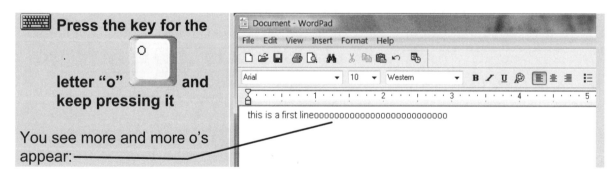

Luckily, it is easy to remove letters you do not need.

3.4 A Typing Error?

In this case, you typed the wrong letters **o** on purpose. But in the future you may press a wrong key by accident. You can remove wrong letters by pressing the **Backspace** key.

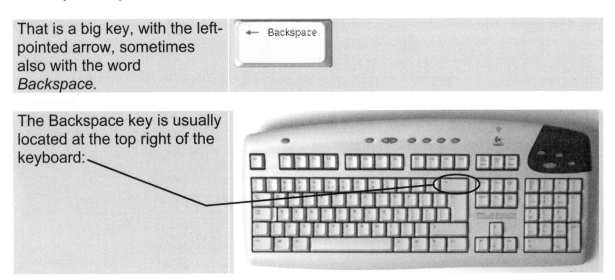

That is a big key, with the left-pointed arrow, sometimes also with the word *Backspace.*

The Backspace key is usually located at the top right of the keyboard:

The Backspace key is used to remove the letter to the left of the cursor. You can use it now to remove the letters o that you do not need, for example:

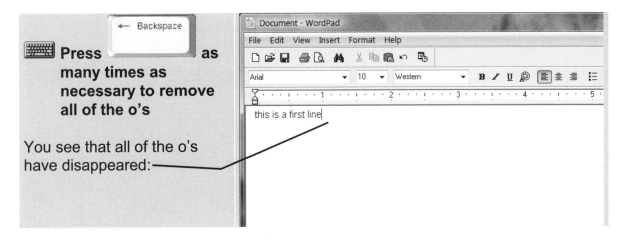

Press ... **as many times as necessary to remove all of the o's**

You see that all of the o's have disappeared:

⇨ **Please note:**

The Backspace key itself is also a repeat key. Do not press it too long or you will have to retype the text.

3.5 Capital Letters

Until now, you have only typed lower-case letters. But you can also type capital letters.

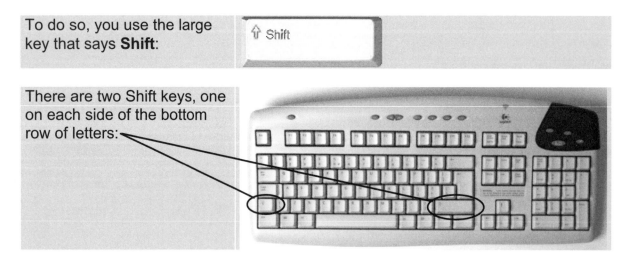

To do so, you use the large key that says **Shift**:	⇧ Shift

There are two Shift keys, one on each side of the bottom row of letters:

The Shift key is always used in combination with a letter, a number or a punctuation mark.

This is how to type a capital letter:
- press the Shift key and keep it pressed
- type the letter
- release the Shift key

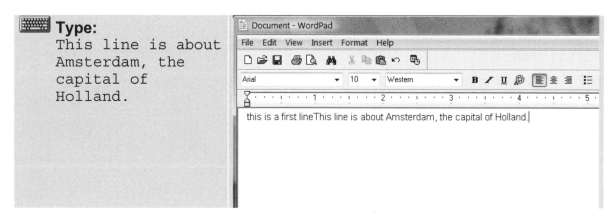

Type:
This line is about Amsterdam, the capital of Holland.

3.6 Words on the Next Line

In word processing programs, the program itself spreads the text over the page. If you type multiple sentences in a row, the text will automatically continue on the next line. Take a look:

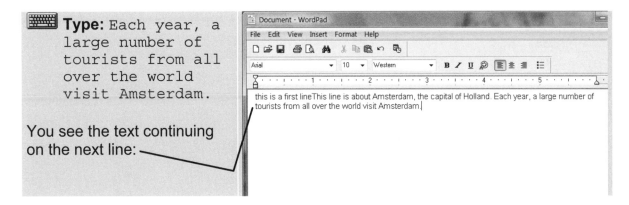

Type: Each year, a large number of tourists from all over the world visit Amsterdam.

You see the text continuing on the next line:

The computer always makes sure that even long sentences will fit nicely on the page. This is done automatically.

3.7 Beginning a New Paragraph

A series of sentences that are grouped together is called a paragraph. A new paragraph starts on a new line.

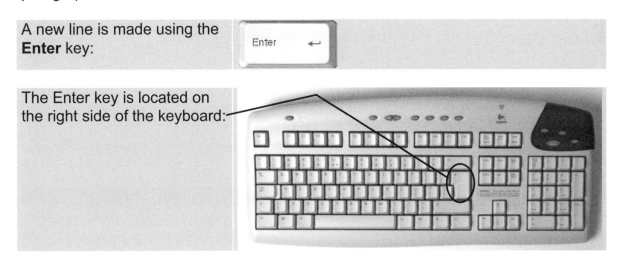

A new line is made using the **Enter** key:

The Enter key is located on the right side of the keyboard:

If you press the Enter key, the cursor (the little blinking line) will move down one line.

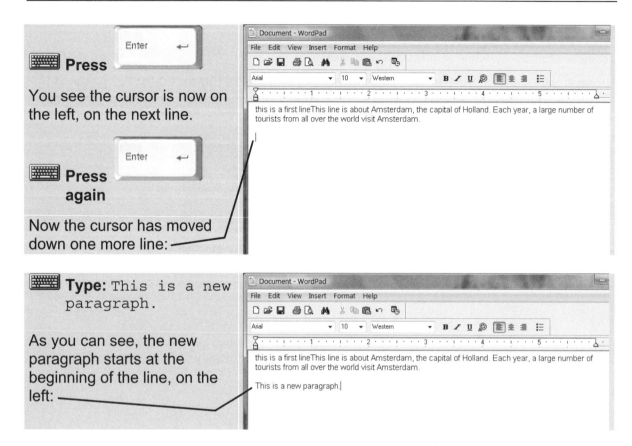

Press | Enter ⏎

You see the cursor is now on the left, on the next line.

Press again | Enter ⏎

Now the cursor has moved down one more line:

Type: This is a new paragraph.

As you can see, the new paragraph starts at the beginning of the line, on the left:

3.8 Colon or @?

The Shift key is also used to type various other characters.

Examples are: : ? @ * % $ + | } < ! ~ & ^

Many of these characters are located at the top of a key:

The character at the top of these keys is typed using the Shift key, just as you do for capital letters.

Type a space (press the spacebar once)

Type: ! ? : @ +

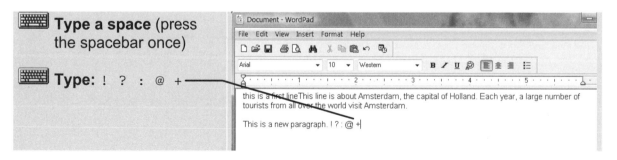

3.9 The Cursor Keys

Everyone makes a typing error now and then. You often do not notice until later, after you have typed more text. To remove the error with the Backspace key, you would have to remove all of the other text as well. Naturally, that is not very convenient. It is better to move the cursor to the place where the error is.

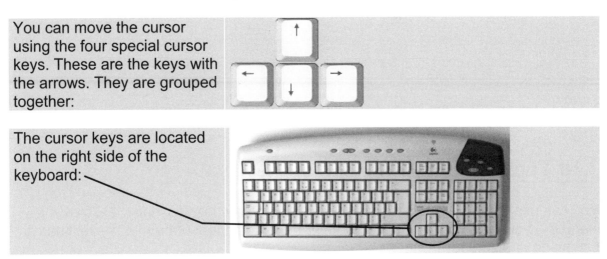

You can move the cursor using the four special cursor keys. These are the keys with the arrows. They are grouped together:

The cursor keys are located on the right side of the keyboard:

You can use these keys to move the cursor to the left or right, up and down, through the text.

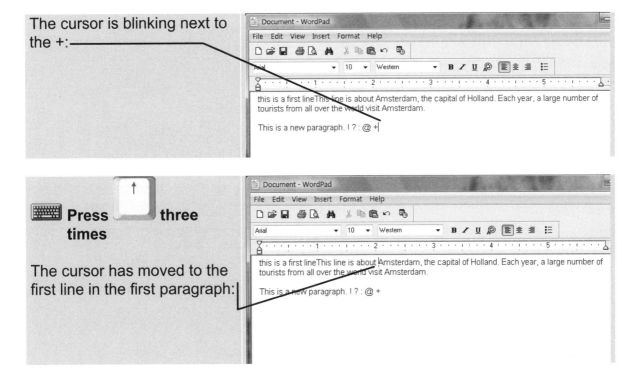

The cursor is blinking next to the +:

Press ↑ three times

The cursor has moved to the first line in the first paragraph:

If you move to the left or right, the cursor follows through the text:

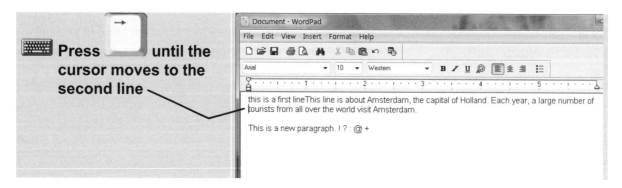

You see the cursor move to the right, through the text, until it jumps to the next line.

3.10 The Beginning and End of the Text

You can use the cursor keys to move the cursor to any position in the text that you want. But you cannot move the cursor over the entire sheet of paper. The text has a beginning and an end. Try it:

The cursor will not move any further than the beginning of the text. On some computers, the program may even sound a warning signal.

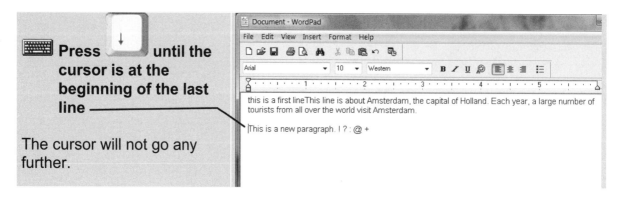

You can not move the cursor any further than the last letter or punctuation mark:

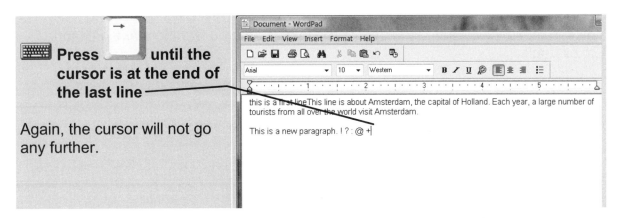

Press until the cursor is at the end of the last line

Again, the cursor will not go any further.

As you have seen, the cursor can not be moved further than the beginning or the end of the text you have typed. You can, of course, type more text there.

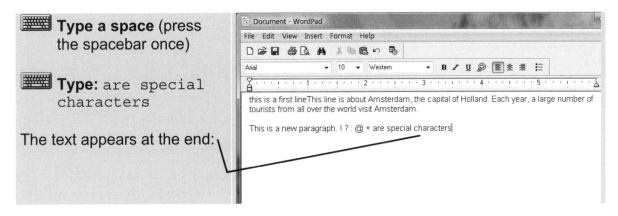

Type a space (press the spacebar once)

Type: are special characters

The text appears at the end:

Of course, you can always add empty lines to the text. The end of the text will then be the last (empty) line:

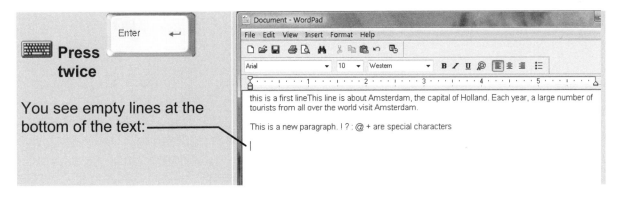

Press twice

You see empty lines at the bottom of the text:

Now you know how to move the cursor through the text. This is very handy when you want to correct errors or change the text.

3.11 Correcting Mistakes

You can move the cursor to the spot in the text where you want to make a change. For example:

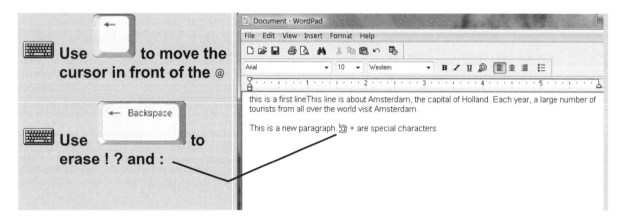

You can also change the first letter of the text into a capital:

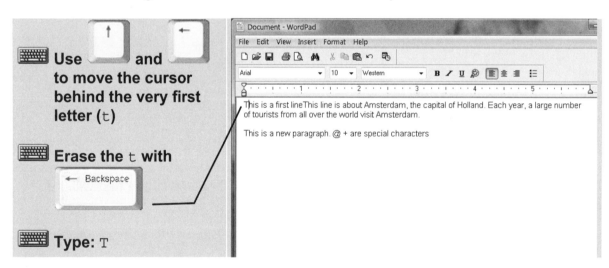

3.12 Removing Empty Lines

You can remove empty lines the same way. Move the cursor to an empty line and press the Backspace key:

Use ↓ and ← to move the cursor to the beginning of the fourth line

Press Backspace

The empty line is removed.

3.13 Moving Quickly through Text

You have now used the most important keys for word processing. However, there are some other very useful keys on your keyboard. There are two special keys that will move the cursor through the text even faster.

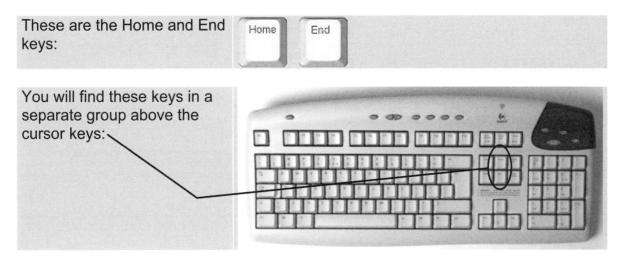

These are the Home and End keys:

You will find these keys in a separate group above the cursor keys:

The Home key is used to move the cursor to the beginning of a line, and the End key is used to move it to the end of a line. In other words: to jump from here to there. Try it:

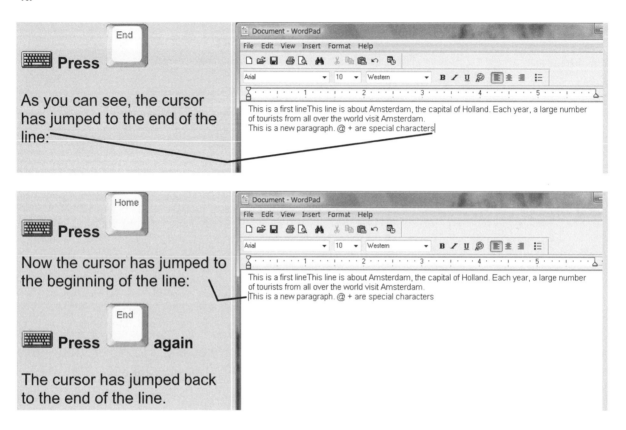

3.14 Starting a New Document

You have now practiced enough with the keyboard. It is time to start with a new, blank document. This is how:

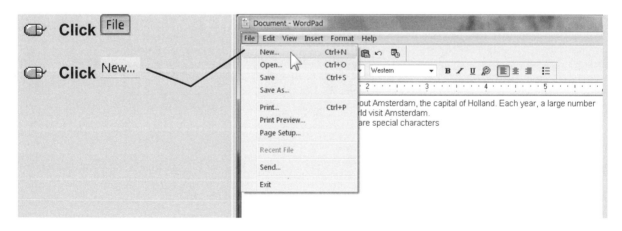

WordPad asks you what kind of file you want.
The standard option *Rich Text Document* is what you want this time.

Click OK

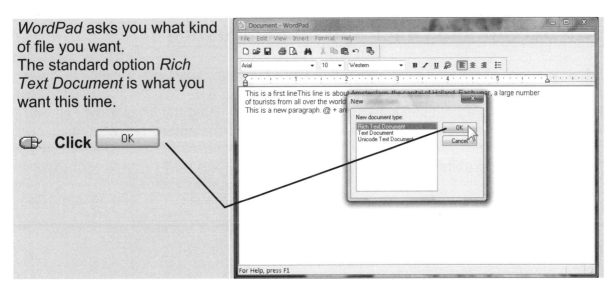

WordPad now asks you whether you want to save the changes to your practice text. You do not need to, so:

Click Don't Save

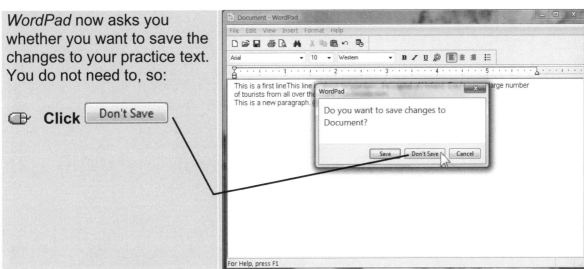

You now have a new, blank document, just like a fresh sheet of paper:

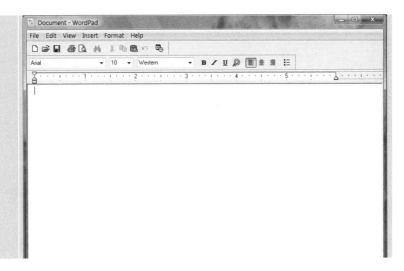

3.15 Accents and Other Special Punctuation

When you look at the keyboard, you will not see any letter keys with accents or other special punctuation such as ç, ñ or é.
But these letters are not difficult to type. You do this by using the keys known as the "dead" keys, they are the keys commonly used to generate letters with accents:

These keys are used in combination with the letter to which the special punctuation is to be added. For example:

Try it:

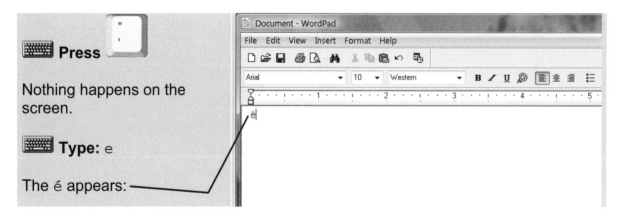

The keys are called "dead" because nothing happens when you press them.
A character does not appear until after you press another key.

Now try to make another letter, such as the ñ. It is a bit more complicated because you have to use the Shift key in order to type the ~.

HELP! It is not working.

If you are not able to type accents, take a look at **Appendix C**, **Changing Your Keyboard Settings**, on page 393.

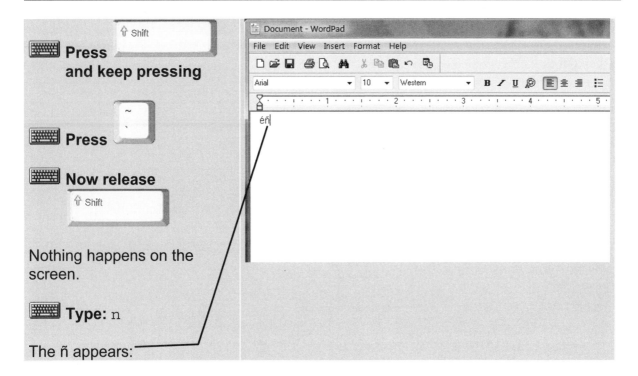

Press and keep pressing

Press

Now release

Nothing happens on the screen.

Type: n

The ñ appears:

This is how you type special letters, such as é, è, ç or ñ.

3.16 Typing Apostrophes

If the key for an apostrophe is dead, how can you type an apostrophe?
This is done using the key together with the space bar. Try it:

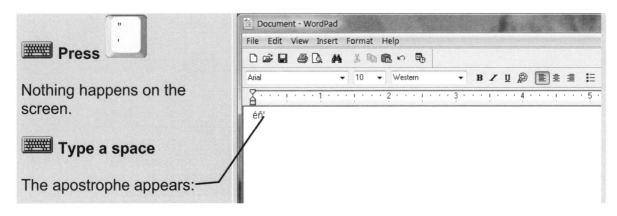

Press

Nothing happens on the screen.

Type a space

The apostrophe appears:

3.17 Closing WordPad

Now you can close the *WordPad* program. This is how:

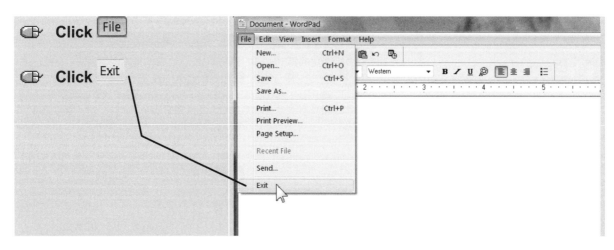

Click File

Click Exit

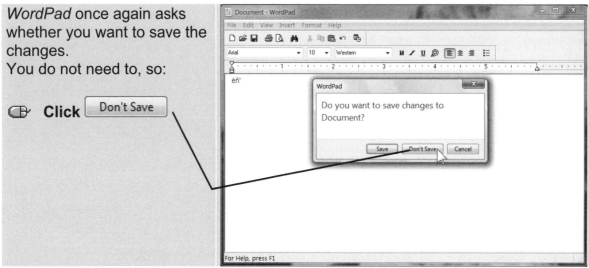

WordPad once again asks whether you want to save the changes.
You do not need to, so:

Click Don't Save

In the next chapter you will learn how to save a document, such as a letter. For the time being, you do not need to save the practice texts.

3.18 Exercises

The following exercises will help you master what you have just learned. Have you forgotten how to do something? Use the number beside the footsteps to look it up in the appendix *How Do I Do That Again?*

Exercise: Typing Text

✔ Open *WordPad*. 14

✔ Type the following text:
```
Canberra is the capital of Australia.
Canberra is exactly halfway between Sydney and Melbourne,
two other large cities.
```

✔ Move the cursor to the end of the paragraph. 41

✔ Now make a new, empty line. 42

✔ Type the following text:
```
Most people think that Sydney is the capital.
```

✔ Move the cursor to the end of the last line of the text. 41 Type a space.

✔ Type the following text:
```
For a long time, people argued about whether Sydney or
Melbourne should be the capital.
They finally decided to pick the city in between the two.
```

✔ In the last sentence, erase the first **the** and type **a** in the same place. 43
```
They finally decided to pick ~~the~~ city in between the two.
```

✔ This is what the practice text looks like now:

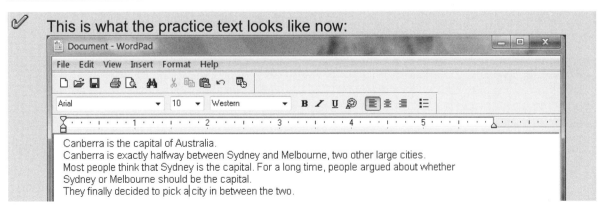

✔ Move the cursor to the beginning of the line. $\ell\ell$40

✔ Move the cursor to the end of the line. $\ell\ell$41

✔ Start a new document and do not save the changes. $\ell\ell$18

✔ Close *WordPad*. $\ell\ell$15

Exercise: Corrections

With this exercise, you can practice correcting typing errors.

✔ Open *WordPad*. $\ell\ell$14

✔ Maximize the *WordPad* window. $\ell\ell$2

✔ Type the following text:
Many people drink tea in the us. It is not as important hear as in other contries where a ceremony is made of drinkingtee, like in japan. They pay much closer attention to the qality of the te. Other exampels of these countries are china and Ingland.

✔ Correct the following mistakes:
Many people drink tea in the **US**. It is not as important he**re** as in other co**u**ntries where a ceremony is made of drinking te**a**, like in **J**apan. They pay much closer attention to the q**u**ality of the te**a**. Other examp**le**s of these countries are **C**hina and **E**ngland.

✔ Start a new text and do not save the changes. $\ell\ell$18

✔ Close *WordPad*. $\ell\ell$15

3.19 Background Information

Dictionary	
Cursor	Short blinking line that signals where text will appear.
Cursor keys	Move the cursor left, right, up or down through a text.
Dead key	A key that produces no output when pressed, but which modifies the output of the next key pressed.
Empty line	Line with no text.
Keyboard	The main input device used to communicate with the computer, similar to a typewriter keyboard but with extra function keys.
Paragraph	A paragraph is a section in a piece of writing, usually highlighting a particular point or topic. The start of a paragraph is indicated by beginning on a new line using the Enter key (or hard return) and may include indentation. The paragraph ends by using the Enter key. It consists of at least one sentence.
Repeat keys	Keys that keep giving characters while being pressed.
Space bar	Large key used to type spaces between words.
WordPad	A text-editing program you can use to create and edit documents.

Source: Windows Help and Support

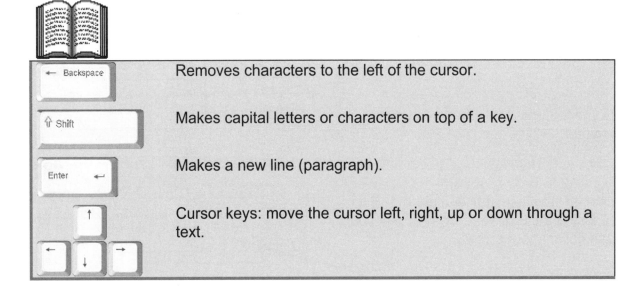

← Backspace	Removes characters to the left of the cursor.
⇧ Shift	Makes capital letters or characters on top of a key.
Enter ↵	Makes a new line (paragraph).
↑ ← ↓ →	Cursor keys: move the cursor left, right, up or down through a text.

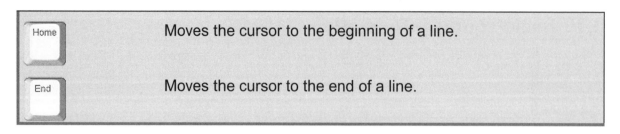 **Home**	Moves the cursor to the beginning of a line.
End	Moves the cursor to the end of a line.

Typing skills

It is certainly not necessary to learn to type like a professional typist in order to work with the computer. Most people have never learned to type, but learn as they go, with two or sometimes four fingers. A time comes when you can quickly find any key and then increase your typing speed.

It is striking that, despite all of the innovations of the computer era, the arrangement of the keyboard is still virtually the same as that of the typewriter.

The normal arrangement used in the United States is still QWERTY. Look at the letters at the top left of the keyboard. A long time ago, the letters were placed in this order to make sure that the typewriter keys would not get stuck even when typing very rapidly.

Apparently, people have become so familiar with this arrangement that they do not want any of it changed.

The keyboard has a separate section for typing numbers. This was designed especially for people who have to enter many numbers and amounts. This section is called the *numeric keypad*.

Some laptops do not have a numeric keypad.

More and more keys are being added. Many of today's keyboards also have special keys used for the Internet. By pressing a single key, for example, you can collect your e-mail.

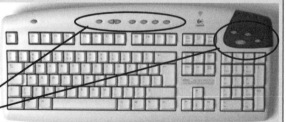

The proper working posture

It is important to arrange your computer properly. This not only makes it more pleasant when you work with your computer, but it also minimizes the risk of various complaints. You will be surprised at the number of hours you will spend working with your PC. A proper working posture is therefore essential. Attention should be devoted to the following:

- You need a table that is sufficiently deep and has the proper height. Your wrists should lie level with the table top when typing and using the mouse.

- An adjustable desk chair with arm rests is ideal because you can adjust it to achieve proper support for your back and legs. If your feet do not touch the ground, put something under them to support them - a few thick books, or a small stool or foot rest, for example.

- The keyboard should be directly in front of you. The mouse should be next to the keyboard on the correct side: on the right if you are right-handed and on the left if you are left-handed.

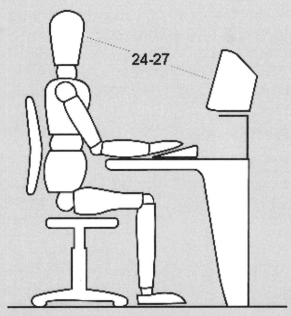

- Place the monitor straight in front of you, at about the same level as your eyes. Do not place the monitor to the left or right because this would force you to constantly strain your neck to turn your head.

- The monitor should be about one arm's length (24 to 27 inches) from your eyes.

- The monitor should not be too low or too high, forcing you to look up or down all the time. If you wear glasses or lenses that are multi-focal (with a special section for reading), having the monitor at the wrong height could force you to use the reading section instead of the "far-off" section of the lenses. You can always raise the monitor by putting something under it (another thick book?).

- Make sure there is no direct or indirect light shining into the monitor that would make it hard to read.

More ways to customize your computer to make it more pleasant to work with are explained in Chapter 10.

3.20 Tips

 Tip

Capitals Only
The keyboard has a special key that is used to type capital letters.
This is the key that says *Caps Lock*:

This key is located on the left side of the keyboard: ——
It is an **on-off** key. That means: if you press it once, the
capitals are on; if you press it again, you turn them off.
An **indicator light** tells you whether capitals have been
switched on or off.

 Tip

Placement of keys on a laptop computer may differ from a desktop keyboard
Keyboards from a laptop computer may differ slightly from those of the desktop
computer. A particular key, for example, the Delete key, may be in a different place.
Most of the descriptions used in this book refer to a desktop keyboard. If you are
using a laptop, you may have to search a bit for the key or key combination being
described.

Desktop keyboard

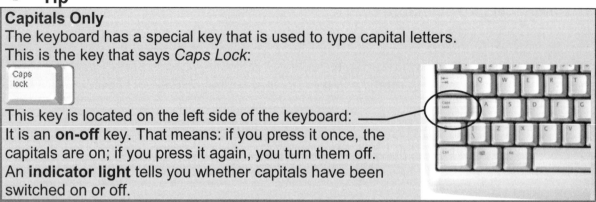

Laptop keyboard

4. Writing a Letter

It is hard to find an office anywhere that still uses a typewriter to type letters. No messy correction fluid or endless retyping, it is easy these days to produce letters, reports and other documents without errors when using a computer. Once created, documents or letters can be used over and over again with just a few changes, or sent via e-mail to people on a mailing list.

Writing documents and letters with the computer is also more practical because you can easily change them until they say exactly what you want them to. You can also save a document and work on it again later.

In this chapter, you will start by writing a letter using the computer. This is also done with the program *WordPad*.

In this chapter, you will learn how to:

- write a letter
- enter the date
- save a letter
- open a letter
- see the print preview
- print the letter
- save changes or not save changes

4.1 Starting a Letter

The easiest way to write a letter is to use the program *WordPad.* You begin by opening this program:

☞ **Open *WordPad*** 𝒞14

You see the empty *WordPad* screen:	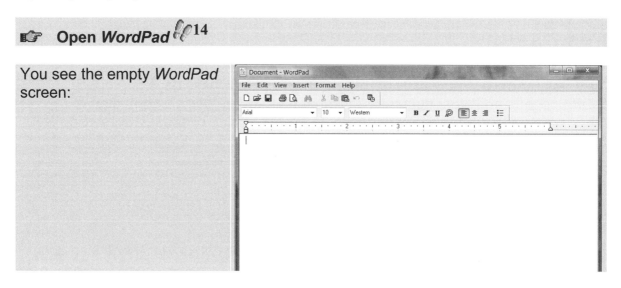

4.2 A Larger Font

A **font** is a complete set of characters in a particular size and style of type, including numerals, symbols and the characters of the alphabet.
When you begin typing in *WordPad*, the font size that is automatically used is rather small, and may be unpleasant to work with. This can be easily changed, just like almost everything else in *Windows Vista.* When typing a letter, it is handy to start by choosing a font size that is a bit bigger. Here is how you do this:

🖯 **Click** ▾

🖯 **Click** 12

You will not see anything happen on the screen. But when you start typing, you will see that the text is somewhat larger and easier to read.

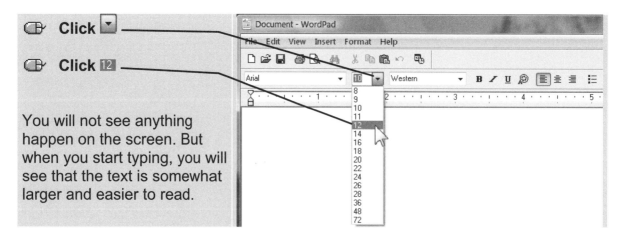

Elsewhere in this book, more information is given about types of *fonts* and *font* sizes.

4.3 Today's Date

We will begin with an informal letter to someone you know. Naturally, a letter starts with the date. You do not have to type the date yourself. *WordPad* has a command that does it for you.

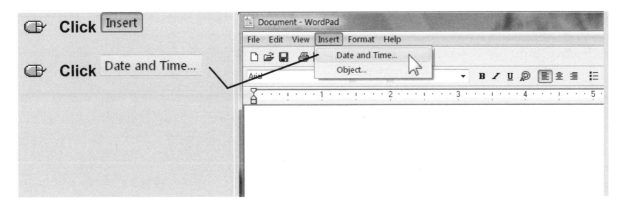

Now you can choose the way you want the date to be written.

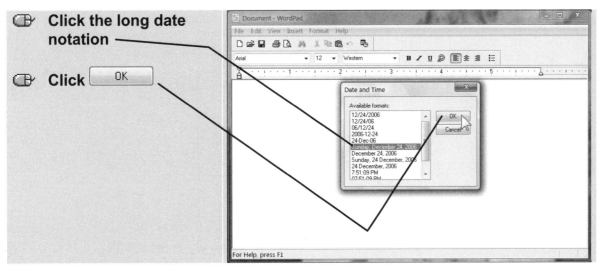

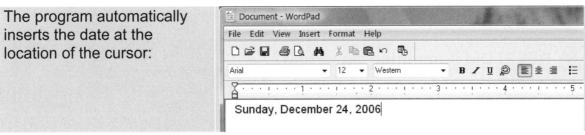

The date in your letter will not be the same as in the illustration.
The program inserts today's actual date.

4.4 Undoing

If something goes wrong while you are writing, or if you accidentally press the wrong key, nearly every *Windows* program has a command that will undo it. Try it:

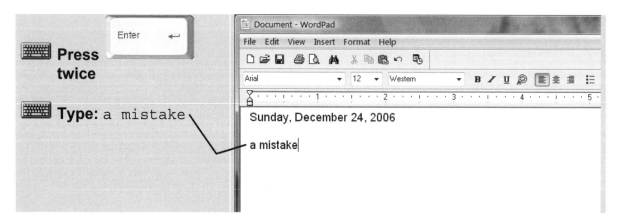

Press twice

Type: a mistake

The program always remembers the last thing you did. So you can always **undo** it:

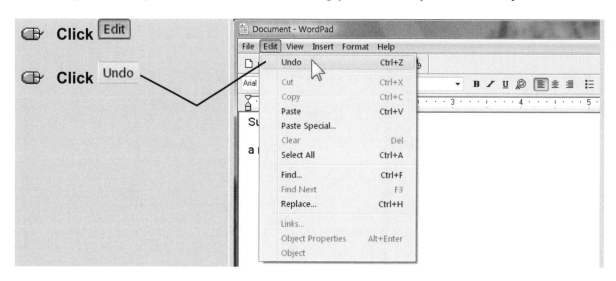

Click Edit

Click Undo

The last line you typed has been removed.

 HELP! Did something go wrong?

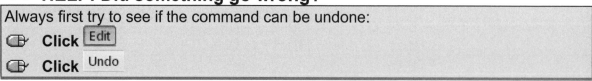

Always first try to see if the command can be undone:

Click Edit

Click Undo

Now you can type the rest of the letter.

4.5 Typing a Letter

 Please note:

> It is important that you type this letter, because this practice letter will be used several times in the rest of this book.

⌨ **Press** **twice**

⌨ **Type:**
```
Dear name,

This week I started
working with Windows
Vista.
This is my first
letter typed on the
computer.

Sincerely,

Your name
```

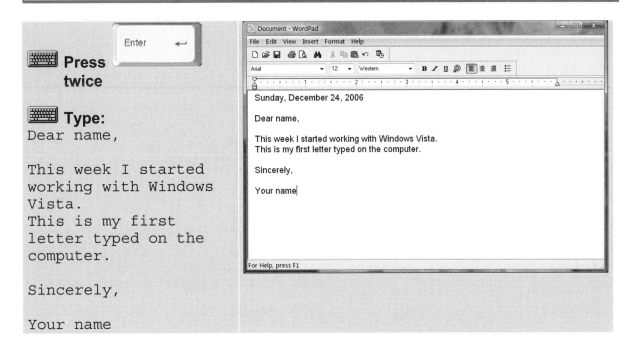

You will save this practice letter on your computer so that you can work on it again later. In daily life, however, you do not necessarily have to save every letter you type. You can also immediately print it and send it.

If you want to save your letter on the computer, you must always tell the computer to do so. If you do not, your letter may be lost. A text is not automatically saved. The text stays in the computer's memory until you stop the program or switch off the computer. The memory that the computer works with is temporary. The text will not be permanently stored until you save it.

4.6 Saving a Document

This first practice letter will be stored on the computer. Storing a document (such as this letter) is called **save** in *Windows*. This is how you save your letter:

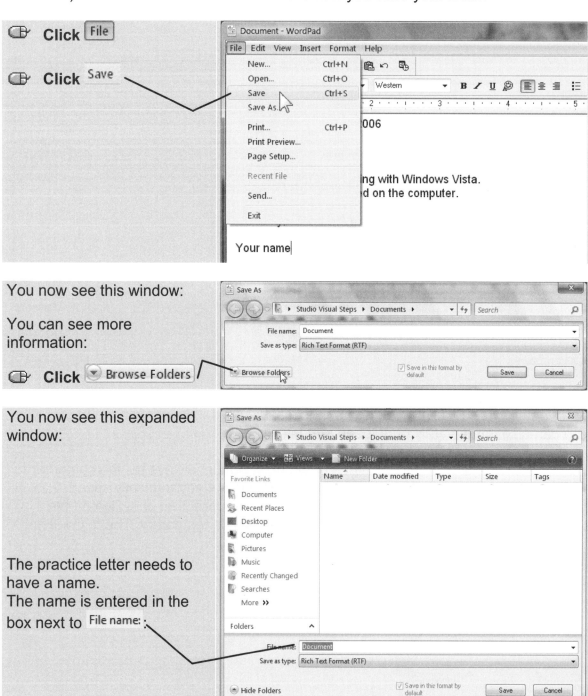

Click File

Click Save

You now see this window:

You can see more information:

Click ⌄ Browse Folders

You now see this expanded window:

The practice letter needs to have a name.
The name is entered in the box next to File name: .

Type: first letter

Click `Save`

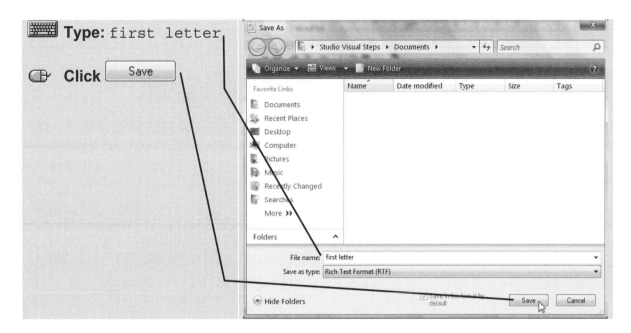

The letter has been saved on your computer's hard disk. How this is done will be explained a bit later.

Now the name of your letter appears at the top of the screen in the *Title bar:*

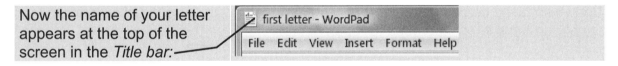

HELP! The file already exists.

Did this window appear?

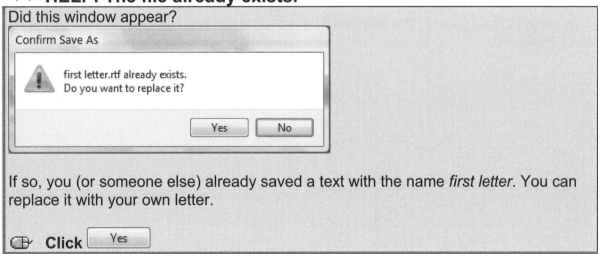

If so, you (or someone else) already saved a text with the name *first letter*. You can replace it with your own letter.

Click `Yes`

4.7 Closing WordPad

Now you must close *WordPad* for the moment. This is done to show you how to retrieve your practice letter so that you can work on it at another time:

☞ **Close *WordPad*** ¹⁵

Now you can open *WordPad* again:

☞ **Open *WordPad* again** ¹⁴

You see an empty screen, without your practice letter.

The name *Document* is shown at the top:

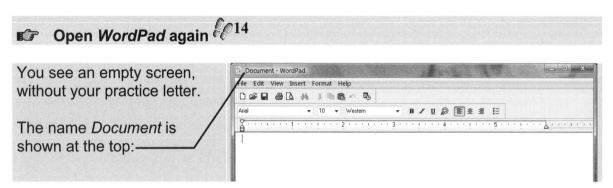

Document is the default name for a new text. In order to get your practice letter to appear on the screen, you need to "open" it first.

4.8 Opening a Document

If you want to use a letter that has been saved on the computer, you must "open" it first. This is how:

👆 **Click** File

👆 **Click** Open...

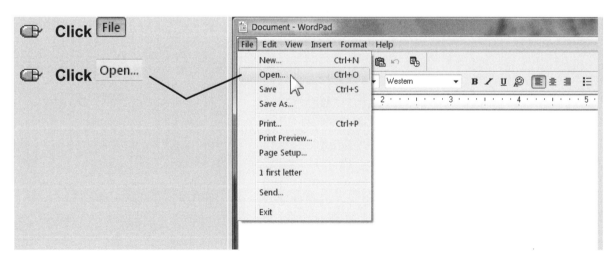

In the big white box in this window, you see the name of your letter:

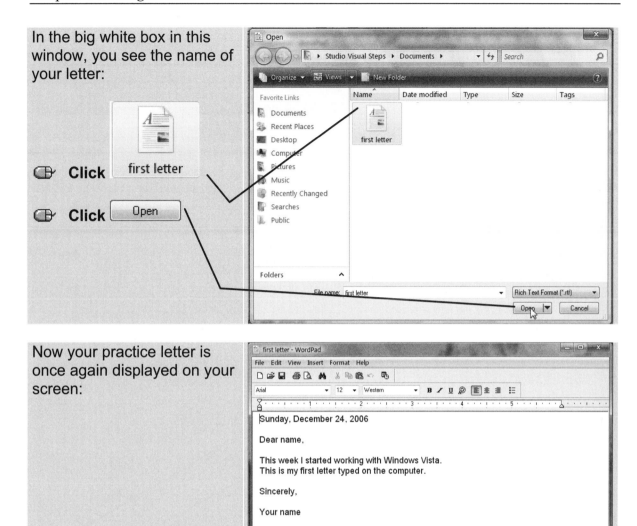

Click first letter

Click Open

Now your practice letter is once again displayed on your screen:

You can continue to work on it now and print it.

HELP! I can not find the practice letter.

You can not find the practice letter in the *Documents* folder?

Maybe *WordPad* is searching for the wrong type of file. In the *Open* dialog box, *WordPad* for instance automatically searches for text documents (*.txt):

In that case:

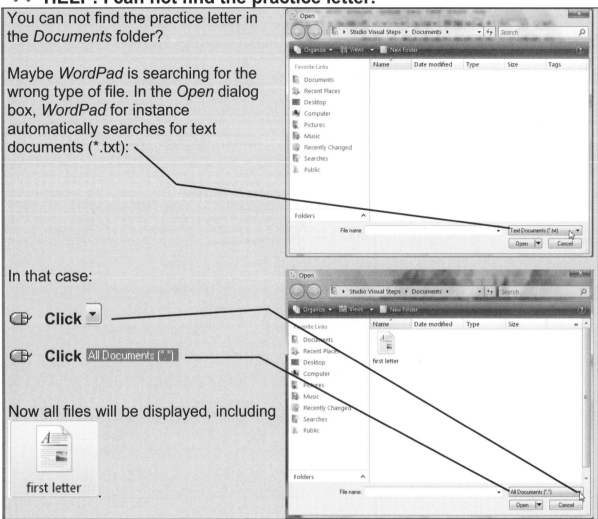

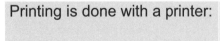 **Click** ▼

 Click All Documents (*.*)

Now all files will be displayed, including

first letter

4.9 Printing the Letter

When you write a letter, most likely you will want it printed on paper.

Printing is done with a printer:

HELP! No printer?

If you do not have a printer, you can skip this section.

Before you actually print a letter, it is wise to have a preview of what it will look like on paper. *WordPad* has a special command for this:

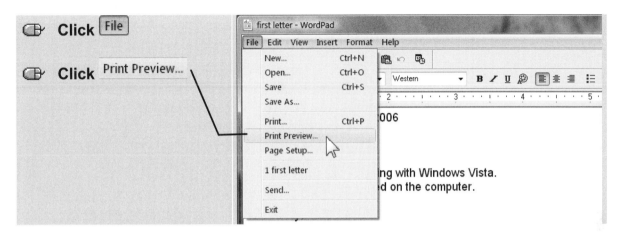

☞ **Click** `File`

☞ **Click** `Print Preview...`

Now this screen appears.
In the middle is a miniature representation of the page as it will be printed:

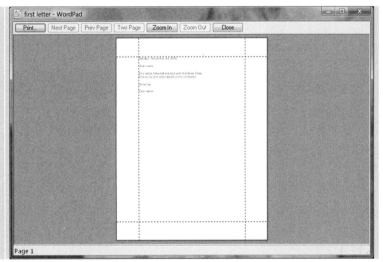

The way the letter is positioned on the page, with the text at the very top left, is not very appealing. You can easily change this by adding some empty lines at the top.

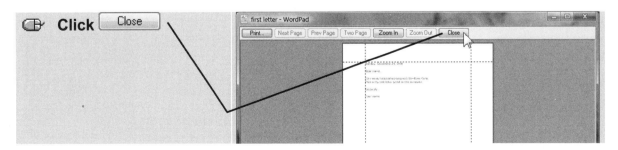

☞ **Click** `Close`

Now you can add the empty lines.

Type 10 empty lines at the top of the letter
✍ 42

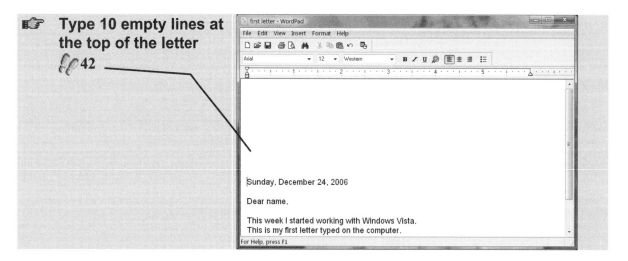

You can see the results using the *Print Preview:*

Click File

Click Print Preview...

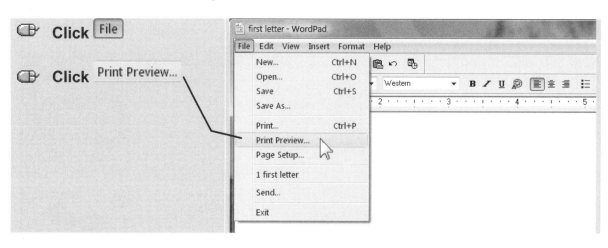

Now the letter has moved down the page a bit:

Click Close

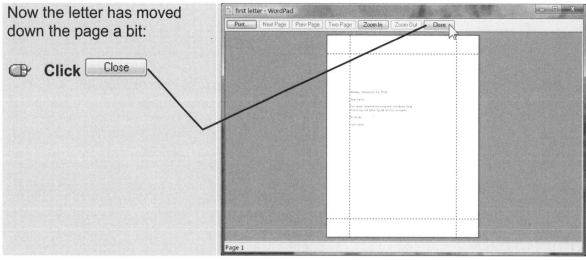

You can print the letter the way it is for now. You can do a lot of other things to make the letter look more appealing, for example by using text effects and a different type of font. This will all be explained a bit further along in the book.

 ## Please note:

It is important to check if your printer is ready for use before you tell the computer to print anything.

☞ Make sure the printer is on

☞ Make sure there is paper in the printer

Is everything ready? Then you can tell the computer to print the letter:

☞ Click `File`

☞ Click `Print...`

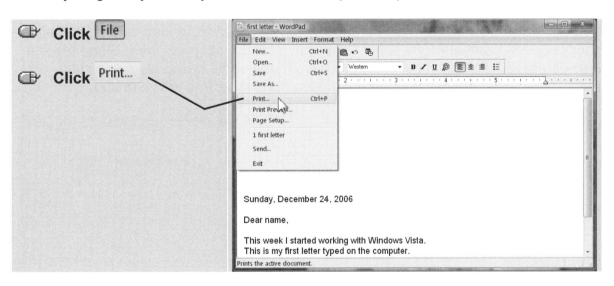

Now you see a screen in which you can choose various print settings:

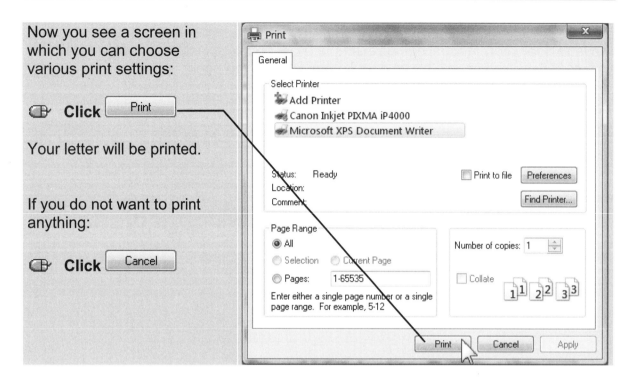

⊞ **Click** Print

Your letter will be printed.

If you do not want to print anything:

⊞ **Click** Cancel

4.10 Save Changes?

You can never accidentally lose something you have saved. *Windows Vista* always checks to see if something is about to be lost. You should give it a try. Since the last time you saved your practice letter, you have made some changes. You added empty lines to the top of the letter. If you stop now, *WordPad* will warn you:

⊞ **Click** File

⊞ **Click** Exit

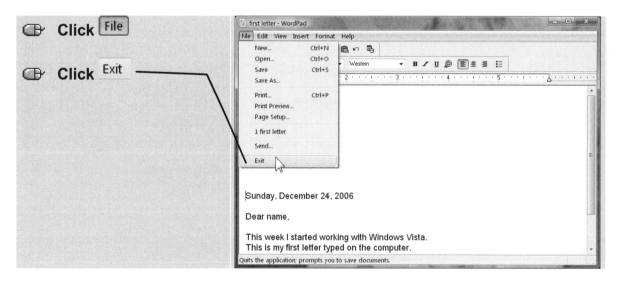

WordPad will ask you whether or not the changes should be saved: ───

In this case, you do want to save them.

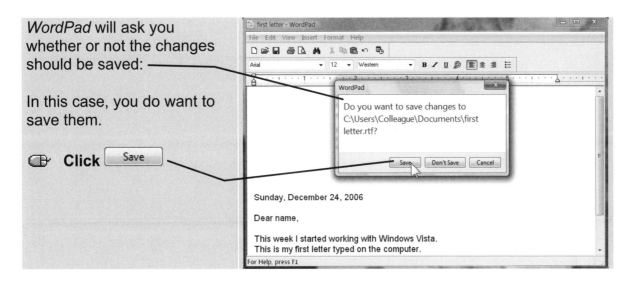

☞ **Click** [Save]

The changes will be saved and *WordPad* will be closed.

💡 **Tip**

To many people, this screen is confusing:

If you unexpectedly see this screen, you apparently made at least one change. No matter how small, even if the change is simply one space, it is still a change to *WordPad*.

- If you click [Save], the changes will be saved.
- If you click [Don't Save], the changes will not be saved.
- If you click [Cancel], you will return to *WordPad*.

Now you can open your practice letter again to see what happens when you save the changes first yourself.

☞ **Open *WordPad* again** ✐14

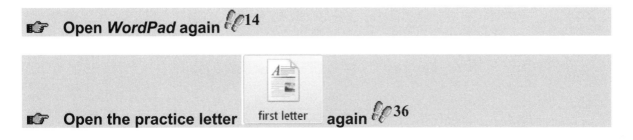

☞ **Open the practice letter** first letter **again** ✐36

First make a small change to the letter:

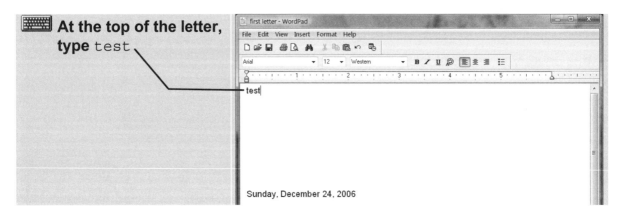

At the top of the letter, type test

Now you can save this small text change:

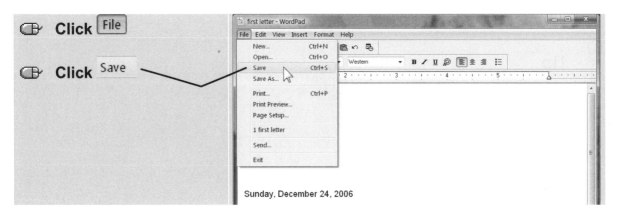

Click File

Click Save

This time you were not asked to select a name. You have already given this document a name: *first letter*.

☞ **Close** *WordPad* 🦶15

Did you notice that the screen asking whether to *save changes* has not appeared? That is because you saved the last changes yourself while you were working.

With the next exercise, you can practice saving documents a little more.

4.11 Exercises

Exercise: Saving Changes

The following exercises will help you master what you have just learned. Have you forgotten how to do something? Use the number beside the footsteps to look it up in the appendix *How Do I Do That Again?*

✔ Open *WordPad*. 🦶14

✔ Type the following short letter:

Date

Dear Sirs,

With this letter I want to thank you for your excellent service.

Sincerely,

Your name

✔ Save this letter and name it *exercise 1*. 🦶27

✔ Start a new letter. 🦶16

✔ Open the letter *exercise 1* again. 🦶35

✔ Add the line printed in bold letters below:

Date

Dear Sirs,

With this letter I want to thank you for your excellent service.
I would also like to inform you that the appliance works perfectly.

Sincerely,

Your name

✔ Print the letter. 🦶19

✔ Start a new letter, and while doing so have the changes saved. 🦶17

4.12 Background Information

Dictionary	
Font	A complete set of characters in a particular size and style of type, including numerals, symbols, punctuation and the characters of the alphabet.
Open	Command to find and retrieve a document which has been saved on a hard drive, CD-ROM or other memory device.
Print	Command to produce a copy of the document on paper with the help of a printer.
Print Preview	A feature that allows the user to view on the computer screen the document as it will appear on the printed page.
Save	Command to store a file on a memory device such as a hard drive or USB stick for future use.
Undo	Command to undo the last thing you did in a program.
Source: Windows Help and Support	

Printers

The printer most commonly used in the home is called an **inkjet** printer.
This type of printer prints characters by spraying very small, precise amounts of ink onto the paper.

Many of these printers can also make color prints. These printers have not only a cartridge with black ink, but also another cartridge with at least three colors. Any color imaginable can be copied by mixing the various colored inks. Each type of printer has different cartridges.

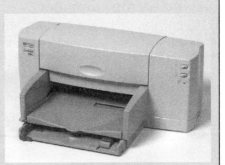

Inkjet printer

Inkjet printers can print on regular paper as well as on special types of paper, depending on the quality of print you want. You can get special photo paper to print photos, for example.

Laser printers are often used in the office sector. They are a non-impact printing device which operates in similar fashion to a photocopier, in which a laser draws the image of a page on a photosensitive drum which then attracts *toner* (an extremely fine-grained powder) on to the paper, where it is subsequently bonded by heating.

Laser printers are known for high quality prints, good print speed, and a low cost-per-copy. Laser printers are available in both color and monochrome varieties.

Laser printer

A recent development is the **photo printer**, which uses special photo paper to print digital photographs.

You can connect this kind of printer to the computer, but there are also models that can print directly from a digital camera's memory card. In this case, the camera's memory card fits into a card reader that is built into the printer.

Photo printer

Saving on the computer

The computer has a certain amount of *working memory.* This working memory consists of chips in which the information is temporarily saved.

When you turn the computer off, however, the memory is emptied. This is why you also need to be able to save information more permanently.

That type of memory exists in various types: the computer's *hard disk* or an external hard disk, but also *diskettes, USB sticks* (*USB memory sticks*), *CD-recordable/-rewritable* and *DVD-recordable/-rewritable.*

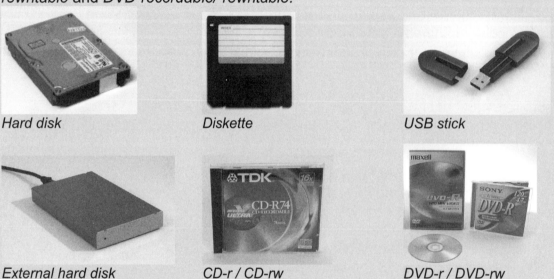

Hard disk   *Diskette*   *USB stick*

External hard disk   *CD-r / CD-rw*   *DVD-r / DVD-rw*

The most important saving method uses the hard (disk) drive on your computer. The hard disk is a small, sealed box that has been built into your computer.

Hard disk   *Inside a computer case*   *Case (housing)*

In this box, a small disk rotates. The disk is magnetic, making it possible to save information on it.

You determine what is saved on the hard drive. You can save documents on it, or drawings, or computer programs. You can copy, move or delete files from the hard drive.

Where to save?

Every desktop computer in use today contains one or more hard disk drives. In addition, many computers will have a CD drive and/or a DVD drive that can read and write (if the drive is a "burner") CDs and/or DVDs. There may also be a floppy drive. If you do not have a floppy drive, you can save your work to a USB stick: the replacement for the floppy. USB sticks connect to the PC's USB ports.

In the *Computer* window, you can see which items your PC contains. In this example, it contains the following items:

Hard disk

DVD RW drive

External hard disk

Removable disk

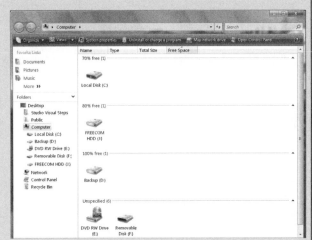

Windows gives every memory device a letter for a name.

- A floppy drive is always named **A**. If the computer does not have a floppy drive, the letter A is not used, like in the example above. The letter **B** is no longer used.
- The hard disk drive always gets the letter **C**. (If there is a second hard disk, it will get the letter **D**.)
- The CD or DVD drive gets the next letter of the alphabet. In the example above, that's **E**. If there are two such drives, the next one will be named **F**.
- The next device gets the letter **G**, and so forth.

In the window above, you see that the letter **F** has been given to a removable disk. In this example, that is a USB stick inserted into the computer. But it could also be an external hard disk connected to the PC, or a digital camera's memory card.

Please note: Other items or devices may be present on your computer. The letters you see on your screen will belong to different devices.

You usually save your work on your computer's hard drive. If you want to take your work with you to another computer, or if you want to make a backup copy of a file, then you can save your work onto a floppy disk, a USB stick or a memory card. Another option for saving your work is to burn it onto a CD or DVD.

CD and DVD

These days, computers come standard with a CD player or DVD player, which you can use to read CDs or DVDs.

CD-roms and DVD-roms are *the* media for distributing computer programs. A CD can hold a large number of files, and a DVD can contain even more.

You can even put files on a CD or DVD yourself. You do need a different type of device for this, however: a *CD writer* or *DVD writer*. This kind of device can "write" onto a special kind of blank disk. This disk is recordable (r).
They can be bought in your local electronics, office supply, and discount department stores.

The *CD rewriter* and *DVD rewriter* are two other devices for reading and writing files to CDs or DVDs. Disks used in these devices are re-recordable (rw), they can be erased and recorded over numerous times without damaging the medium. They are a little more expensive however and in the case of DVD-rw may not be compatible with certain DVD players.

You can not play DVDs in a CD-drive, but the other way around works just fine.

4.13 Tips

 Tip

Regularly save your work
If you work for a lengthy period of time, you should regularly save your work. It is also wise to save your work first before making large changes. If anything goes wrong, you then have a spare copy that has been saved.

 Tip

When not to save changes?
When you close a program window, the computer shows you this question:

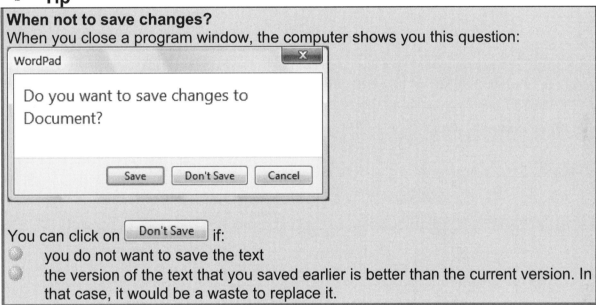

You can click on **Don't Save** if:

- you do not want to save the text
- the version of the text that you saved earlier is better than the current version. In that case, it would be a waste to replace it.

 Tip

Rules for file names
What rules apply to naming a text?

File name: | ▼

A file name may not:

- be longer than 255 letters or numbers, including spaces
- contain one of the following characters: \ / : * ? " < > . |

Tip

Did something go wrong with your printer?
When this happens, be sure to check:
- whether the printer is turned on
- whether the printer has paper
- whether something else is wrong, such as an empty ink cartridge or a jammed piece of paper. If necessary, consult the printer manual.

Did you fix what was wrong?
Then *WordPad* will try again and the printing will start automatically.

 Tip

The buttons in *WordPad*
You see various buttons at the top of the screen. These can be used to enter a command with a single click of the mouse:

These buttons have the following functions:

		Command:
☐	Start a new document	`File`, `New...`
☞	Open a document	`File`, `Open...`
☐	Save a document	`File`, `Save`
☐	Print the text	`File`, `Print...`
☐	See the print preview	`File`, `Print Preview...`

5. Word Processing

It is very easy to modify a text using your computer. You can select a word, copy it and move it somewhere else, move sentences or paragraphs, or save the text for future use.

Because so many people use word processing programs, many standard letters (*templates*) exist. It is easy to make your own template. You might start by creating a simple, new document about a certain subject, like an invitation. You add a place for a name and other bits here and there to make the invitation more personal. The recipient's name is inserted and the invitation is printed. The recipient of such an invitation will think you have written a unique and a personal message, but most of the document was typed just one time.

This chapter primarily focuses on word processing. You will discover how easy it is to change sentences: sometimes all you have to do is click and drag with your mouse.

In this chapter, you will learn how to:

- move the cursor with the mouse
- select a single word or paragraph
- delete a word
- move a word or paragraph
- split a paragraph and paste it back together

5.1 The Cursor and the Mouse

☞ **Open** *WordPad* 📖 14

You can move the cursor with the cursor keys on the keyboard, or by using the mouse. In order to practice this, type the following words to a popular nursery rhyme.

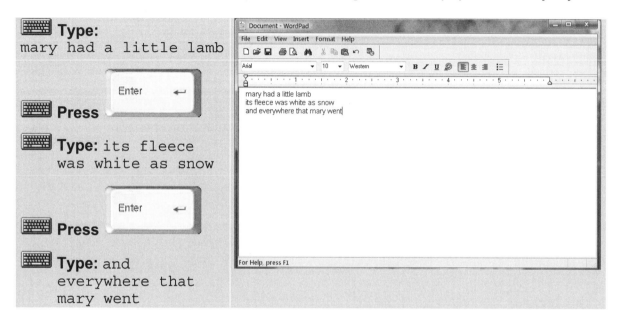

⌨ **Type:**
mary had a little lamb

⌨ **Press** `Enter ←`

⌨ **Type:** its fleece
was white as snow

⌨ **Press** `Enter ←`

⌨ **Type:** and
everywhere that
mary went

When you slide your mouse pointer over text, the pointer changes its appearance from an ⬚ (arrow) into this ⌶. When you click the mouse somewhere in the text, the cursor will move immediately to that spot.

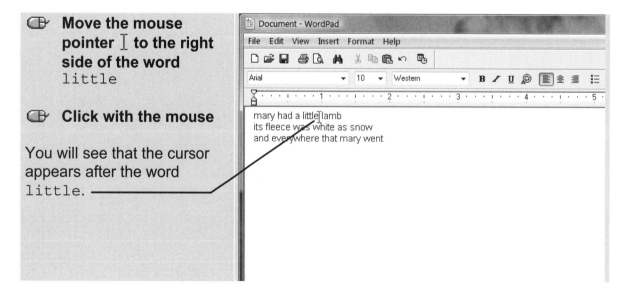

🖰 **Move the mouse pointer ⌶ to the right side of the word** little

🖰 **Click with the mouse**

You will see that the cursor appears after the word little. ——

Now you can delete the word *little* using the Backspace key:

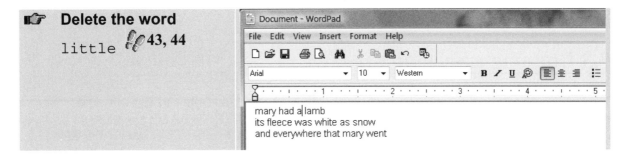

Delete the word

little ✍ 43, 44

5.2 Selecting a Word

Using the Backspace key to delete a word is not very efficient. There are faster ways to delete a word or even an entire paragraph all at once.
In order to do so, you must first *select* the portion that you want to delete. Selecting is done with the mouse.

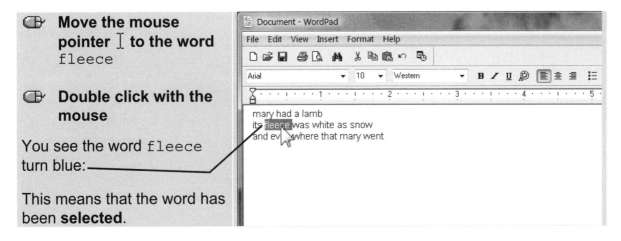

☞ **Move the mouse pointer ⌶ to the word** fleece

☞ **Double click with the mouse**

You see the word fleece turn blue:————

This means that the word has been **selected**.

You can select a different word in the same way.

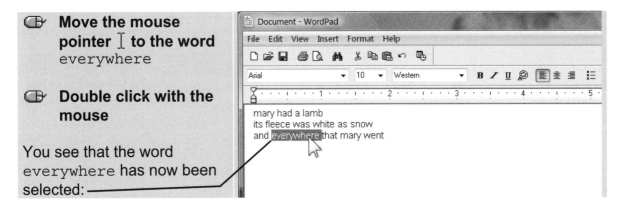

☞ **Move the mouse pointer ⌶ to the word** everywhere

☞ **Double click with the mouse**

You see that the word everywhere has now been selected: ————

As you can see, this method allows you to select one word at a time. The word `fleece` is no longer selected after you select `everywhere`.

5.3 Undoing a Selection

It is very easy to undo a selection. Simply click somewhere else in the window:

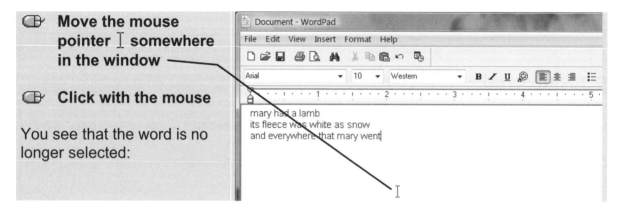

☞ **Move the mouse pointer I somewhere in the window**

☞ **Click with the mouse**

You see that the word is no longer selected:

5.4 Deleting a Word

Once you have selected a word, you can do many things with it. You can delete it, for example. Later, you will see some more things you can do with a selected word.

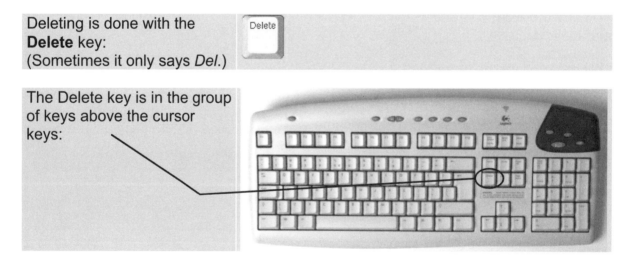

Deleting is done with the **Delete** key:
(Sometimes it only says *Del.*)

The Delete key is in the group of keys above the cursor keys:

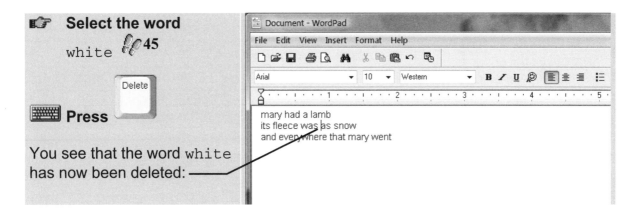

5.5 Dragging a Word

You can drag a selected word to another place in the text. To practice this, first type the last line of the nursery rhyme. The words are in the right order now, but will not be after this exercise.

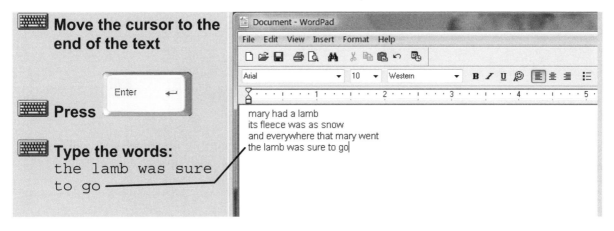

Before you can drag a word, you must select it:

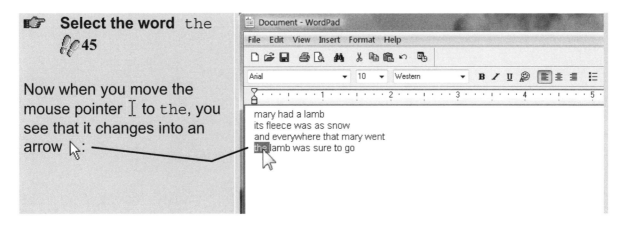

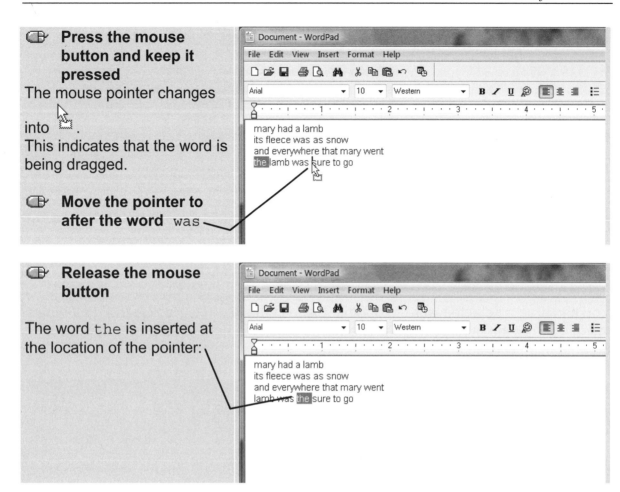

⊕ Press the mouse button and keep it pressed

The mouse pointer changes

into 🐁 .
This indicates that the word is being dragged.

⊕ Move the pointer to after the word was

⊕ Release the mouse button

The word the is inserted at the location of the pointer:

Learning to drag words will take some time. At the end of this chapter, you will find an exercise to practice dragging. You need to save the text for this:

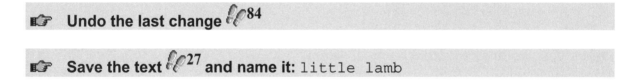

☞ **Undo the last change** 👣[84]

☞ **Save the text** 👣[27] **and name it:** little lamb

5.6 Typing Over a Word

If you want to replace one word with another, it is not always necessary to delete the word first. You can simply type over a word that has been selected. Try it:

☞ **Select the word** go
𝕃𝟺𝟻

⌨ **Type:** walk

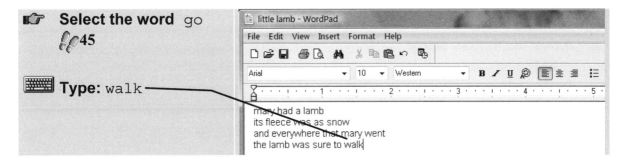

As you can see, the selected word is replaced by the new word you typed.

☞ **Start a new text; do not save the changes** 𝕃18

Now you have an empty screen again, without text.

5.7 Selecting a Paragraph

You can also select a paragraph and delete it or drag it. You can easily practice by placing the words of the national anthem in the right order. Type the first four lines. They have been put in the wrong order on purpose:

⌨ **Type:** what so
proudly we hailed

⌨ **Press** `Enter ↵`

⌨ **Type:** Oh, say can
you see

⌨ **Press** `Enter ↵`

⌨ **Type:** at the
twilight's last
gleaming

⌨ **Press** `Enter ↵`

⌨ **Type:** by the dawn's
early light

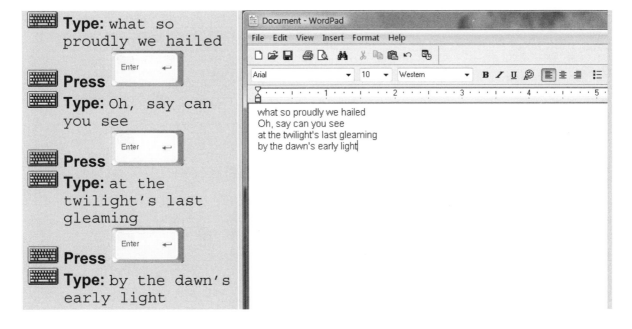

The start of a paragraph is indicated by beginning on a new line (using the Enter key). The paragraph ends by using the Enter key. A paragraph can be a group of sentences, one sentence alone or even just one line of text. In the text above every line is a paragraph.

It is easy to select a paragraph. Double-clicking with the mouse selects a word. Triple-clicking selects the paragraph:

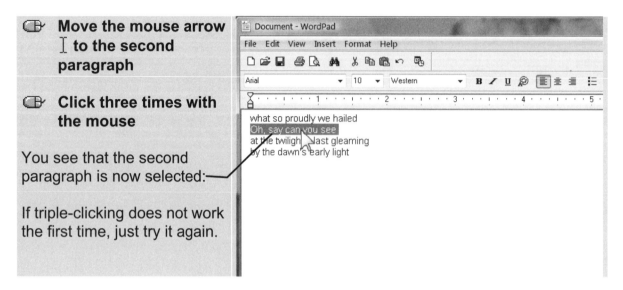

☞ Move the mouse arrow ⌶ to the second paragraph

☞ Click three times with the mouse

You see that the second paragraph is now selected:

If triple-clicking does not work the first time, just try it again.

5.8 Dragging a Paragraph

Dragging a paragraph is done the same way as dragging a word. You can point to the selected paragraph and drag it to the place where it should be:

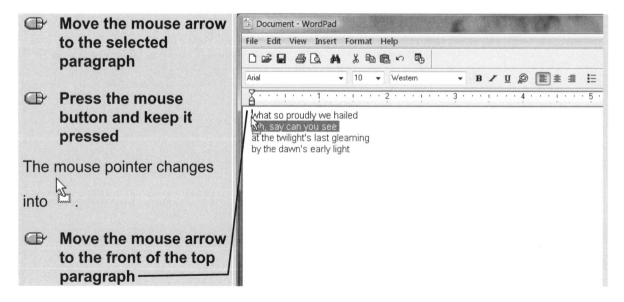

☞ Move the mouse arrow to the selected paragraph

☞ Press the mouse button and keep it pressed

The mouse pointer changes into ⬚.

☞ Move the mouse arrow to the front of the top paragraph

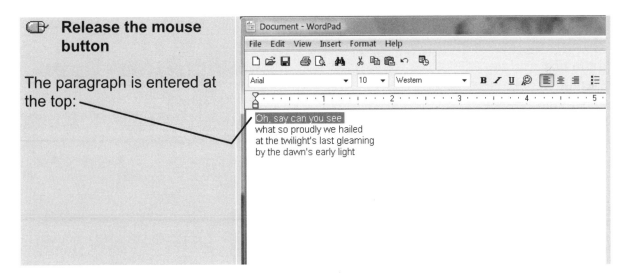

Dragging paragraphs will be easier once you give it some practice. See the relevant exercise at the end of this chapter. There you can put the entire anthem in the right order. You will be saving the text for this purpose shortly.

5.9 Mini Word Processing

Now you have learned the most important actions in word processing. Actually, *WordPad* is not the only program where these actions are useful. These same actions can be used in various other situations in *Windows Vista*, for example when you are saving a document. Take a look:

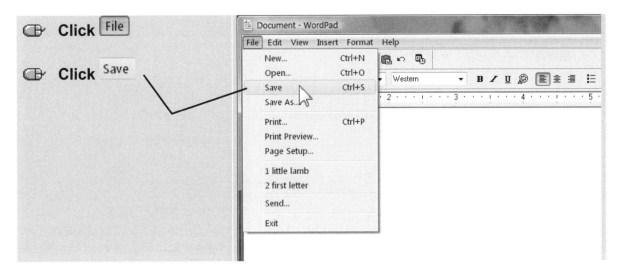

You now see this window:

In the box next to File name: , a tentative name is already shown, namely: Document

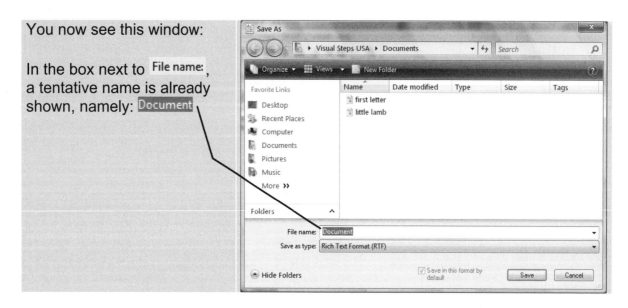

This box acts like a kind of mini word processor. You can use all of the actions that you learned in *WordPad* in these boxes as well. Examples are:

- if the word is selected, you can delete it using the Delete key
- if you press the cursor keys, the cursor will move through the word
- if the word is not selected, you can add letters or delete them

Go ahead and try:

Press ←

The cursor moves to the left.

Press Home

The cursor moves to the beginning of the line:

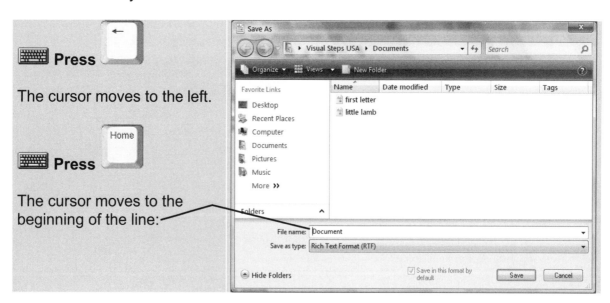

As you can see, the cursor acts the same way it does in *WordPad*. Selecting is also done the same way:

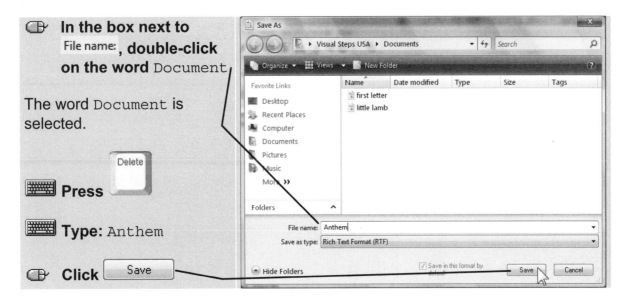

In the box next to File name: **, double-click on the word** Document

The word Document is selected.

Press Delete

Type: Anthem

Click Save

The text is saved as *Anthem.rtf*.

☞ **Start a new text** ℓℓ16

Now you have an empty screen again, without text.

5.10 Splitting and Pasting Paragraphs

You have already seen that you can make empty lines (in fact empty paragraphs) by pressing the Enter key. You can also split a paragraph the same way. Sometimes this will happen accidentally when you press the Enter key. It is useful to know that you can **undo** this.

Type:
The Everglades are in Florida.

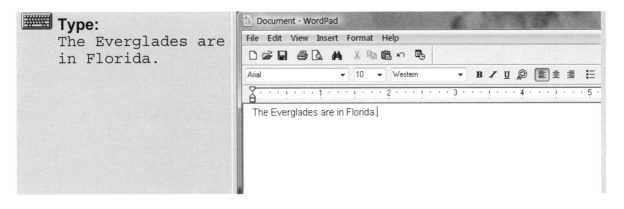

Move the pointer to the word `are`

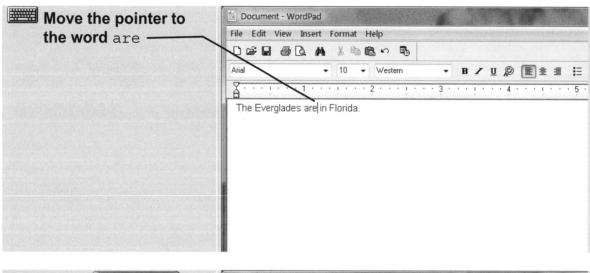

Press Enter

Now the sentence is split into two lines:

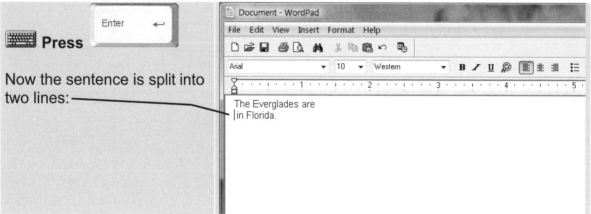

Both lines are in fact separate paragraphs. The bottom paragraph can easily be pasted back to the top paragraph using the Backspace key. In this instance, the cursor is still in the right place, at the beginning of the line.

Press Backspace

Now the sentence is pasted back together:

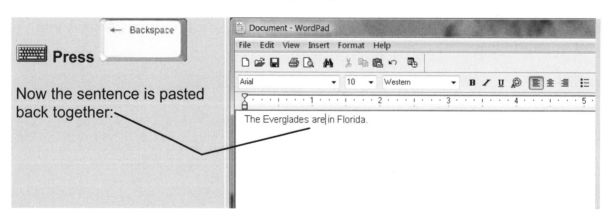

☞ **Start a new text; do not save the changes** 🦶18

5.11 Copying, Cutting and Pasting

Windows has three very useful commands: *copying, cutting* and *pasting.* Once you have copied or cut something, you can paste it somewhere else.
You can copy or cut in one program, and paste into a different program. A text created in an e-mail program can be pasted in a letter in *WordPad*, for example.

You can practice doing this in *WordPad*. Type the following three lines:

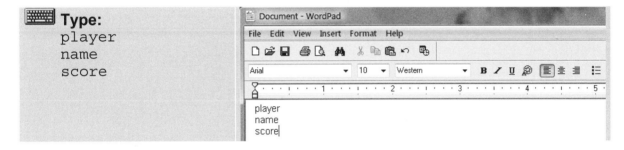

Type:
player
name
score

A portion of text, such as a word, is easy to copy and paste somewhere else in the text. But before you can copy something, you must select it first. Remember this rule:

➡ **Please note:**

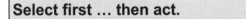

Select first ... then act.

Select the word name
45

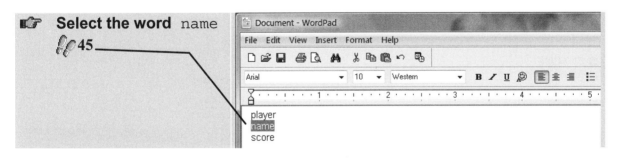

Click Edit

Click Copy

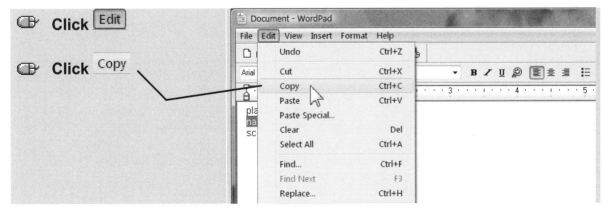

You can not see anything happening, but the word `name` has now been copied to the *Clipboard*. *Windows Clipboard* is a temporary storage area.
You can paste the word `name` somewhere else. The cursor is used to indicate where to paste.

Move the cursor to the end of the last line

☞ **Make an empty line at the bottom**

⸤⸥42

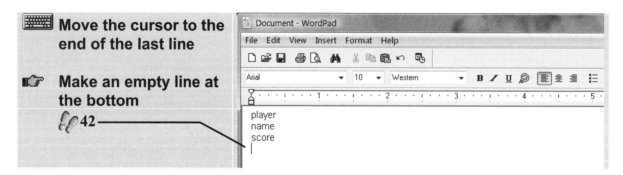

Now you can paste the word*:*

🖰 **Click** Edit

🖰 **Click** Paste

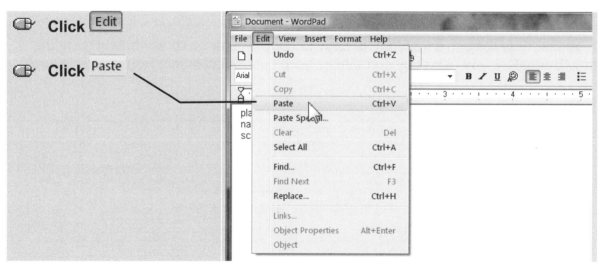

The word `name` now appears at the bottom:

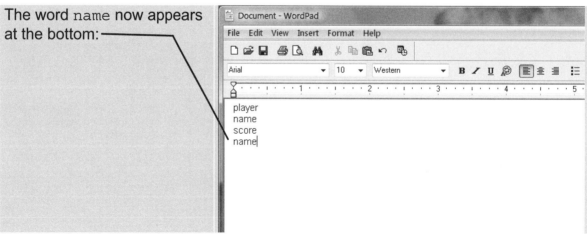

A word that you *select* and *copy* can be pasted as many times as you want. Take a look:

Click Edit again

Click Paste again

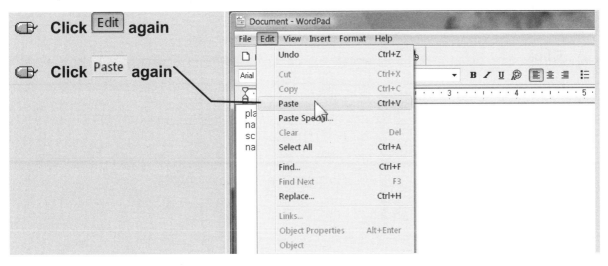

The word `name` appears again:

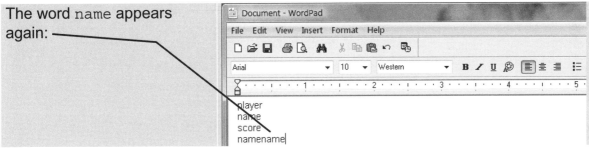

⇨ **Please note:**

You can only paste the last text you copied. Each time you copy a text, any previously copied text is removed from the computer's memory.

You can also *cut* a word and paste it somewhere else. Give it a try, but remember the rule:

⇨ **Please note:**

Select first ... then act.

Select the word

player 45

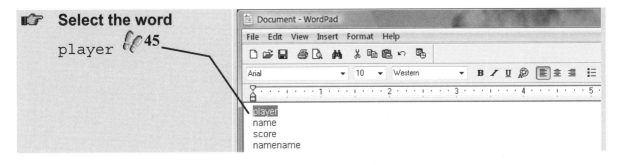

Now you can cut the word `player`:

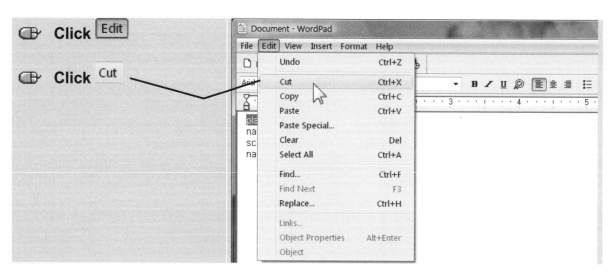

Click `Edit`

Click `Cut`

Now the word `player` has disappeared:

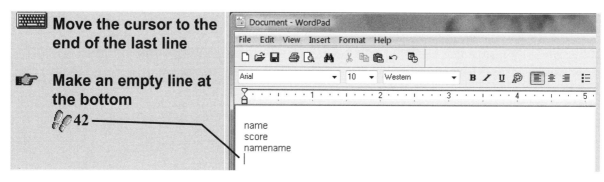

Move the cursor to the end of the last line

Make an empty line at the bottom

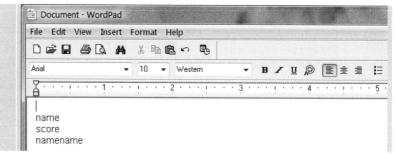

42

Now you can paste the word `player`:

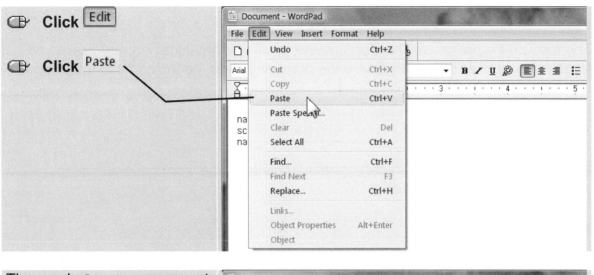

Click Edit

Click Paste

The word `player` appears at the bottom:

In this the way you see how easily words or sentences can be moved. First select, then cut, then paste your selection somewhere else. Please note that in this example, you'd have to type a space in the middle of the pasted word "namename".

➡ Please note:

You can only paste the last text you cut. If you cut a new text, the text you cut previously will be lost. You can always **undo** your last step, if you do not want to lose that portion of text.

☞ **Start a new text; do not save the changes** 18

With the next exercises you can practice what you have learned in this chapter.

5.12 Exercises

The following exercises will help you master what you have just learned. Have you forgotten how to do something? Use the number beside the footsteps to look it up in the appendix *How Do I Do That Again?*

Exercise: The Song

This exercise will help you practice deleting and dragging words and attaching portions of text to one another.

✔   Open the document with the name: 📄 little lamb . 👣**36**

✔   Select the word that. 👣**45**

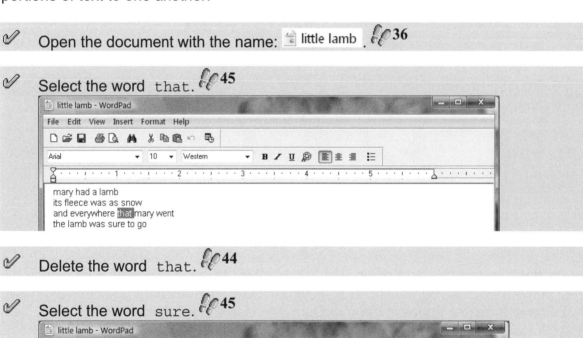

✔   Delete the word that. 👣**44**

✔   Select the word sure. 👣**45**

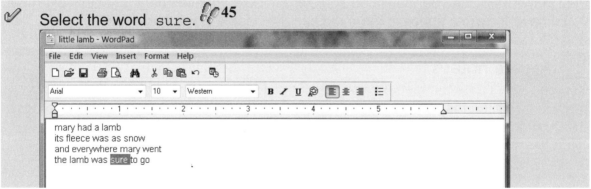

✓ Drag the word `sure` and position it after the word `lamb`:

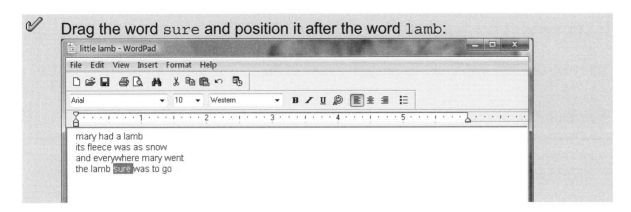

Now you can put the song on a single line:

✓ Attach the four paragraphs to make a single line. 🖐46 Add a space and a comma in the correct places.

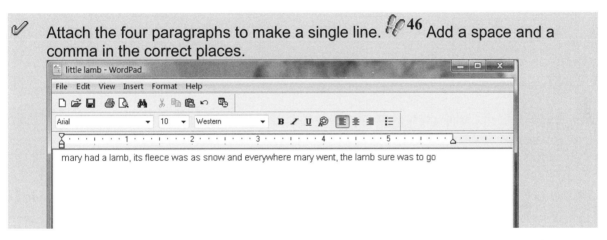

✓ Save this document. 🖐28

Exercise: The National Anthem

This exercise lets you practice dragging lines of text.

Open the document with the name: 📄 Anthem . 👣36

Drag the paragraphs so that they are in the correct order:

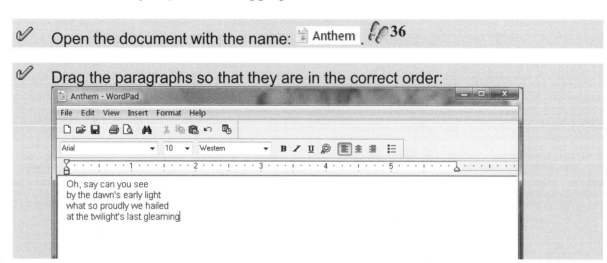

Now add the following four paragraphs:
```
through the perilous fight
whose bright stars and broad stripes
were so gallantly streaming
o'er the ramparts we watched
```

Now drag these paragraphs so that they are also in the correct order:

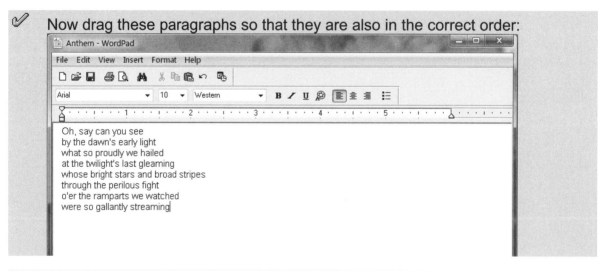

Save the document. 👣28

Start a new text. 👣16

Exercise: Copying and Pasting

✔ Type the following three lines (paragraphs):
```
two
three
points
```

✔ Select `points`. ✔ 45

✔ Copy the word `points`. ✔ 22

✔ Move the cursor after the word `two` ✔ 39 and type a space.

✔ Now paste the word: `points`. ✔ 23

✔ Move the cursor after the word `three` ✔ 39 and type a space.

✔ Now paste the word `points` here. ✔ 23

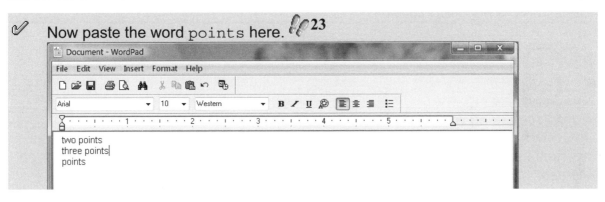

✔ At the bottom, select the word `points`. ✔ 45

✔ Cut the word `points`. ✔ 24

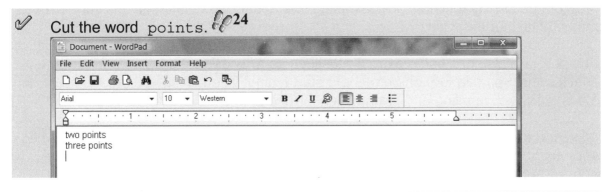

✔ Close *WordPad*; you do not need to save the changes from above. ✔ 18

5.13 Background Information

Dictionary	
Copy	Command to duplicate a selected portion of a document, so that it can be inserted somewhere else.
Cut	Command to remove a selected portion of a document, so that it can be inserted somewhere else.
Delete	Action that removes a selected portion of a document.
Paste	Command to insert a previously selected portion of a document which had been copied or cut.
Select	Action with the mouse that highlights a portion of a document.

Source: Windows Help and support

Word Processing programs

Until now, you have worked with *WordPad*. It is a simple program that is more than sufficient for learning the basic principles of word processing. Its big brother is called *Microsoft Word*. This is a highly-detailed program that offers numerous functions.

You can make virtually anything you want with *Microsoft Word*: letters, minutes of meetings, folders, posters, flyers, cards, and other types of printed matter. The program has many functions for designing the layout of these items. It is very easy to make tables, for example.

The program also has some extra *Tools* such as an excellent spelling and grammar checker that you can turn on before you start typing. Then while you are typing, it alerts you when spelling and grammatical errors occur.

Microsoft Word is available as a separate program, but is usually sold as part of the *Microsoft Office* package. This package has a number of programs, including the popular spreadsheet *Excel* (a program for making calculations).

5.14 Tips

 Tip

Correcting on-screen?

Many people find it difficult to correct texts on their screens since it is easy to overlook typing errors. They often print their work first so that they can add corrections on paper. However, nearly every word processing program, such as *Microsoft Word*, has an excellent spelling checker that will find most of the typing errors for you and offer suggestions for improvement.

 Tip

The buttons in *WordPad*

You can see various buttons on the *WordPad* tool bar. These can be used to perform the commands *copy, cut, paste* and *undo* with a single click of the mouse:

These buttons have the following functions:

		Command:
✂	Cut a selection	Edit, Cut
📋	Copy a selection	Edit, Copy
📋	Paste a selection	Edit, Paste
↶	Undo the last thing done	Edit, Undo

 Tip

Did something go wrong?

Always try to undo what went wrong first:

☞ **Click** Edit, Undo

or:

☞ **Click** ↶

In almost all cases you can undo the last action you performed. In some programs you even can undo more than one action.

Tip

Selecting by dragging
You can select not only a whole word or an entire sentence, but any section of text you want:

☞ Move the cursor to the beginning of the section you want to select

one two three four five
six seven eight nine

☞ Keep pressing the mouse button and drag the mouse to the right

one two three four five
six seven eight nine

You will see that the letters are selected one after the other:

☞ Keep pressing the mouse button and drag the mouse downward

one two three four five
six seven eight nine

This makes it possible to select multiple words or lines:

It takes some practice, but soon you will be able to select any portion of the text that you want.

 Tip

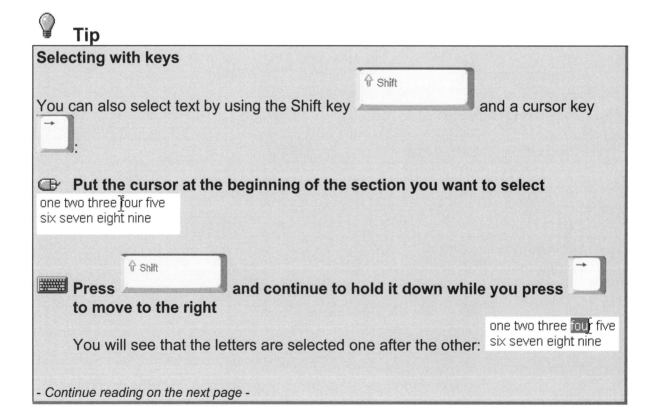

Selecting with keys

You can also select text by using the Shift key 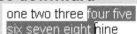 and a cursor key

→ :

☞ Put the cursor at the beginning of the section you want to select

one two three four five
six seven eight nine

⌨ Press ⇧ Shift **and continue to hold it down while you press** → **to move to the right**

one two three four five
six seven eight nine

You will see that the letters are selected one after the other:

- Continue reading on the next page -

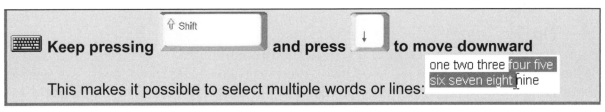

Keep pressing ⇧ Shift **and press** ↓ **to move downward**

This makes it possible to select multiple words or lines: one two three four five six seven eight nine

💡 Tip

Selecting lines by clicking and dragging

You can also select lines or paragraphs by clicking and dragging in the margin of the text:

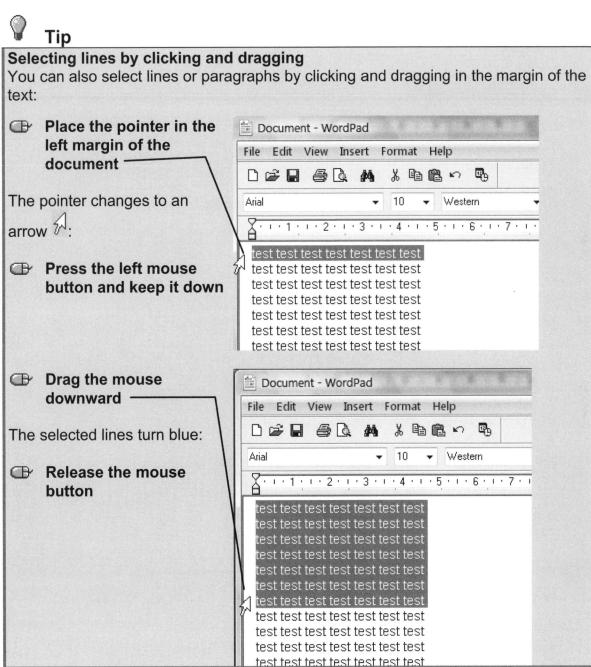

👉 **Place the pointer in the left margin of the document**

The pointer changes to an arrow 🔖:

👉 **Press the left mouse button and keep it down**

👉 **Drag the mouse downward**

The selected lines turn blue:

👉 **Release the mouse button**

Tip

Windows Vista Demos: Learning to use the mouse
Windows Vista Demos are narrated video demonstrations, designed to introduce you to personal computing. Watch as tasks are performed on screen. This is how you start a demo:

☞ **Click**

In the *Start menu*:

☞ **Click** Help and Support

At the top of the window:

⌨ **Type:** demo

☞ **Click** 🔍

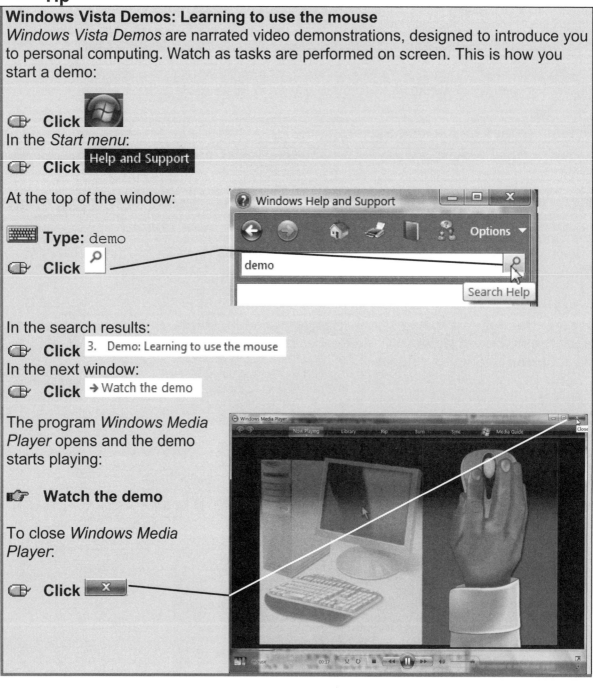

In the search results:

☞ **Click** 3. Demo: Learning to use the mouse

In the next window:

☞ **Click** → Watch the demo

The program *Windows Media Player* opens and the demo starts playing:

☞ **Watch the demo**

To close *Windows Media Player*:

☞ **Click** ✕

6. Folders and Files

In this chapter you will learn to work with *folders* and *files*. A *file* is the generic name for everything saved on the computer. A file can be a program, a data file with names, text you have written, or a photo. Actually, everything that is on the hard disk of your computer is called a *file*.

A *folder* is little more than a container in which you store files. If you put thousands of paper files on someone's desk, it would be virtually impossible to find any particular one when you needed it. That is why people often store paper files in folders inside a filing cabinet. Arranging files into logical groups makes it easy to locate any particular file. Folders on your computer work exactly the same way.
Not only do folders hold files, but they also can hold other folders. A folder within a folder is usually called a *subfolder*. You can create any number of subfolders, and each can hold any number of files and additional subfolders.

When it comes to getting organized, you do not need to start from scratch. *Windows Vista* comes with a handful of common folders that you can use as anchors to begin organizing your files. Here is a list of some of the most common folders to store your files and folders in: *Documents, Pictures, Music, Videos, Downloads.*
In the previous chapters you have already saved some of your work in the folder *Documents*.

Using a folder window, you can work with files and folders that are on the hard disk of your computer. You can delete, copy and move files or folders there.
Perhaps at one time you will want to put a text or another file on a USB memory stick. You can do that in this folder window too.

In this chapter, you will learn how to:

- use the folder window *Document*
- make a new folder
- move and copy a file to another folder
- copy and delete files
- change the name of a file or folder
- empty the *Recycle Bin*
- copy a file to a USB memory stick

6.1 Opening Your Personal Folder

Your *Personal Folder* is a folder containing your folders *Documents, Pictures, Music, Contacts* and other folders. The *Personal Folder* is labeled with the name you use to log on to your computer. The *Personal Folder* is located at the top of the *Start menu*. Take a look:

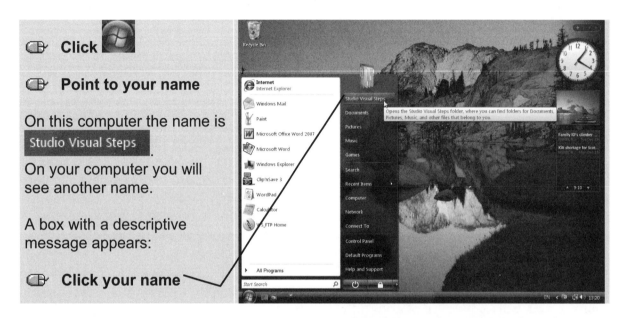

☞ **Click** [Windows logo]

☞ **Point to your name**

On this computer the name is
`Studio Visual Steps`.
On your computer you will
see another name.

A box with a descriptive
message appears:

☞ **Click your name**

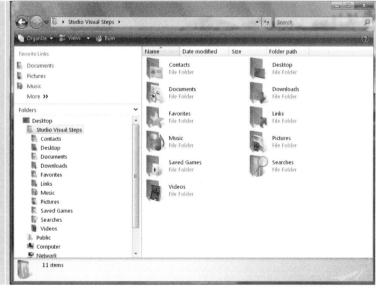

You now see this window with
all your folders:

This window is called a *folder
window*.

The content of the *Personal
Folder* can be slightly
different on every computer.

HELP! I do not see all the folders in the left pane.

If the left pane of your window does not show folders like those in the figure on the previous page:

👆 **Click** Folders

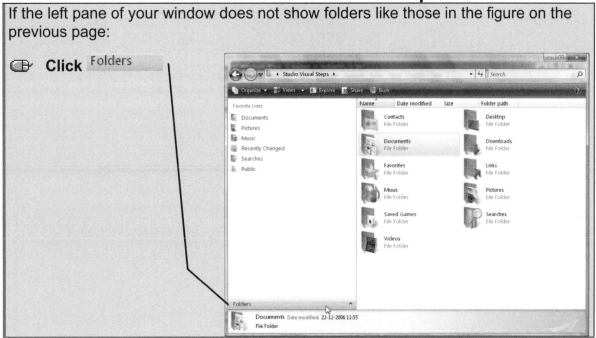

6.2 Changing the Display of the Folder Window

There are several ways to view your folders in the folder window. Take a look at the display settings of your folder window:

👆 **Click** next to Views

A menu appears:

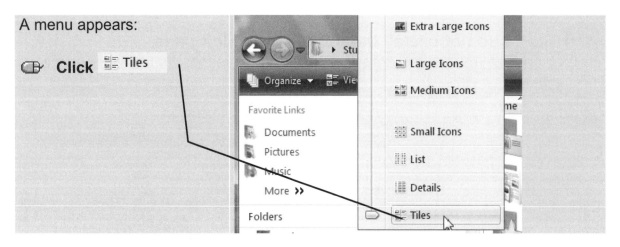

Click ‖≣ Tiles

Click 🗇 Organize ▾

A menu appears:

Click 🖵 Layout

A second menu appears:

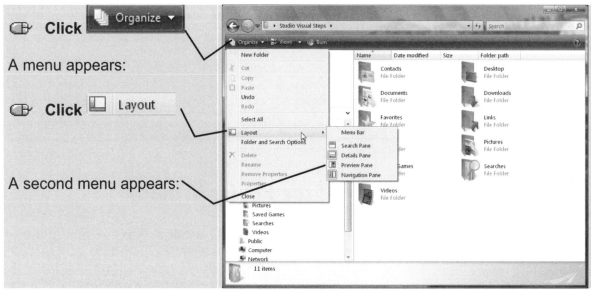

In this second menu only the options 🔲 Details Pane and 🔲 Navigation Pane should be active. If an option is active (or *highlighted*), you will see a light blue box around the icon. If the icon is not highlighted, you can activate the option by clicking it.

Click (if necessary) 🔲 Details Pane

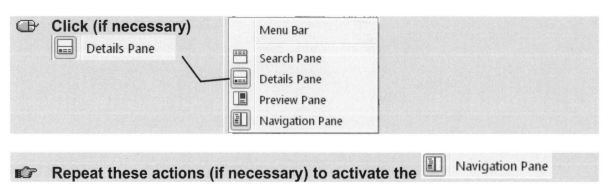

☞ **Repeat these actions (if necessary) to activate the** 🔲 Navigation Pane

Deactivating an option is done in the same way, by clicking the option in the list.

☞ **Repeat the actions (if necessary) to deactivate the other options**
▭ Search Pane **and** ▭ Preview Pane

Now the folder window on your computer displays the same as the figure shown below:

🖝 **Click** 📁 Documents

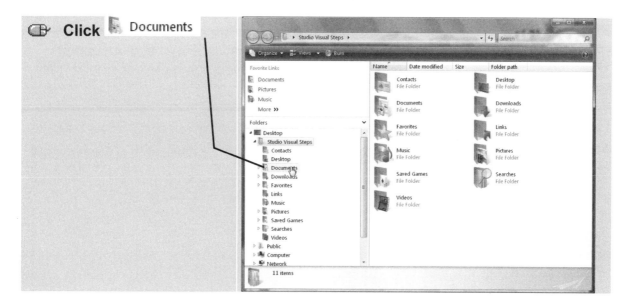

6.3 Understanding the Different Parts of a Folder Window

In addition to showing the contents of the folder, a folder window has specific areas that are designed to help you navigate around the folders on the hard disk of your computer or work with files and folders more easily. Take a look now:

Navigation pane:
It shows all folders on your computer.

Notice how the *Address bar*
📁 ▸ Studio Visual Steps ▸ Documents
identifies the folder you are in:

The files contained in this folder are shown as icons in the *File list:*

When you select a file, you can see information about it in the *Details pane*, here:

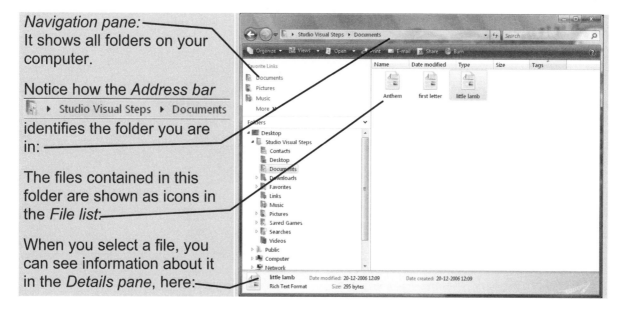

By using the *Navigation pane* on the left side, you can quickly navigate to any folder on your computer. When you click a folder in the *Navigation pane*, the folder contents in the *File list* will now display the contents of the folder you clicked.

6.4 The Folder Documents

Windows Vista has a special folder where you can save all of your text documents. This folder is named *Documents*. You have already saved some of your work in the folder *Documents* in the previous chapters.

The *Address bar* of the folder window shows your current location on the computer:

On your computer the name Studio Visual Steps will be another name.

You now see the content of the folder *Documents:*

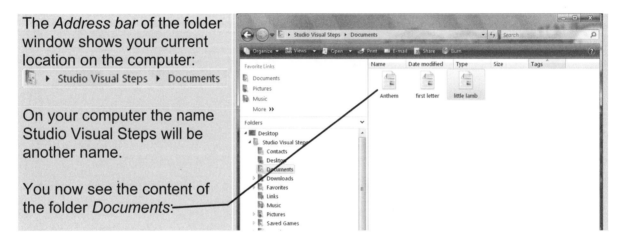

There are at least three files in the folder *Documents:* your practice texts.

Look closely at these files:

Each file is represented by an icon.

6.5 File and Folder Icons

Windows Vista represents files and folders with icons.
You may see one or more of the following icons for folders:

A folder.
A folder may contain other subfolders or files, but it can also be empty.

You may see one or more of the following icons for files:

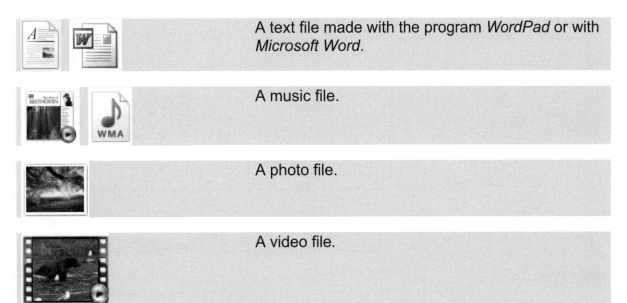

A text file made with the program *WordPad* or with *Microsoft Word*.

A music file.

A photo file.

A video file.

These are only a few examples. There are many, many more icons because every program has its own icon for files.

6.6 Making a New Folder

A folder is a container that helps you organize your files. Every file on your computer is stored in a folder, and folders can also hold other folders. Folders located inside other folders are often called *subfolders*.
You can make new folders yourself. This can be handy, for example, to keep your letters separate from all of your other documents. In this exercise, you will make a new folder inside the folder Documents.

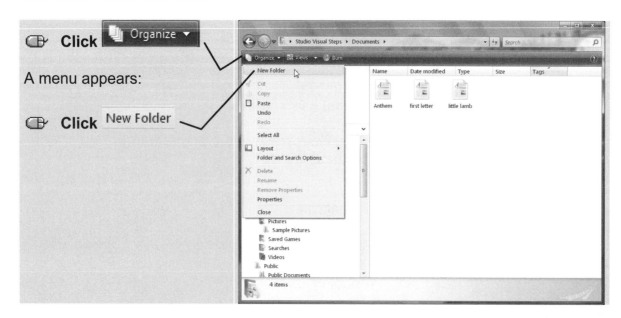

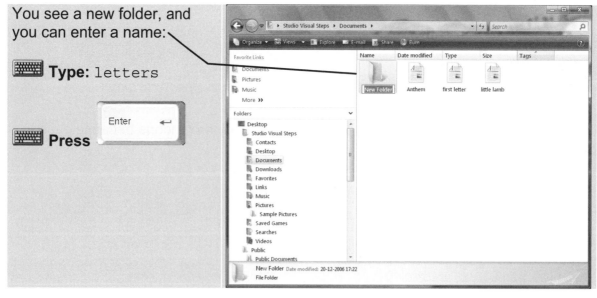

Now you have made a new

subfolder **letters** inside the folder **Documents**:

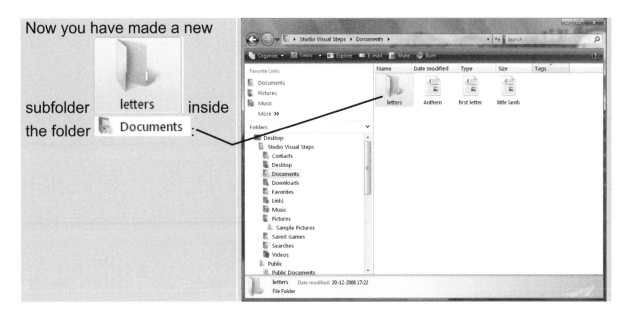

You can use this folder *letters* to save a letter that you have written in *WordPad*, for example.
To do so, you can minimize the folder window *Documents* and then start the program *WordPad*.

☞ **Minimize the folder window *Documents*** 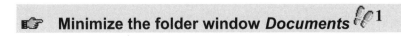1

6.7 Saving in a Folder

As an exercise, you will first write a letter in *WordPad* and then you will save it in the

subfolder you just made, 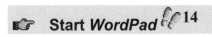 .

☞ **Start *WordPad*** 14

Add some "content" to your letter, type the following short sentence fragment:

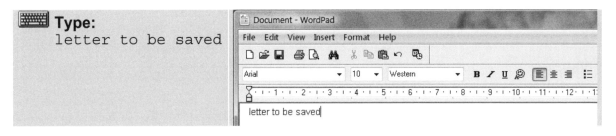

⌨ **Type:**
letter to be saved

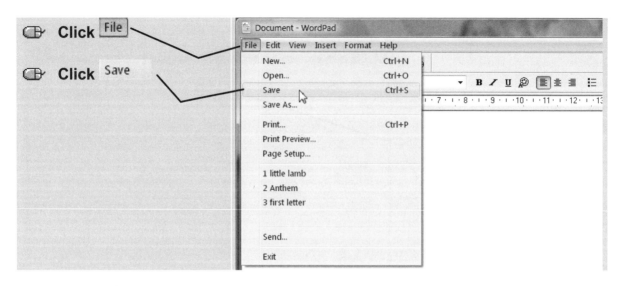

You now see the *Save As* window:

In the *Address bar* (on top) you see the folder

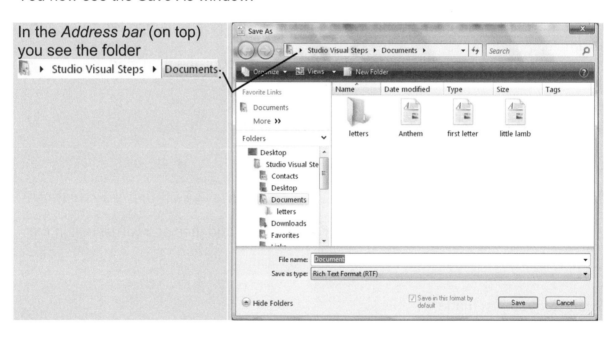

HELP! My Save As window is different.

Do you see a window without the *Navigation pane*?

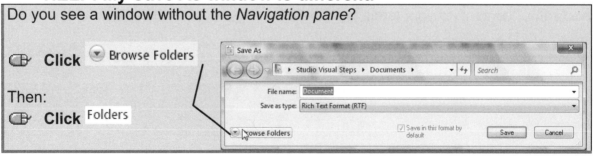

You want to save your new letter in the subfolder [letters]. First, you will need to open the subfolder [letters]. This is the easiest way to do it:

On the left side of the *Save As* window in the *Navigation pane*:

☞ **Click** [letters]

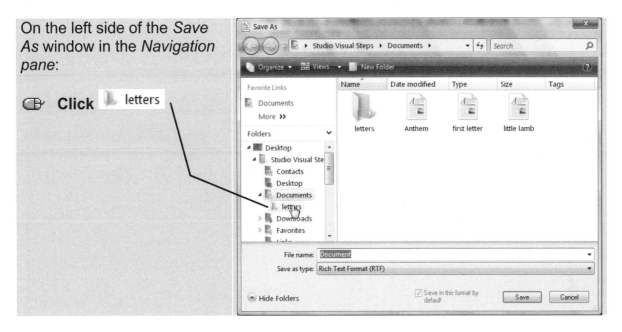

The folder *letters* will be opened. Notice that the folder name *letters* now appears in the *Address bar* to the right of *Documents.* The file list is currently empty.
In the lower part of the window, a file name is already shown: Document . That is the *default* name the program always shows. You can change the name like this:

☞ **Click next to** File name: : Document

☞ **Delete the name** 𝒶𝒶44

⌨ **Type:** note

Then:

☞ **Click** [Save]

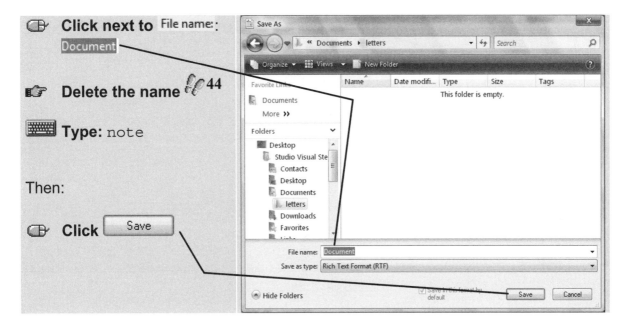

The file *note* is saved in the folder *letter.*

☞ **Close the program** *WordPad* ✌15

Now you can reopen the folder window *Documents*, to verify that your file has been saved in the subfolder *letters*.

☞ **Open the folder** *Documents* **with the button on the** *Taskbar* ✌26

⊞ **Double-click**

letters

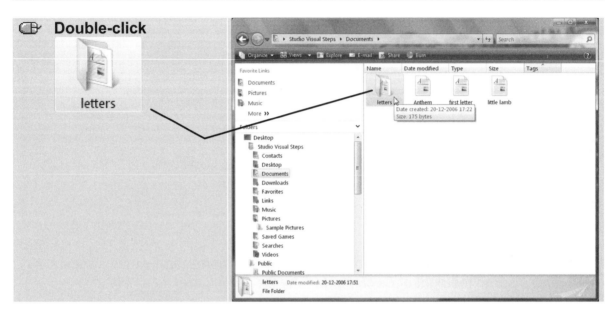

In the *Address bar* you can see the folder *letters* is now opened:

In the file list you now see your saved *WordPad* file:

note

To go back to the folder
📄 Documents:

⊞ **Click** 📄 Documents

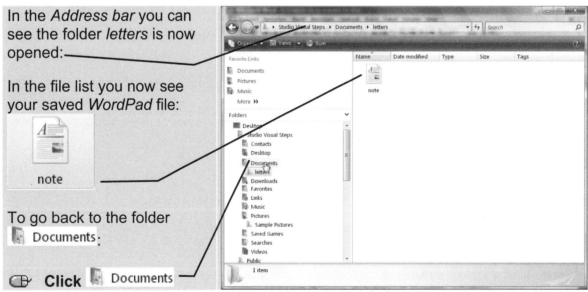

6.8 Copying Files

You can also copy files. For example, you can make a second copy of a letter that you want to change slightly. To practice, you can copy your practice texts.

Now you see the files in the Documents folder:

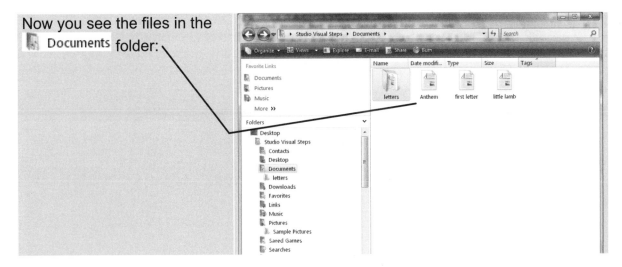

You can now copy one of the practice texts, but remember the rule: select first, then act.

⇨ **Please note:**

Select first ... then act.

Selecting a file is easy: simply click its icon or name.

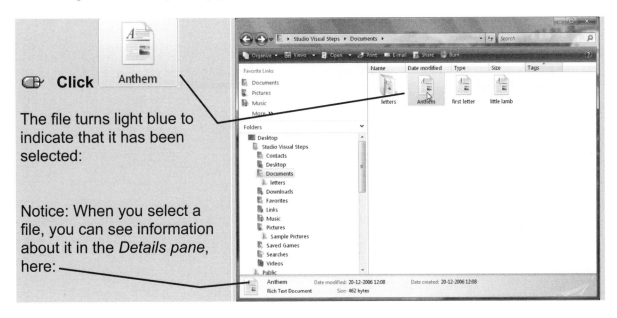

🖱 **Click** Anthem

The file turns light blue to indicate that it has been selected:

Notice: When you select a file, you can see information about it in the *Details pane*, here:

HELP! There is a blue box around the name.

Do you see a light blue box around the name? Has the mouse pointer changed into I?

For example: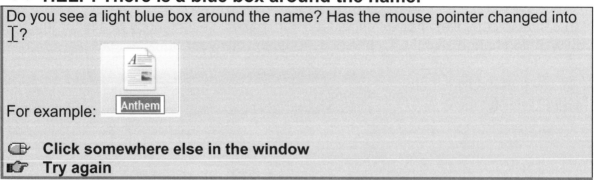

☞ **Click somewhere else in the window**
☞ **Try again**

☞ **Click** *Organize ▼*

☞ **Click** *Copy*

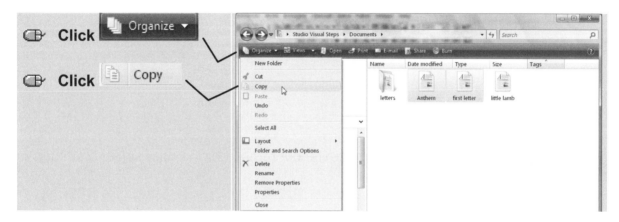

Windows Vista now knows you want to copy the file. The next step is pasting the

copied file into the folder *letters* :

To open the folder *letters*:

☞ **Double-click**

letters

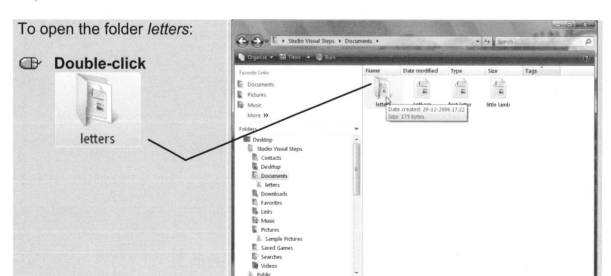

Now you see the content of
the folder *letters:*

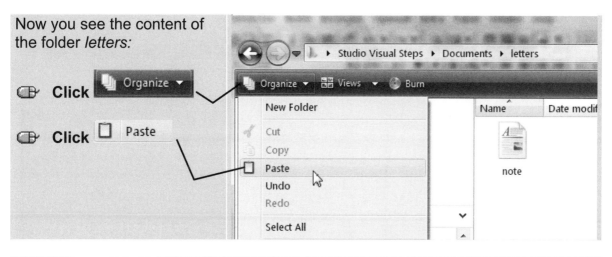

☞ **Click** Organize ▼

☞ **Click** ☐ Paste

The file Anthem has
been pasted:

There are more ways to copy a file. For example by using the right mouse button.
Try it:

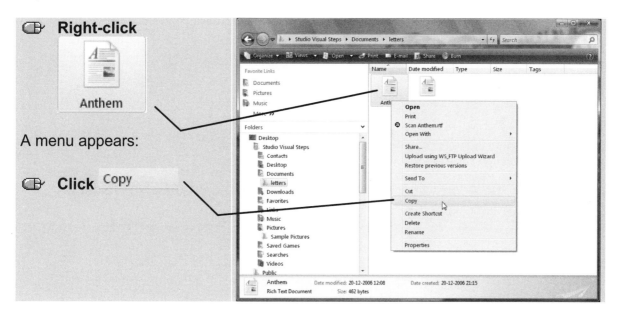

☞ **Right-click**
Anthem

A menu appears:

☞ **Click** Copy

☞ **Right-click a blank area of the folder window**

A menu appears:

☞ **Click** Paste

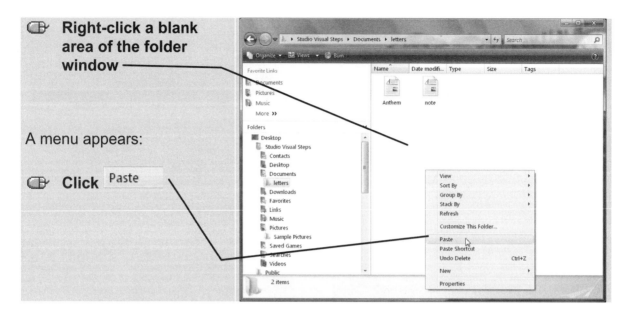

There is a copy Anthem - Copy of the file in the same folder. Notice, the word "Copy" is added automatically to the name. This is because files with duplicate names are not allowed inside the same folder. Even though the content of the file is the same, the name of the file has to be different if it is located in the same folder.

☞ **Click** ←

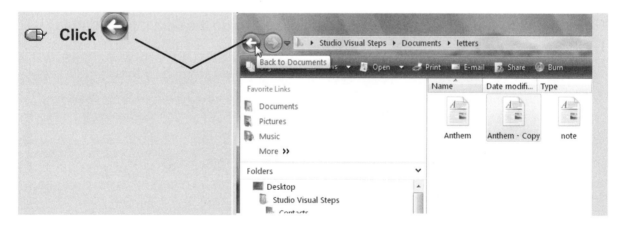

Remember: in the *Address bar* of the folder window you can see which folder is opened: ▸ Studio Visual Steps ▸ Documents ▸ letters .

6.9 Moving a File

You can also cut a file and paste it into another folder. The file will then be moved to the destination folder.

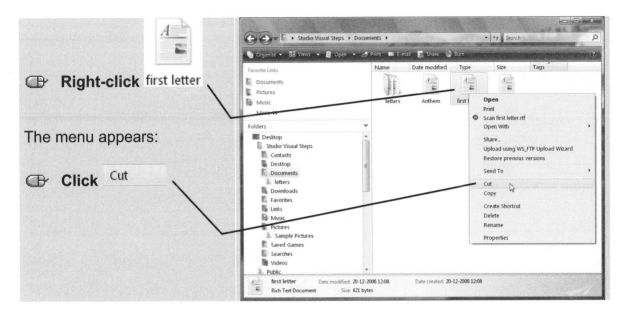

Right-click first letter

The menu appears:

Click Cut

You are going to paste the file into the folder *letters*:

To open the folder *letters*:

Double-click letters

Now you see the folder *letters*:

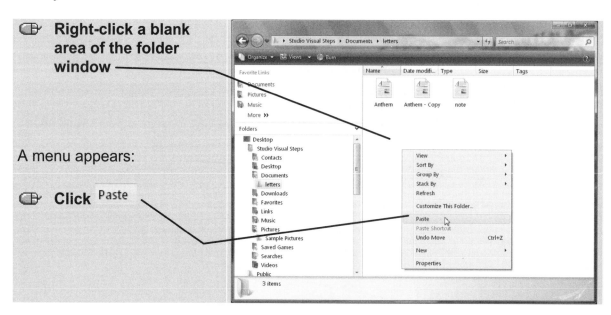

☞ **Right-click a blank area of the folder window**

A menu appears:

☞ **Click** Paste

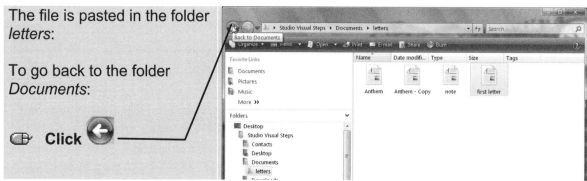

The file is pasted in the folder *letters*:

To go back to the folder *Documents*:

☞ **Click** ⬅

In the folder *Documents* the file *first letter* has indeed disappeared:

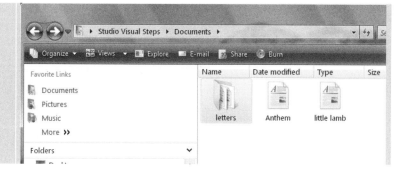

6.10 Dragging and Dropping Files

The easiest way to move files to another folder is by *dragging and dropping*.
Try it:

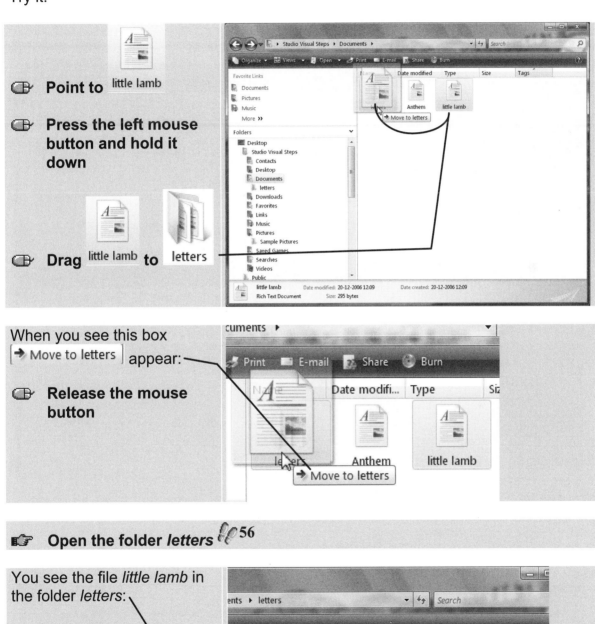

☞ Point to little lamb

**☞ Press the left mouse
button and hold it
down**

☞ Drag little lamb **to** letters

When you see this box
→ Move to letters appear:

**☞ Release the mouse
button**

☞ Open the folder *letters* 🦶56

You see the file *little lamb* in
the folder *letters*:

6.11 Selecting Multiple Files

You can also copy more than one file at a time. To do this, you must select them first. Go ahead and try:

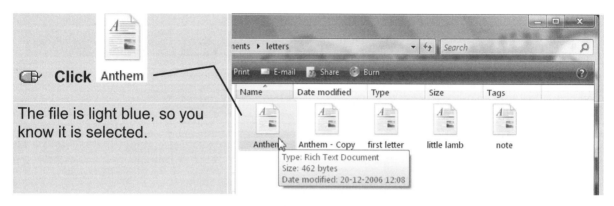

Click Anthem

The file is light blue, so you know it is selected.

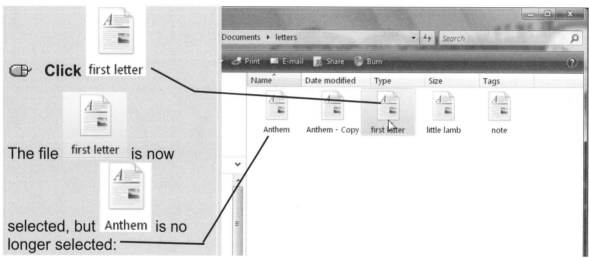

Click first letter

The file *first letter* is now

selected, but *Anthem* is no longer selected:

You can select only one file at a time by clicking. But you can select more than one file if you use a special key on your keyboard:

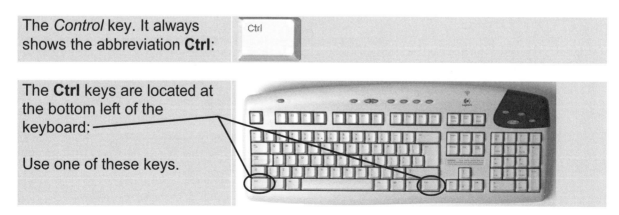

The *Control* key. It always shows the abbreviation **Ctrl**:

The **Ctrl** keys are located at the bottom left of the keyboard:

Use one of these keys.

The Ctrl key is used together with the mouse. The file first letter is still selected.

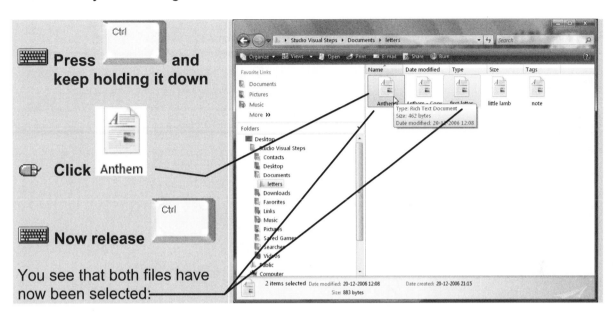

Press and **keep holding it down**

Click Anthem

Now release

You see that both files have now been selected:

You can select even more files by using the Ctrl key. Then you can copy and paste, or cut and paste, or drag the group of selected files to their destination folder. For now, that is not necessary. This is how you clear the selection:

Click on any blank area of the folder window

The selection is cleared.

 Tip

To select a consecutive group of files (or folders when you are working with folders):

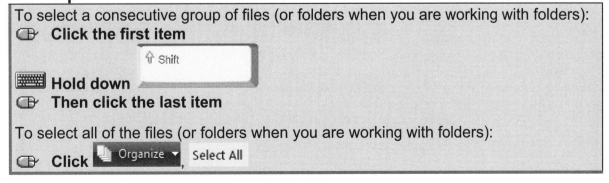

Click the first item

Hold down ⇧ Shift

Then click the last item

To select all of the files (or folders when you are working with folders):

Click Organize ▼ , Select All

6.12 Changing the File Name

Sometimes you may want to give a file a different name. Perhaps, you have several documents about the same subject, for example, and you want to be able to clearly distinguish one document from another.
You can try changing the name of a file with one of the two practice letters.

 Right-click note

A menu appears:

 Click Rename

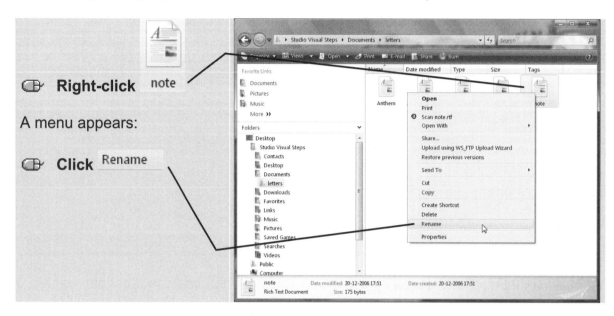

HELP!

Do you unexpectedly see the window for *WordPad* or *Microsoft Word?*
If so, you double-clicked on the file name, and opened the program. To close the program:

 Click [X]

☞ **Try again**

Now the word *note* is highlighted with a blue background color:

⌨ **Type the new name:**
exercise do not save

⌨ **Press** [Enter ↵]

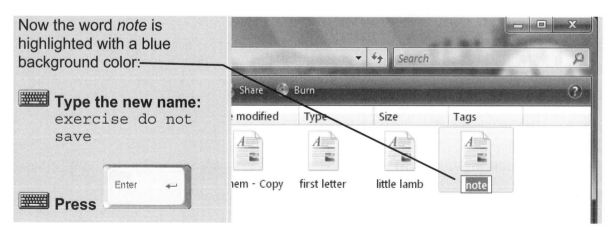

The name has changed:

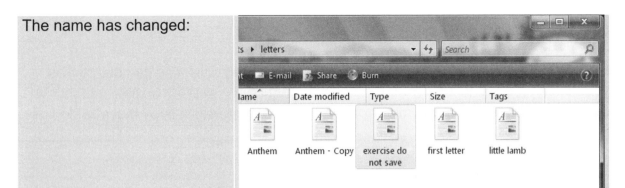

 HELP!

You can not put more than one file with the same name in a folder.
If you try to give a file a name that already exists, you will see:

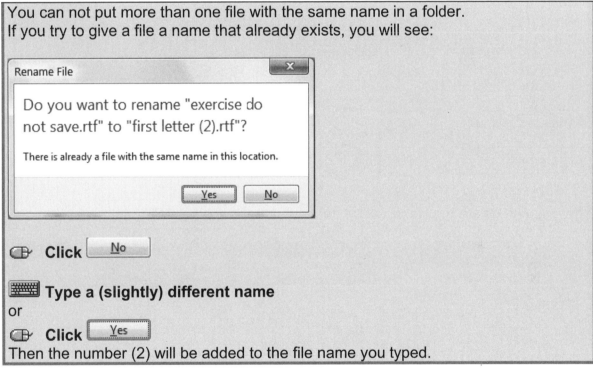

👆 **Click** No

⌨ **Type a (slightly) different name**
or
👆 **Click** Yes
Then the number (2) will be added to the file name you typed.

6.13 Deleting Files

It is wise to regularly do a "spring cleaning" on your hard disk. You can delete files you no longer need to keep your hard disk manageable. To practice, you can delete the file *Anthem - Copy* in the folder , because this is a copy that you do not really need.

⇨ **Please note:**

Select first ... then act.

It is important to select carefully, so that you do not delete the wrong files.

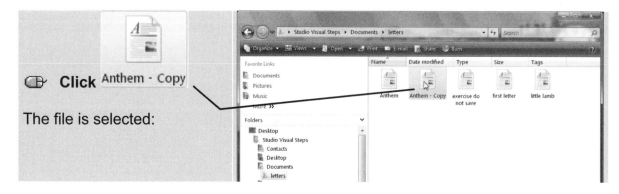

Click Anthem - Copy

The file is selected:

Now you can delete the file. It will be "tossed" into the *Recycle Bin*.

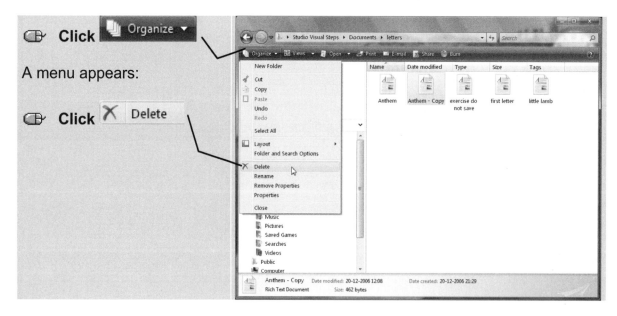

Click Organize ▾

A menu appears:

Click ✕ Delete

Windows Vista will ask whether the file should be put in the *Recycle Bin*:

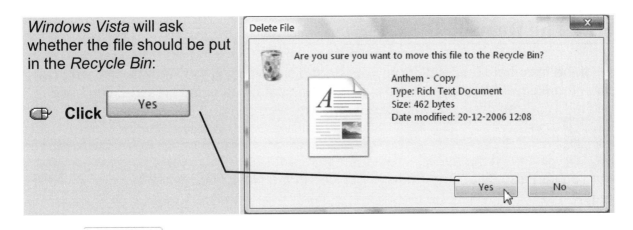

Delete File

Are you sure you want to move this file to the Recycle Bin?

Anthem - Copy
Type: Rich Text Document
Size: 462 bytes
Date modified: 20-12-2006 12:08

Yes   No

 Click [Yes]

The file Anthem - Copy has now disappeared from the folder window *letters*. Files that have been deleted are not gone forever. As a kind of safety catch, they are put into the *Recycle Bin* first. They are not really gone forever until you empty the *Recycle Bin*. As long as a file is in the *Recycle Bin*, you can retrieve it later if you need it.

 Tip

Selecting multiple files
You can also delete multiple files at the same time. You must select them first by clicking them while pressing the Ctrl key or the Shift key. Then you can delete them.

Tip

Selecting an entire folder

You can also select an entire folder   to delete. You can select a folder by clicking it; then you can delete it.

Tip

Only your files
Be careful when deleting files. Only delete files that you yourself have made.
If you did not create the file, you might not be able to delete it.
Also, you cannot delete a file (or the folder that contains it) if the file is currently open in a program. Make sure that the file is not open in any program, and then try to delete the file or folder again.
Never delete files or folders for programs that you do not use. Program files must be deleted in a different way.

6.14 The Recycle Bin

All of the files that you delete from your hard disk end up in the *Recycle Bin*. You can open the *Recycle Bin* to see what is in it. It will contain all of the files that you have deleted. You can open the *Recycle Bin* with its own icon on the *Desktop:*

But you can also select the *Recycle Bin* icon in the *Navigation pane:*

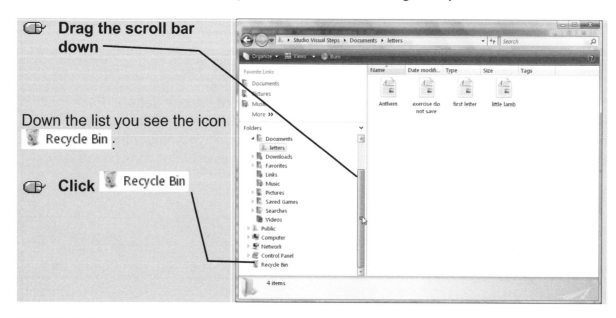

☞ **Drag the scroll bar down**

Down the list you see the icon
Recycle Bin .

☞ **Click** Recycle Bin

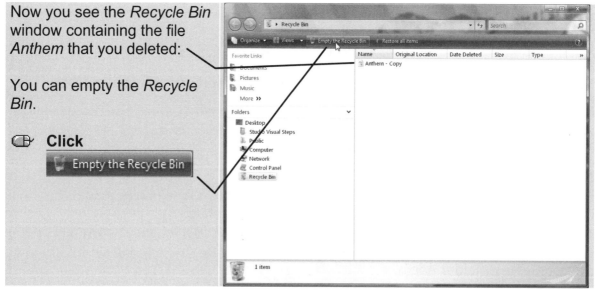

Now you see the *Recycle Bin* window containing the file *Anthem* that you deleted:

You can empty the *Recycle Bin.*

☞ **Click** Empty the Recycle Bin

To be certain, you will be asked to confirm that you want to permanently delete this file.

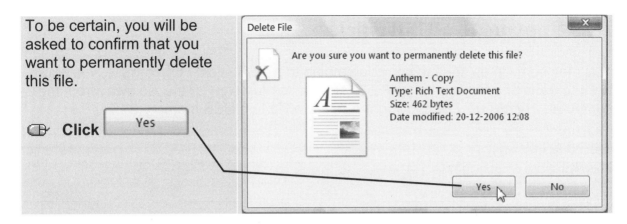

Delete File

Are you sure you want to permanently delete this file?

Anthem - Copy
Type: Rich Text Document
Size: 462 bytes
Date modified: 20-12-2006 12:08

Yes   No

 Click | Yes |

Now the file has been permanently deleted and cannot be retrieved.

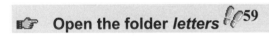 **Open the folder *letters*** $\ell\ell$59

 Tip

When to empty the Recycle Bin?
You do not have to empty the *Recycle Bin* every time you delete a file. You only need to empty it when you want to permanently delete a file. It is better to collect your deleted files in the *Recycle Bin* and to wait to empty it until you do your "spring cleaning".

 Tip

Is there anything in the Recycle Bin?
You can tell by the icon for the *Recycle Bin* on the *Desktop* whether there is anything in it. The icon changes its appearance:

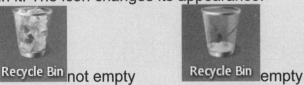

Recycle Bin not empty   Recycle Bin empty

6.15 Copying to a USB Stick

You may sometimes need to copy something to a USB stick. For example, you might want to transfer a file to another PC or store a backup copy of the file away from the computer. Try this now by copying the *Anthem* file to a USB memory stick.

 Please note:

In order to work through this section, you need a USB stick.
A USB stick is a small, portable device that plugs into a computer's USB port. Like a hard disk, a USB flash drive stores information, but with a flash drive you can easily transfer that information from one computer to another.
If you do not have a USB stick, you can skip this section.

First you have to insert the USB stick into the computer.

☞ Locate the USB port on your computer

A USB port can be on the front or the back of the computer, or both.
On a laptop, a USB port could also be on one of its sides.

☞ Insert the USB stick into the USB port and gently press it in

Having trouble?
☞ Then turn the stick over and try again

The first time you use the USB stick you will see this:

On the right side of the *Taskbar* you see this notification:

Installing device driver software
Click here for status.

Wait a moment until you see this text balloon appear:

The USB stick is ready to use.

A second folder window appears on top of the folder window Documents ▸ letters :

In the *Address bar* you see this is the folder window of the USB stick:

▸ Computer ▸ Removable Disk (K:)

In this figure the USB stick is called *Removable Disk (K:)*. On your computer that might be a different letter.

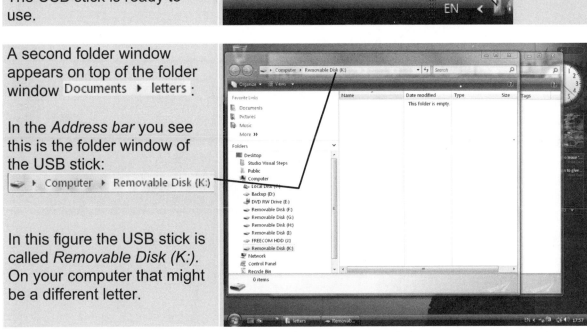

The easiest way to copy files from the folder Documents ▸ letters to the USB stick folder Removable Disk (K:) is by using both folder windows. You must reduce the size of the folder windows on the *Desktop* so you can see the contents of both of them. You can change the size of the windows by dragging the edge of the frame with the mouse. In Chapter 2 you have already learned how to do that.

☞ **Place the mouse pointer precisely on the right edge of the window's frame**

☞ **Hold the mouse button down and drag to the left**

You will see the size of the window reduce.

☞ **Release the mouse button**

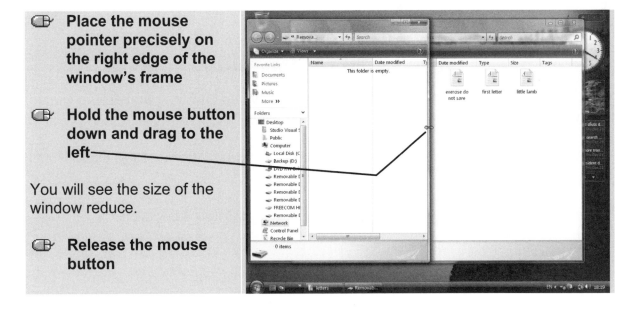

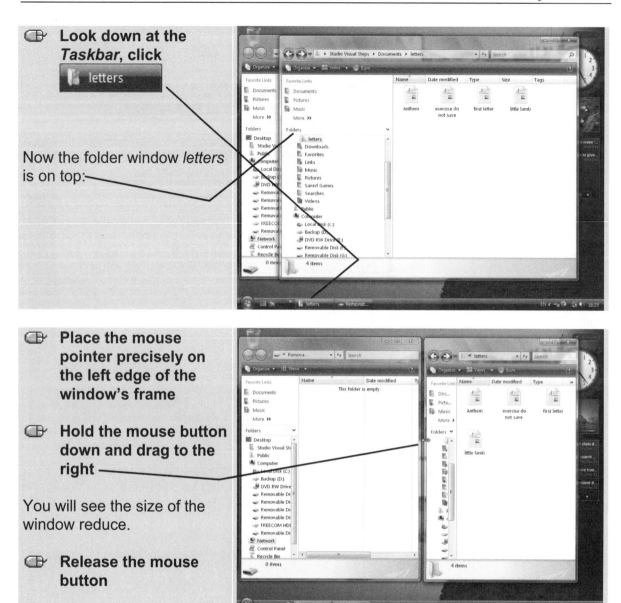

☞ Look down at the *Taskbar*, click

📁 letters

Now the folder window *letters* is on top:

☞ Place the mouse pointer precisely on the left edge of the window's frame

☞ Hold the mouse button down and drag to the right

You will see the size of the window reduce.

☞ Release the mouse button

You can see the content of both folder windows. Now you can drag and drop a file from the folder window Documents ▸ letters to the folder Removable Disk (K:) .

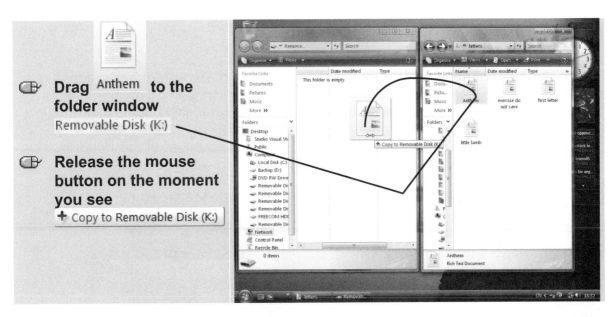

Drag Anthem to the folder window
Removable Disk (K:)

Release the mouse button on the moment you see
➕ Copy to Removable Disk (K:)

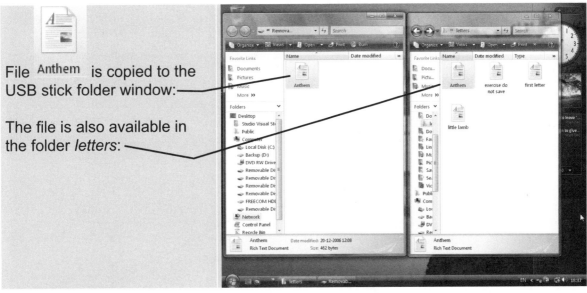

File Anthem is copied to the USB stick folder window:

The file is also available in the folder *letters*:

➡️ **Please note:**

When you drag a file (or folder) into a folder on same hard disk (your own computer), the file (or folder) is **moved** to the destination folder.

When you drag a file (or folder) into a folder on a different hard disk or USB stick, the file is **copied** to the folder on the destination disk or stick.

☞ **Restore the size of both folder windows** 𝒪𝒪12

☞ **Close both folder windows** 𝒪𝒪4

6.16 Safely Removing a USB Stick

Before removing storage devices, such as USB sticks, make sure that the computer has finished saving any information to the device. If the device has an activity light flashing, wait for a few seconds until the light has finished flashing before removing it.

If you see the *Safely Remove Hardware* icon at the far right of the *Windows Taskbar*, you can use this to ensure that the USB stick is ready to be removed:

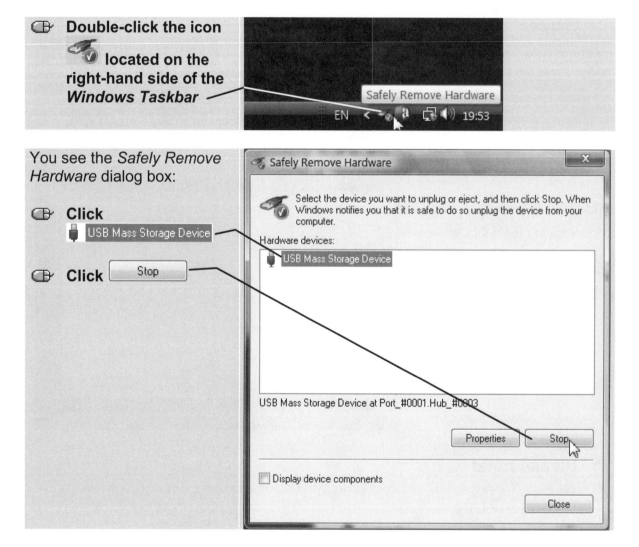

☞ **Remove the USB stick from the computer**

In this chapter you have learned how to use the folder windows. You practiced moving, deleting and copying files and dragging files to a USB stick.

You can practice a little more by doing the exercises in this chapter.

6.17 Exercises

The following exercises will help you master what you have just learned. Have you forgotten how to do something? Use the number beside the footsteps to look it up in the appendix *How Do I Do That Again?*

Exercise: Opening Folder Windows

- ✓ Open your *Personal Folder.* 86
- ✓ Open the folder *Documents.* 59
- ✓ Open the folder *letters.* 56
- ✓ Go back to the folder *Documents* using the *Back button.* 57
- ✓ Go to the folder *letters* using the *Forward button.* 57
- ✓ Close the folder window. 4

Exercise: Working with the Navigation Pane

In this exercise, use the *Navigation pane* (not the *Back and Forward buttons*).

- ✓ Open your *Personal Folder.* 86
- ✓ Open the folder *Documents.* 59
- ✓ Open the *Recycle Bin* folder. 59
- ✓ Open the folder *Documents.* 59
- ✓ Open your *Personal Folder.* 59
- ✓ Close the folder window. 4

Exercise: Making a New Folder

✔ Open your *Personal Folder*. 🐾86

✔ Open the folder *Documents*. 🐾59

✔ Create a new folder with the name *practice*. 🐾58

✔ Open the new folder *practice*. 🐾59

✔ Close the folder window. 🐾4

Exercise: Copying Files

Please note: you need to do the exercise above in order to do this exercise.

✔ Open your *Personal Folder*. 🐾86

✔ Open the folder *Documents*. 🐾59

✔ Copy the file *Anthem* to the folder *practice*. 🐾60

✔ Close the folder window. 🐾4

Exercise: Renaming a File

Please note: you need to do the exercises above in order to do this exercise.

✔ Open your *Personal Folder*. 🐾86

✔ Open the folder *Documents*. 🐾59

✔ Open the folder *practice*. 🐾59

✔ Change the name of the file *Anthem* to *song*. 🐾61

✔ Close the folder window. 🐾4

Exercise: Deleting Files

Please note: you need to do the previous exercises in order to do this exercise.

☑ Open your *Personal Folder*. №*86*

☑ Open the folder *Documents*. №*59*

☑ Open the new folder *practice*. №*59*

☑ Delete the file *song* in this folder. №*62*

☑ Close the folder window. №*4*

Exercise: Renaming and Deleting a Folder

Renaming and deleting folders is done just like renaming and deleting files. Try it:

☑ Open your *Personal Folder*. №*86*

☑ Open the folder *Documents*. №*59*

☑ Rename the folder *practice* into *my letters*. №*61*

☑ Delete the folder *my letters*. №*62*

☑ Close the folder window. №*4*

Exercise: Copying a File to a USB Stick

☑ Open the folder *Documents*. №*55*

☑ Insert the USB stick into the computer.

☑ Copy file *Anthem* to the USB stick (drag and drop - two folder windows). №*60*

☑ Safely remove the USB stick. №*85*

☑ Close both folder windows. №*4*

6.18 Background Information

Dictionary

Address bar	The *Address bar* appears at the top of every folder window and displays your current location as a series of links separated by arrows. Using the *Address bar*, you can see which folder is opened.
File	The generic name for everything saved on the computer. A file can be a program, a data file with names, text you have written, or a photo. Actually, everything that is on the hard disk of your computer is called a *file*.
File list	This is where the contents of the current folder are displayed.
Folder	A folder is a container that helps you to organize your files. Every file on your computer is stored in a folder, and folders can also hold other folders.
Folder list	List of folders in the *Navigation pane*. Using the folder list in the *Navigation pane*, you can navigate directly to the folder you're interested in by clicking on this folder.
Folder window	When you open a folder on the desktop, a folder window appears. A folder window has specific areas that are designed to help you navigate around the folders on the hard disk of your computer or work with files and folders more easily.
Hard disk	The primary storage device located inside a computer. Also called a hard drive or hard disk drive, it is where your files and programs are typically stored.
Navigation pane	Shows a list of folders that can be opened in the folder window.
Recycle Bin	When you delete a file or folder, it goes to the *Recycle Bin*. You can retrieve a file from the *Recycle Bin*. But if you empty the *Recycle Bin*, all of its contents are permanently gone.
Search box	Box you find in a folder window. As you type in the *Search box*, the contents of the folder are immediately filtered to show only those files that match what you typed. The *Search box* does not automatically search your entire computer, however. It only searches the current folder and any of its subfolders.

- Continue reading on the next page -

USB port	A narrow, rectangular connection point on a computer where you can connect a universal serial bus (USB) device such as a USB stick.
USB stick	Small portable device, to store files and folders. Plugs into a computer's USB port. *Windows Vista* will show a USB stick as a removable disk.

Source: Windows Help and Support

Diskettes, USB sticks, CDs, DVDs

Diskettes, USB sticks, CDs and DVDs are storage media often used to store files outside the computer. For example, you can use them to transfer files to another computer or to save a *backup* copy. Software manufacturers often provide their products on CD-ROM or DVD-ROM.

Diskette

Diskettes, also called floppy disks, are 3.5 inches in size. They can store up to 1.44 MB. You can write files directly to a diskette in *Windows Vista*. The memory can be reused. To use a diskette, you need to have a floppy drive in your PC.

USB stick

A USB stick is a small storage medium with a large storage capacity. You can insert it directly into your PC's USB port. The storage capacity can vary from 16 MB to 16 GB or more. The price depends on the capacity. You can write files directly to a USB stick in *Windows Vista*. The memory can be reused.

CD-ROM and DVD-ROM

Many software manufacturers deliver their software on CD-ROMs. These days, software manufacturers deliver very large programs on DVD-ROMs. Large files like movies are also released on DVD-ROM. You can play these CD-ROMs and DVD-ROMs in your CD player or DVD player, but you can not write to them. ROM means Read Only Memory.

Writable CDs and DVDs

If your computer includes a CD or DVD recorder, you can copy files to a writable disc.

The parts of the Open window

This is the window that you use in *WordPad*, for example, to open a file from your hard disk. It looks like the *Save As* window. *Windows* such as these are easy to use.

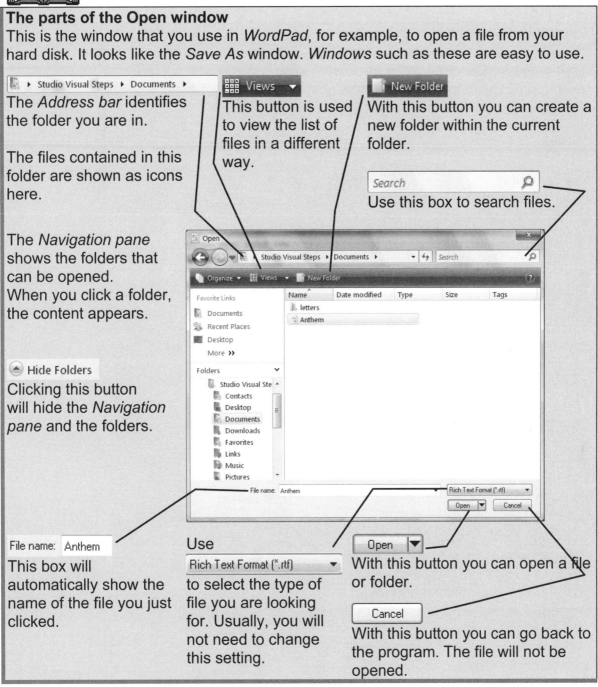

The *Address bar* identifies the folder you are in.

The files contained in this folder are shown as icons here.

The *Navigation pane* shows the folders that can be opened.
When you click a folder, the content appears.

Clicking this button will hide the *Navigation pane* and the folders.

This button is used to view the list of files in a different way.

With this button you can create a new folder within the current folder.

Use this box to search files.

This box will automatically show the name of the file you just clicked.

Use to select the type of file you are looking for. Usually, you will not need to change this setting.

With this button you can open a file or folder.

With this button you can go back to the program. The file will not be opened.

6.19 Tips

 Tip

The folder list in the Navigation pane

When you use the folder list in the *Navigation pane* in the folder window, you can navigate directly to the folder that contains the (sub)folders or files you are interested in.

The only thing you have to do is click a folder name and the content will be displayed in the file list.
Here you see the content of the *Personal Folder.*

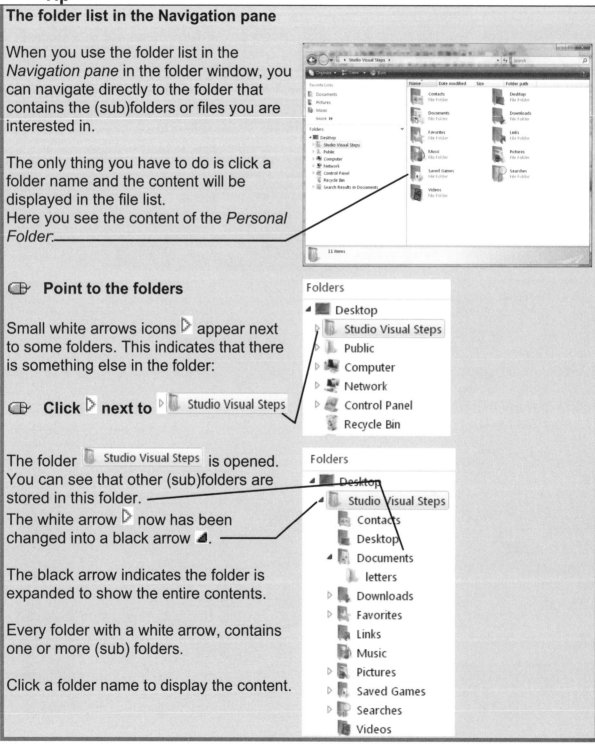

Point to the folders

Small white arrows icons ▷ appear next to some folders. This indicates that there is something else in the folder:

Click ▷ next to ▷ 🗋 Studio Visual Steps

The folder 🗋 Studio Visual Steps is opened. You can see that other (sub)folders are stored in this folder.
The white arrow ▷ now has been changed into a black arrow ◢.

The black arrow indicates the folder is expanded to show the entire contents.

Every folder with a white arrow, contains one or more (sub) folders.

Click a folder name to display the content.

Tip

Searching files in a folder
There are many ways to find your files on your computer. Most of the time, you will start by using the *Search box* that is available within any folder.

☞ **Click in the *Search box***

⌨ **Start typing**

As you type, the search results appear above the *File list*.
Just click a file name to open it.

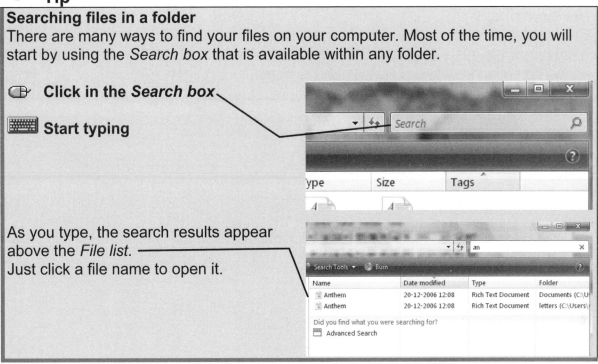

 Tip

Finding a file
Have you forgotten where you saved an important file?
Then you can use the *Windows Vista Search box*:

☞ **Click**

The *Start menu* with the *Search box* appears. You do not need to click inside the box first.

⌨ **Start typing**

As you type, the search results appear above the *Search box* in the left pane of the *Start menu*.
Just click a file name to open it.
The *Search box* is one of the most convenient ways to find things on your computer. The exact location of the items does not matter. The *Search box* will scour your programs and all of the folders in your personal folder. It will also search your e-mail messages, saved instant messages, appointments, and contacts.

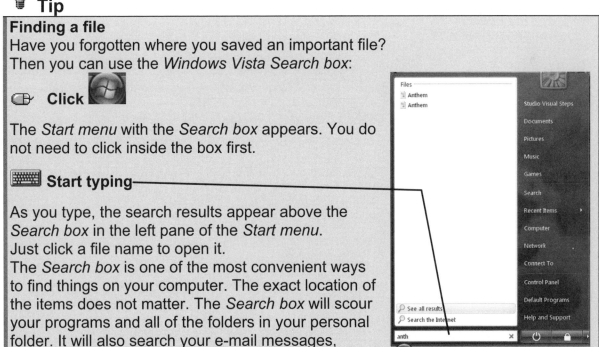

Tip

The Search folder
There are more ways to search files. The *Search folder* is one of them.
The *Search folder* is a good choice when:
- You do not know where a file or folder is located.
- You want the search results to include files from more than one folder, such as *Pictures* and *Music*.
- You want to search by using more than a single file name.

To open the *Search folder*:

⊂⟩ **Click**

⊂⟩ **Click** Search in the *Start menu*

When you want to
search in your
computer:

⊂⟩ **Click**

⊂⟩ **Click**
 Computer

⌨ **Start typing in
the search box**

The search results
appear almost
immediately:

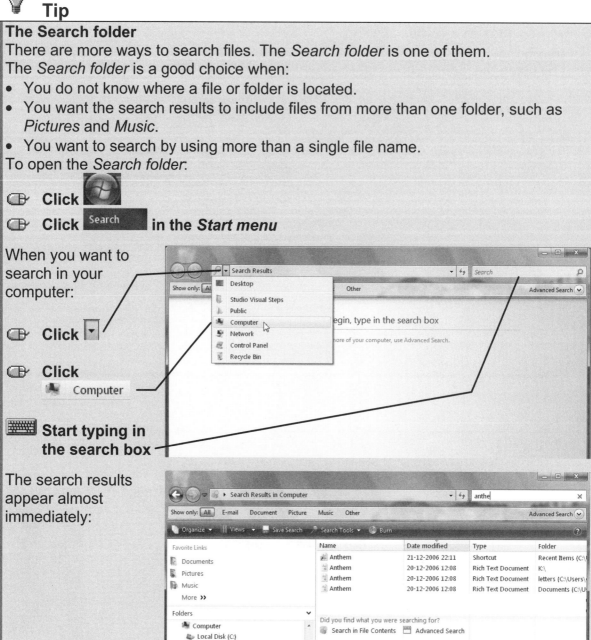

 Tip

File names
You can not use any of the following characters in a file name: \ / ? : * " > < |

Tip

Windows Vista Demos

Windows Vista Demos are narrated video demonstrations, designed to introduce you to personal computing. Watch as tasks are performed on screen. This is how you start the demo *Working with files and folders*:

Click , Help and Support

At the top of the window:

Type: demo

Click

In the search results:

Click 4. Demo: Working with files and folders

In the next window:

Click → Watch the demo

The program *Windows Media Player* opens and the demo starts playing:

☞ **Watch the demo**

To close *Windows Media Player*:

Click X

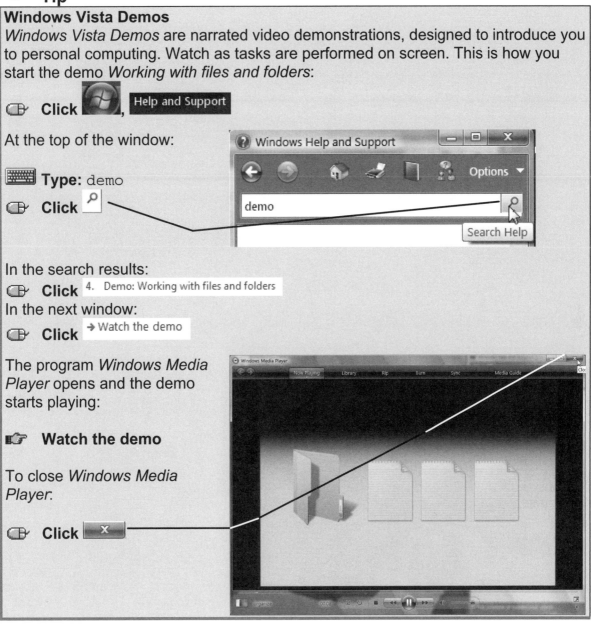

7. Text Layout

Since the arrival of word processing programs, much has changed in the way that people work with text when writing books and magazine articles. Before word processing was used, a text was written by hand by the author, or typed, and submitted to the publishing house. The typesetter or layout staff was responsible for the layout of the text. The printing company took care of the printing.

Nowadays, word processing programs and printers are so well developed that the average computer user can determine the text layout of any document and select different printing options when a printer is available.

A text can be laid out in various ways. You can experiment with simple character formatting such as underline, boldface, and italicized text. Then you can try a variety of other formatting options, such as changing the font or adding color to your text.

You can decide on a particular layout after you have typed your text, or you can choose the layout characteristics you want before you start typing.

In this chapter, you will learn:

- what laying out a text is
- how to make words bold, italicized, or underlined
- how to apply a different color
- how to select a different font
- how to make letters larger or smaller
- how to apply layout options before or after the text has been typed

7.1 Text Layout

You can layout a text in order to make it clearer or more appealing. When displayed as a simple text, driving directions might look like this:

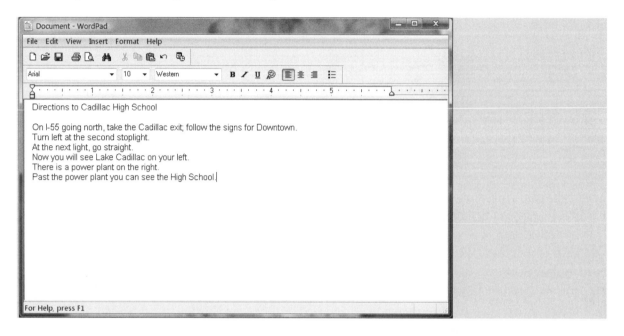

Below, a variety of character formatting is used, including boldface, italicized text and underlining. The same driving directions look very different now:

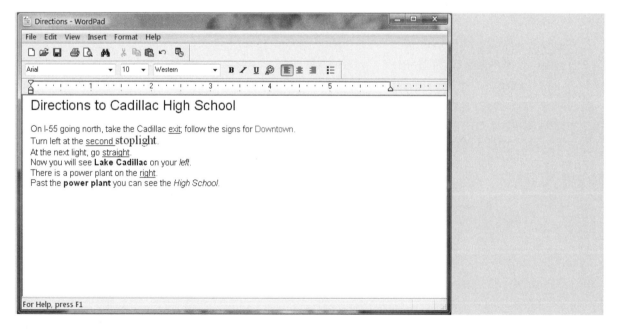

In this chapter, you will learn how to apply the layout effects as shown above.

7.2 Text Layout in WordPad

☞ **Open** *WordPad* 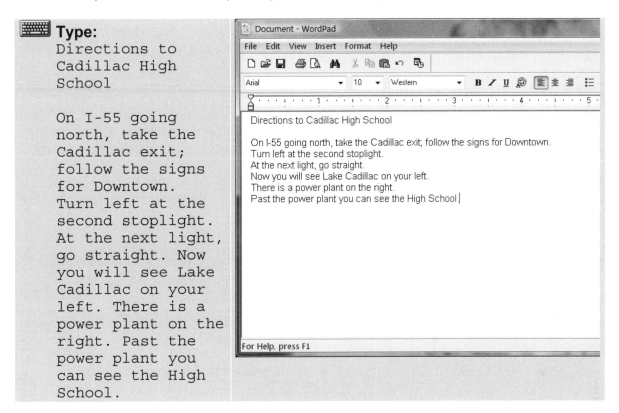14

In order to practice with text layout, type the following directions:

Type:
Directions to
Cadillac High
School

On I-55 going
north, take the
Cadillac exit;
follow the signs
for Downtown.
Turn left at the
second stoplight.
At the next light,
go straight. Now
you will see Lake
Cadillac on your
left. There is a
power plant on the
right. Past the
power plant you
can see the High
School.

It is a good idea to save your document before changing it.

☞ **Save the text and name it** *Directions* 27

Now you can change the appearance of your text. Start by changing the way the words are displayed. You can give emphasis by underlining words, or using boldface or italics.

7.3 Selecting Text

You must first *select* the text before you can make any changes.
Remember the rule:

Select first ... then act.

You learned how to select text in Chapter 5.

7.4 Underlining Words

You can start, for example, by <u>underlining</u> words. Nowadays people do not underline words very often, but it is still a way to make a word stand out. First select the word.

Select first ... then act.

You can select a word by double-clicking on it.

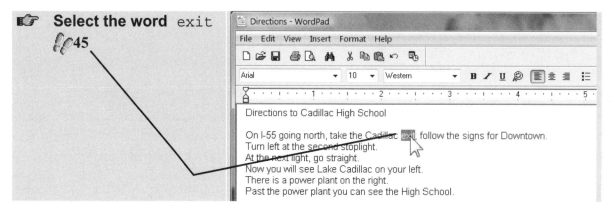

Now that you have selected the word, you can underline it. There are various buttons for character formatting.

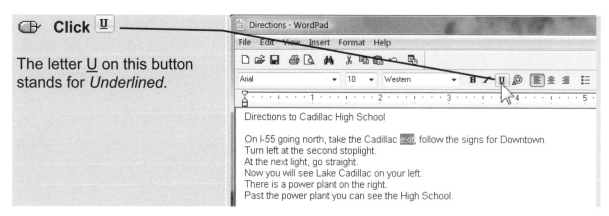

You will not be able to see the underlining clearly until you remove the selection.

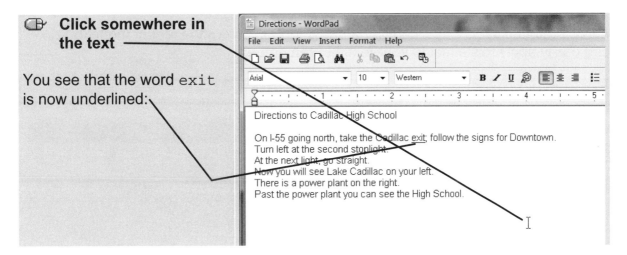

☞ Click somewhere in the text ———

You see that the word `exit` is now underlined:

7.5 Boldface

You can use the same method to print letters in **boldface**. Letters in bold clearly stand out in a text. But first you must select the relevant word again:

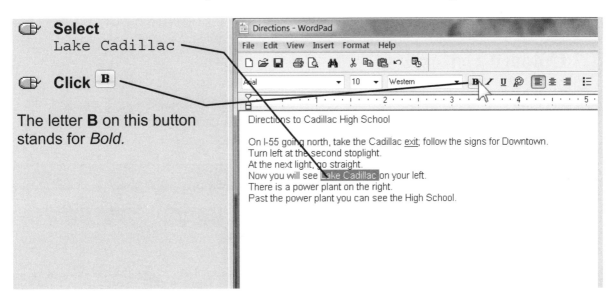

☞ Select
`Lake Cadillac` ———

☞ Click B —

The letter **B** on this button stands for *Bold*.

Lake Cadillac is now displayed in boldface.

7.6 Italics

Italics are often used to distinguish names or phrases from the rest of the text. You can easily apply this effect to your text, but remember:

Select first ... then act.

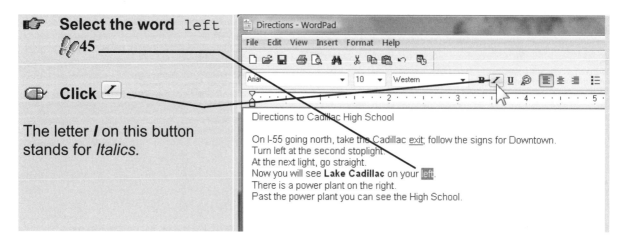

The letter *I* on this button stands for *Italics*.

The word *left* is now displayed in italicized text.

7.7 Colored Letters

You can also change the color of your text. You will see the color on your screen. If you want to print this document in color, you will need a color printer at hand. Adding color is done in the same way as the previous formatting styles.

Select first ... then act.

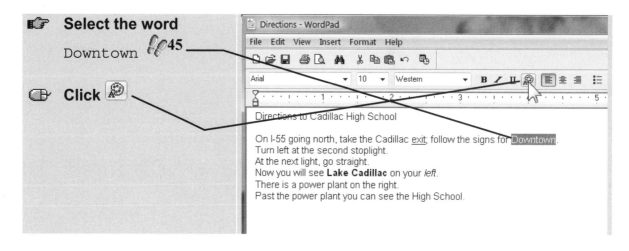

Traffic signs are often green, so why not make the letters green:

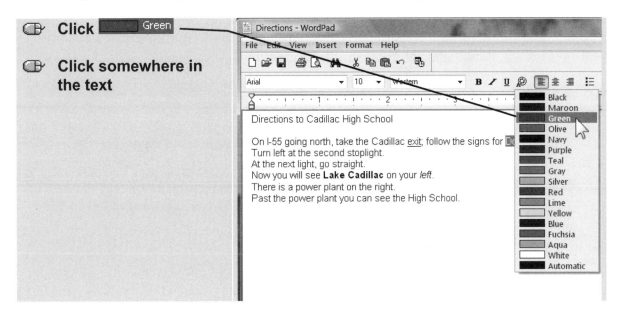

Now the word *Downtown* is green.

7.8 Other Types of Layout Effects

You can format your text in numerous ways. You can even apply more than one effect to a single word: underlining, boldface and italics. Try it:

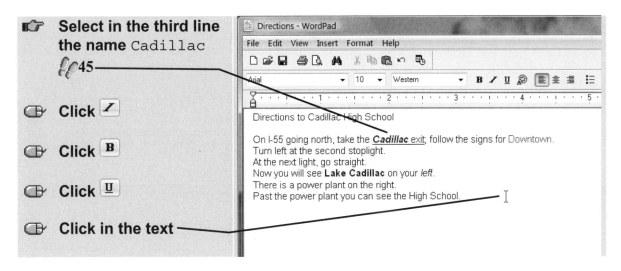

Now you can see that Cadillac is underlined and displayed in boldface italics.

7.9 Undoing Effects

You can also remove the text effects. The character formatting buttons are like on-and-off buttons. Italics are either on or off, for example.

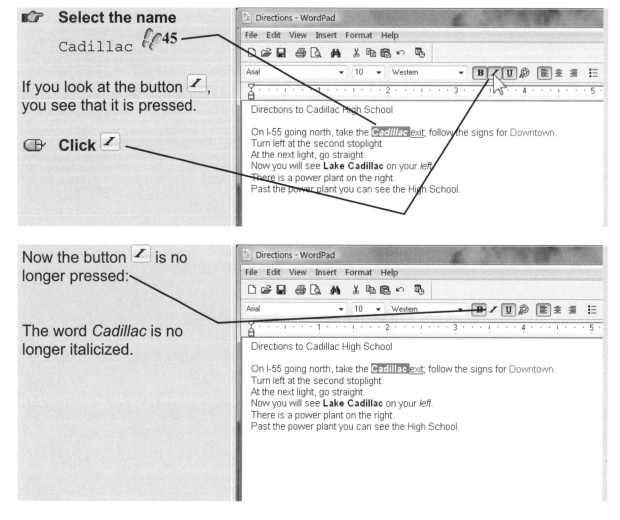

☞ **Select the name**

   Cadillac *45*

If you look at the button ✐,
you see that it is pressed.

☞ **Click** ✐

Now the button ✐ is no
longer pressed:

The word *Cadillac* is no
longer italicized.

You can use this method to change the appearance of your text whenever you want.

7.10 The Font

There are many, many *typefaces*. They vary from straight and modern to classical newspaper print. In *Windows Vista*, two typefaces - called fonts - are used as a kind of standard:

Times New Roman. This is the font that is often used in newspapers.

Arial. This is a *sans-serif* font. That means that there are no little lines or curls on the individual characters.

When you start *WordPad*, the font setting is *Arial*. You can change your entire text to a different font. But first, you must select the entire text. *WordPad* has a special command for this.

Click `Edit`

Click `Select All`

Now the entire text is selected.

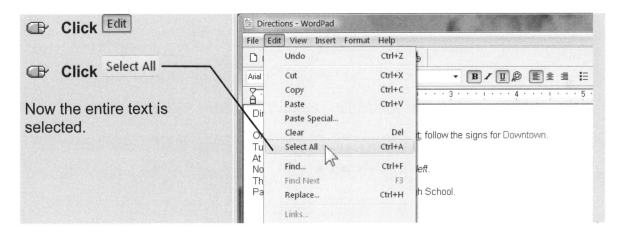

Now you can change the font. This is how:

Click ▾

You see a list of the various fonts:

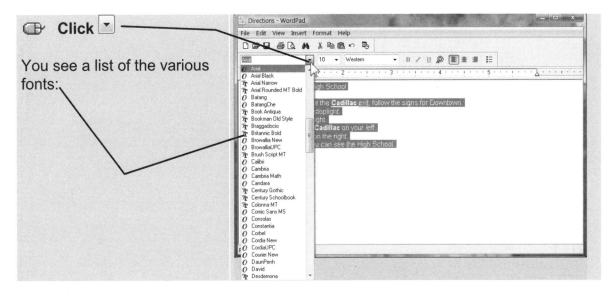

You can use the sliding bar to scroll through this list. If you want to see the bottom part of the list, use the button ⊡ next to it:

☞ Click ⊡ at the bottom a few times

The list will scroll up.

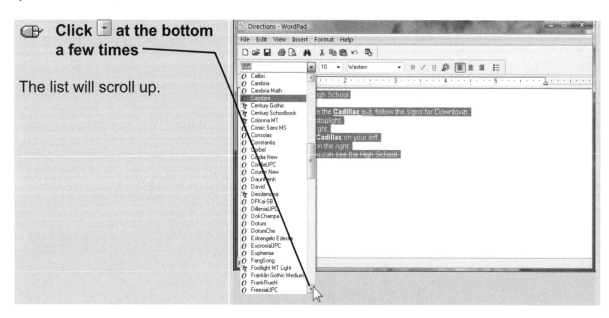

Continue through the list until you find the name *Times New Roman*:

☞ Click ⊡ as many times as necessary until you can see *O* Times New Roman

Now you can select this font:

☞ Click *O* Times New Roman

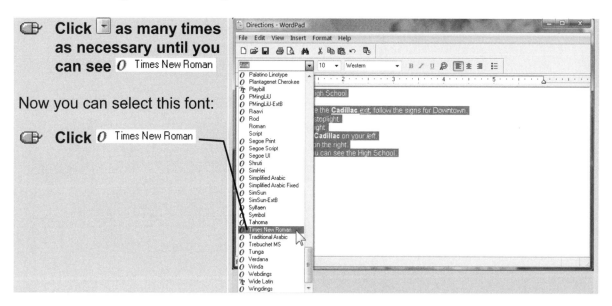

You can see that the font has changed.

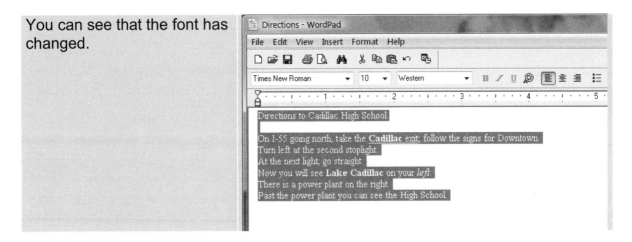

If you do not like this effect, you can always undo it:

Click Edit

Click Undo

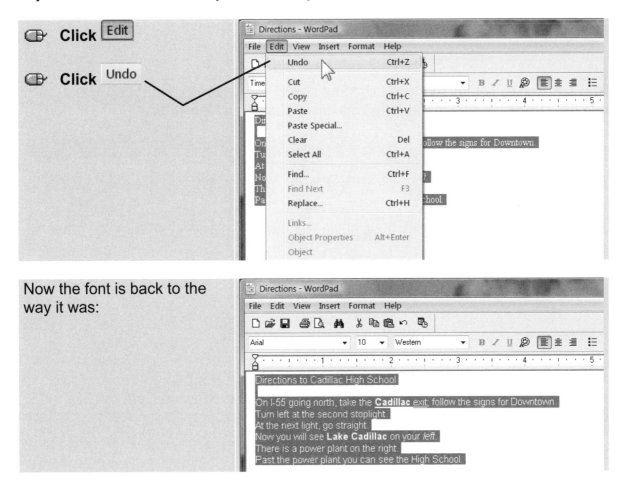

Now the font is back to the way it was:

Normally, the same font will be used for the layout of the entire text. You might use a different font when you want to add emphasis to a particular word. This is possible. You can also change the font for one or more words after you have selected them.

7.11 The Font Size

Fonts can be used in various sizes from extremely small to extremely large. You can give a title a larger font size, for example. First you must select the line. This is done by clicking on it three times.

Select the top line
47

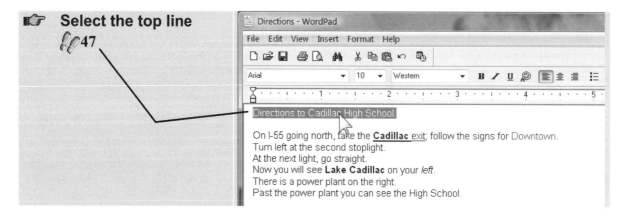

Now you can select the font size. The font size is expressed in a number. The number stands for the number of points used to construct the letters.

Click ▼

You see a row of numbers.

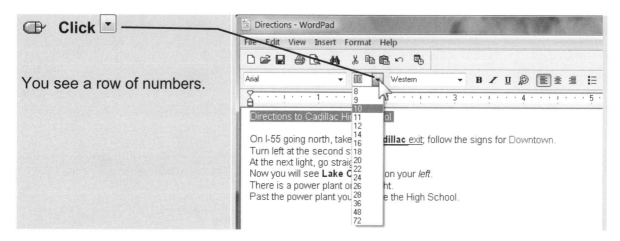

A small number means a small number of points, thus a small letter. The font size that *WordPad* normally uses is relatively small: 10 points. Now you can select a different font size from the list.

Click 16

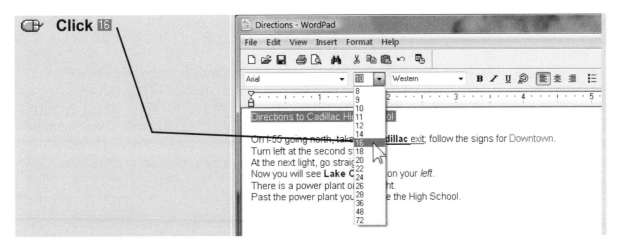

The selected letters are much larger now:

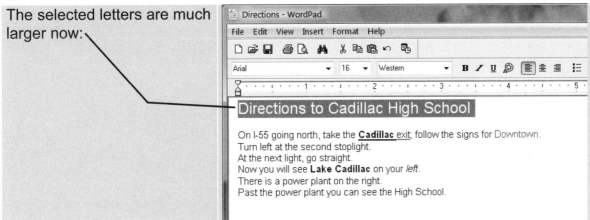

You can change the font size of the entire text, of whole paragraphs, or of individual words this way. Now you need to save the text and start a new one.

Save the text $\ell\ell^{28}$

Start a new text $\ell\ell^{16}$

7.12 Determining Layout in Advance

Until now, you typed the text first and then made changes to the layout afterwards. You can also set up your layout before you start typing. You can choose a larger letter (font) size, for example, making it more pleasant for you to work. The standard font size in *WordPad* is relatively small: only 10 points. A 12-point font is much easier to read on the screen.

If you select a larger font size before you start typing your text, it will automatically be used for the rest of the text.

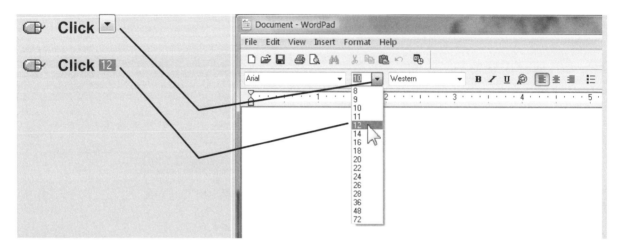

☞ **Click** ▾

☞ **Click** 12

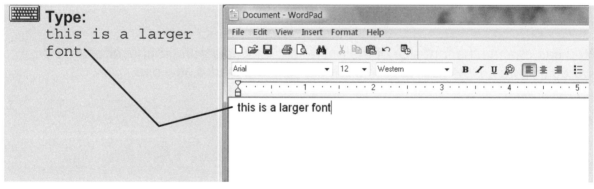

⌨ **Type:**
this is a larger
font

This is how to select a different font or font size in advance so that you do not have to change them when you are done.

☞ **Start a new text; do not save the changes** 🖐18

As an exercise, you can finish the layout of the driving directions.

7.13 Exercises

The following exercises will help you master what you have just learned. Have you forgotten how to do something? Use the number beside the footsteps to look it up in the appendix *How Do I Do That Again?*

Exercise: The Directions

☑ Open the text with the name: `Directions`. 🐾**36**

☑ Select the word `straight`. 🐾**45**

☑ Underline the word `straight`. 🐾**48**

☑ Select the word `second`. 🐾**45**

☑ Underline the word `second`. 🐾**48**

☑ Select the word `right`. 🐾**45**

☑ Underline the word `right`. 🐾**48**

☑ Click somewhere in the text.

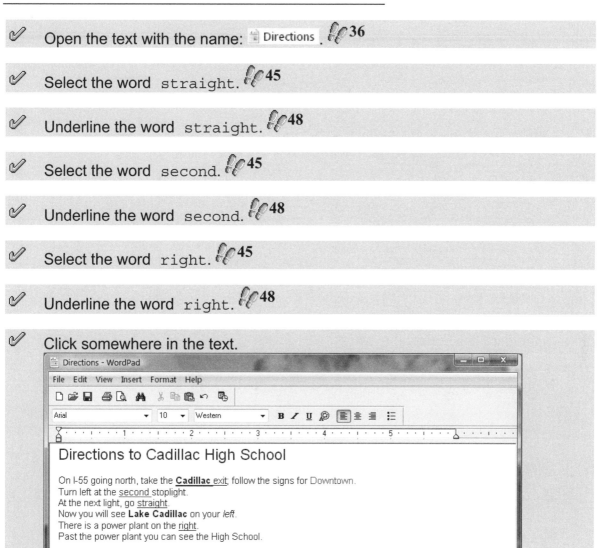

☑ Go to the last sentence, and select the words `power plant`. 🐾**45**

☑ Apply boldface to the words `power plant`. 🐾**50**

Click somewhere in the text.

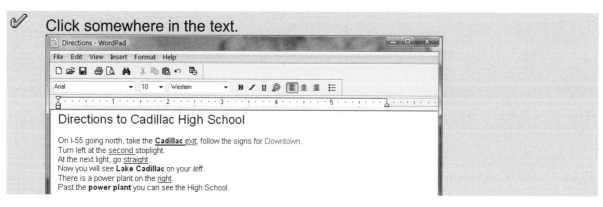

Select the words `High School`. 45

Italicize the words `High School`. 49

Click somewhere in the text.

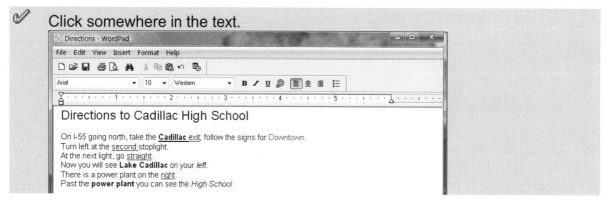

In the third line, select the name `Cadillac`. 45

Remove the boldface from the word `Cadillac`. 50

Remove the underlining from the word `Cadillac`. 48

Click somewhere in the text.

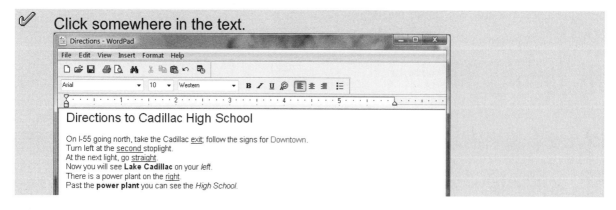

✓ Select the word `stoplight`. 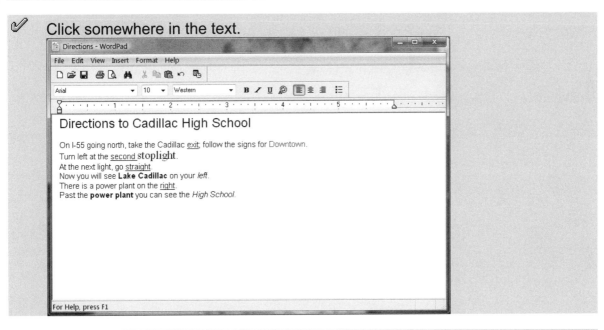45

✓ Change the color of the word `stoplight` to blue. 51

✓ Make sure that the word `stoplight` is still selected. 45

✓ Change the font to *Times New Roman*. 52

✓ Make sure that the word `stoplight` is still selected. 45

✓ Change the font size to 14 points. 53

✓ Click somewhere in the text.

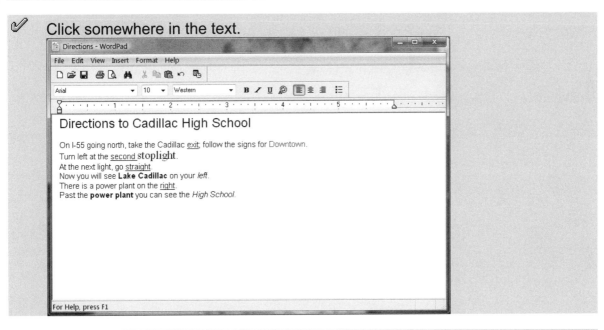

✓ Save the text. 28

✓ Close *WordPad*. 4

7.14 Background Information

Dictionary	
Bold	Makes text darker and thicker.
Font	A complete set of characters in a particular size and style of type, including numerals, symbols, punctuation and the characters of the alphabet.
Italic	Makes text slant.
Layout	The overall design of a document including elements such as font size, typeface, the arrangement of titles, alignment, letter-spacing and margins.
Underline	Puts a line underneath a text.
Source: Windows Help and support	

Fonts

A large number of fonts have been developed for the PC. You can see which fonts have been installed on your computer by viewing the list in *WordPad*:

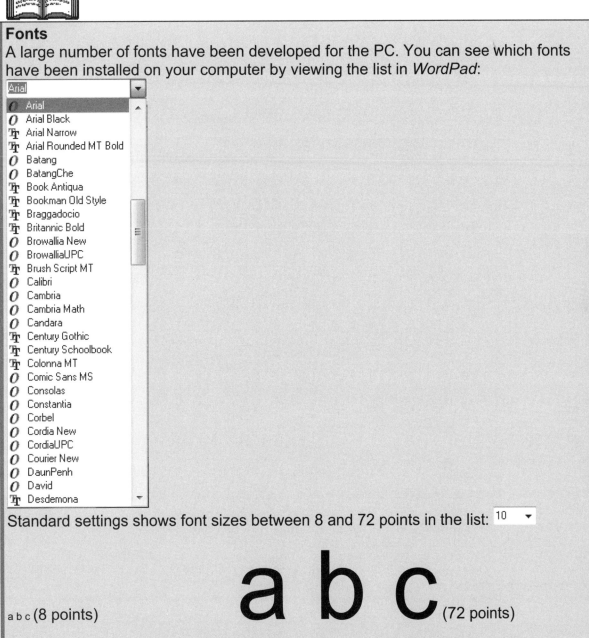

Standard settings shows font sizes between 8 and 72 points in the list: 10 ▾

a b c (8 points)

a b c (72 points)

But you can also enter a smaller or larger number of points yourself. Actually, you can choose any size letter you want, even letters that are as large as a regular sheet of paper. You can use these large letters if you want to make a poster, for example. You do this by typing a number in the font size box: 32 ▾ .

Characters

In addition to the letters of the alphabet, numbers, and punctuation marks, every font also has symbols that are not included on the keyboard, for example: ®, ¼ or §:

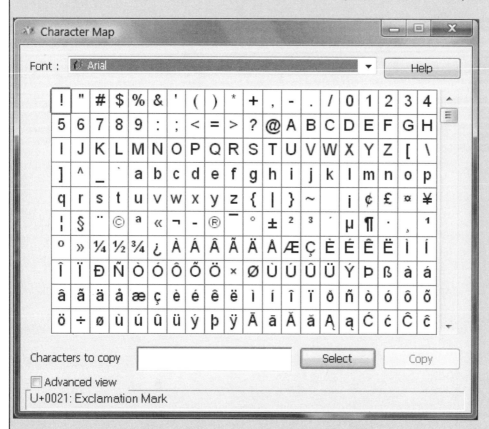

Besides regular typefaces, *Windows Vista* also has fonts that consist solely of symbols such as √, ©, ♣, Σ, or π.

Read also the Tip on page 248.

No need to type

There are various ways of inputting text into a computer without having to type it yourself. If a text is *digital*, meaning that it has already been made available for the computer, you can open it on your computer from a diskette, CD, USB memory stick, or via your e-mail program.

If you have an existing text that is on paper, you can read the text into the computer using a **scanner.**

Many scanners are supplied with what is known as an *OCR program*. OCR is an abbreviation that stands for *Optical Character Recognition*. You lay the paper on the scanner and the OCR program scans it and translates it into editable text.

The text can then be used in a word processing program such as *WordPad* or *Microsoft Word*.

Scanner

Are you tired of typing? You can use your voice to dictate text to your computer. You can install a *voice recognition program.*
You will need a microphone connected to your computer in order to do this.
You start the voice recognition program and then issue a short command to open another program, such as *WordPad*. You can then dictate your text.

The program automatically converts your spoken words into text that appears on your screen as if you were typing it yourself.

Microphone

Windows Vista has a speech recognition option with which you can operate *Windows* on a basic level and dictate text into a program such as *WordPad*.
You can find more information about speech recognition in *Windows Vista* by doing the following steps:

 Click , Help and Support

 Type in the *Search* box: `speech recognition`

 Click 🔎

7.15 Tips

 Tip

WordPad has three buttons that you can use to work with files: ☐ 🖆 🖬.

		Commands:
☐	Start a new text	[File], New...
🖆	Open a document	[File], Open...
🖬	Save a document	[File], Save

 Tip

Using the program *Character Map* you can insert these symbols into a *WordPad* text. This is how to start this program if it has been installed on your computer:

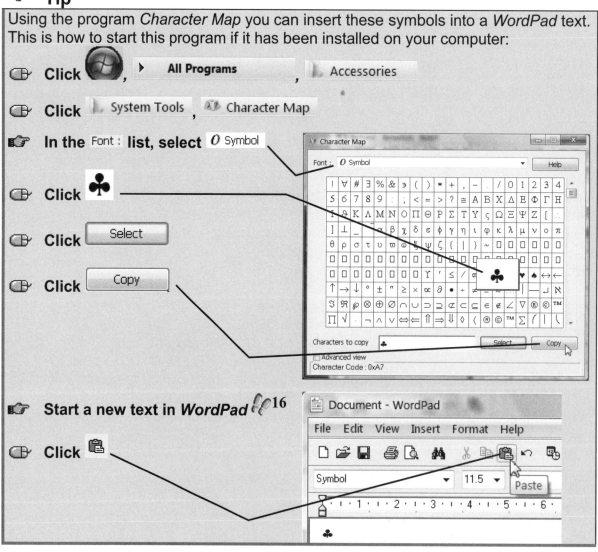

☞ **Click** 🪟 , ▶ **All Programs** , 📁 **Accessories**

☞ **Click** 📁 **System Tools** , 🔤 **Character Map**

☞ **In the** Font : **list, select** *O* Symbol

☞ **Click** ♣

☞ **Click** Select

☞ **Click** Copy

☞ **Start a new text in** *WordPad* 🖉16

☞ **Click** 📋

8. Surfing the Internet

The Internet consists of millions of computers that are all interconnected. The *World Wide Web* is one of the most exciting parts of the Internet. *World Wide Web* means exactly what it says: a web of computers where an infinite amount of information is located regarding every imaginable topic. No matter where you are in the world, you can access that information with your computer.

On the Internet, a source of information is called a *website*. It is a site somewhere on the Web. Within the website, you can browse from one page to another by clicking with your mouse. You can even jump from one website to another. This is called *surfing*. The type of program you need to surf the Internet, is called a *browser*. You might browse through a printed catalog, but these days you can also *browse* just as easily through the company's online catalog.

In order to get on the Internet, you must initiate a connection with a computer that is permanently connected to the Internet. This is done by means of an *Internet Service Provider* (ISP). If you want to use the provider's services, you must subscribe to them or pay for them in another way. The provider then assigns you a *username* and a *password*. The username and password will give you access to the Internet.

If you are connected to the Internet, you are **online.** In this chapter, first you will learn to go *online* and then how to *surf*.

In this chapter, you will learn how to:

- open *Internet Explorer*
- contact your *Internet Service Provider*
- use a web address
- browse forward and backward
- save a web address
- use a *favorite*
- stop using the Internet

 Please note:

For the exercises in this chapter, you must have an Internet connection that works. If necessary, contact your *Internet Service Provider* or your computer supplier.

8.1 Some Information First: The Modem

The modem
Telephone networks are used to connect computers which may be hundreds or thousands of miles apart from one another. This makes sense, since nearly everyone has a telephone. It is also not uncommon for cable television providers to offer Internet services, using their cable network to connect to the Internet.

In order to connect to the Internet via the telephone line or cable, you need a special piece of equipment: called a **modem.** A modem makes it possible for your computer to communicate with the *Internet Service Provider*. There are two different types of modems: internal and external.

An **external modem** is a separate box that is connected to your computer with a cable.
Another cable leads from the modem to the plug for the telephone line or the cable connection.

External modem

Nearly all new computers, however, have a modem that is built in. This is called an **internal modem**.
The only thing you see in this type of modem is a contact point for a telephone plug or the cable connection, located at the back of your computer.

Internal modem

Modems that are connected to the telephone line also have a cable that leads to the telephone's plug. Sometimes a double plug is used, so that your telephone can remain plugged into the same contact point.

Laptop computer with external modem and double plug

8.2 Is Your Modem Ready?

Before you continue with this chapter, you need to make sure your modem is ready.

☞ **Check to make sure your modem is connected to the telephone or cable network**

Do you have an external modem?
☞ **If so, turn the modem on**

Do you have an internal modem?
☞ **If so, you do not need to take any action**

8.3 Starting Internet Explorer

The program that is used to connect to the Internet in *Windows Vista* is called *Internet Explorer.*
This is how to open the program:

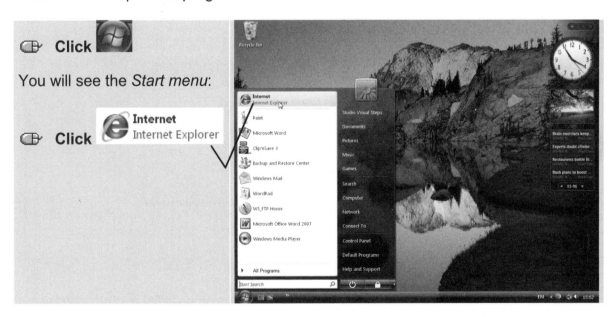

🖱 **Click**

You will see the *Start menu*:

🖱 **Click** **Internet** Internet Explorer

The program will open, after which an Internet connection can be established.

If you are using *Internet Explorer* for the first time and you have a *broadband* connection to the Internet (DSL or cable), you will probably see a window like this floating on top of the *Internet Explorer* window:

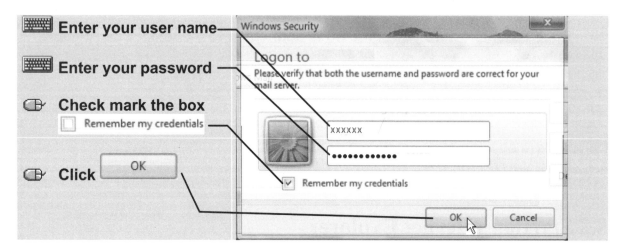

If you are using *dial-up networking* to connect to the Internet, you will see a *Dial-up Connection* window.

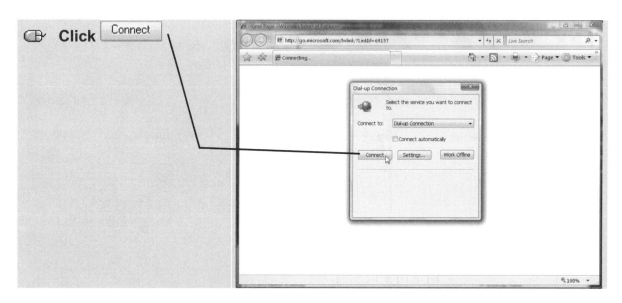

If you have an Internet access subscription, your ISP has given you a **username** and a **password**. If everything is set up properly, both of these will already be displayed in the next window.

If your username and password are **not** displayed:

⌨ **Type your user name and password in the appropriate boxes**

🖰 **Check mark the box**

☐ Save this user name and password fo

🖰 **Click** ○ Me only

🖰 **Click** [Dial]

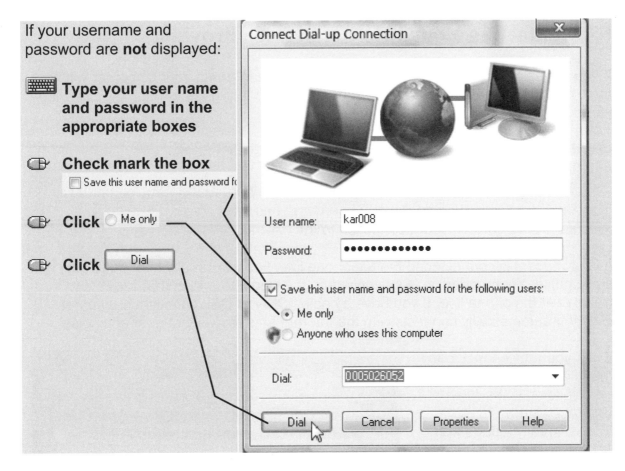

Connect Dial-up Connection

User name: kar008

Password: ••••••••••••••

☑ Save this user name and password for the following users:

● Me only

○ Anyone who uses this computer

Dial: 0005026052

[Dial] [Cancel] [Properties] [Help]

A connection is made to your ISP (*Internet Service Provider*).

 HELP! I do not see windows like these.

Are these windows not shown on your screen? If you are connected to the internet by cable or DSL, then this *Dial-Up Connection* window will not appear. You will have a different set up on your computer. *Internet Explorer* automatically connects with the Internet when you open it.

☞ **Just continue reading**

8.4 Contacting Your Internet Service Provider

If you are using dial-up networking to connect to the Internet, your computer will now try to contact your ISP by using the modem. The modem goes through the following steps:

- the modem dials the number of the internet provider
- then it connects to your ISP's computer
- your computer sends your username and password to the ISP's computer
- the ISP's computer checks your username and password
- if they are correct, your connection to the Internet is established

If your modem is connected to the telephone line, you will usually hear quite a bit of static noise. Your modem is busy converting the signal to a form that allows it to travel over the phone line. If you have a cable, ISDN or DSL connection, *Internet Explorer* automatically connects with the Internet and you will not hear any noise.

Once you are connected to the Internet, a home page will be displayed in the *Internet Explorer* window.
This is usually a page from *Microsoft*, the company that makes *Internet Explorer*.

Down in the right corner of the *Taskbar*, you will see an

icon with two computers: indicating that you are *online*.

The modem is busy doing something if the computer displays this icon .

⇨ **Please note:**

The initial start page on your computer may not be the same as the one in the illustration. You might, for example, see a web page that someone else has specified in your browser's settings.

HELP! No connection?

Were you unable to connect to the Internet?
This could be because your ISP's number is "busy":

> Dialing...
> Dialing attempt 1.
> Unable to establish a connection.

When that happens, try again later.

 HELP! Still no connection?

If you have tried to connect to the Internet a number of times and you still unable to do so, it is probable that the settings on your computer are not correct.
Contact your ISP for assistance.

8.5 Typing an Address

Every website has its own web address on the *World Wide Web*. These are the addresses that start with www that you see everywhere.
You can use these addresses to find a website on any computer that is connected to the Internet. The web address of Visual Steps publishing company is:

www.visualsteps.com

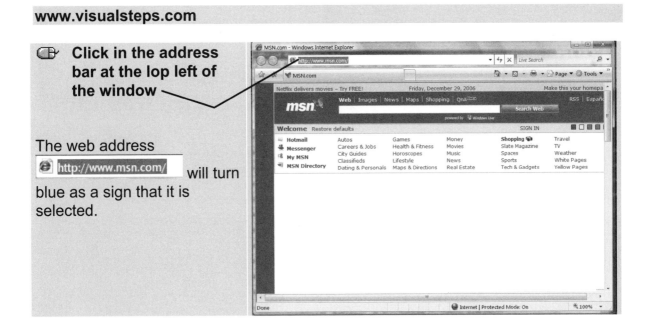

☞ Click in the address bar at the lop left of the window

The web address `http://www.msn.com/` will turn blue as a sign that it is selected.

Now you can type the address in this address bar:

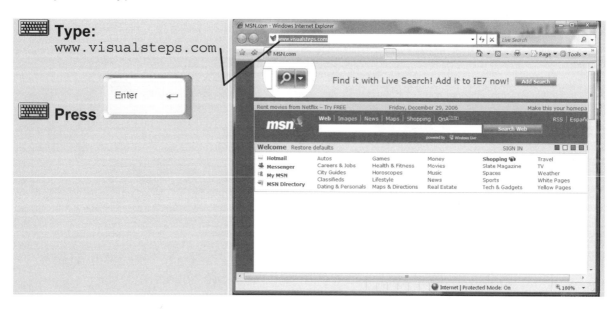

Type:
www.visualsteps.com

Press Enter

After a few moments, you see the opening page for this website:

This web page is updated frequently. You may see other pictures in your window.

8.6 Wrong Address

Once in a while a typing error is made when typing an address, or a certain address no longer exists. This is especially true because the Internet is highly dynamic, changing every day. Private individuals may change their web addresses. Sometimes you will see an address that starts with **http://**. That is additional information, indicating that the address is for a website. With *Internet Explorer*, you do not need to type **http://**. The program automatically understands that you want a website and will add it to the address.
When typing a web address, you should take note of the following:

> Make sure that any dots (.) or forward slashes (/) are typed in the correct places. If they are not, you will receive an error message.
> Never type spaces in a web address.

If even one dot is missing, an error message will appear. Try it:

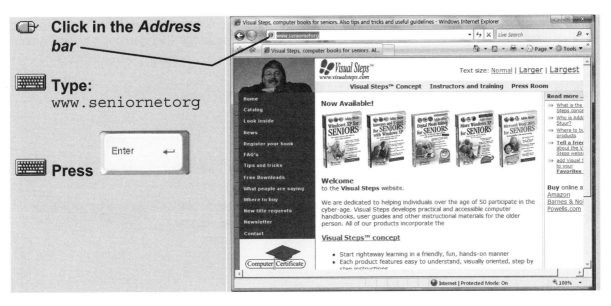

Click in the *Address bar*

Type:
www.seniornetorg

Press Enter

After some time, the following web page is displayed:

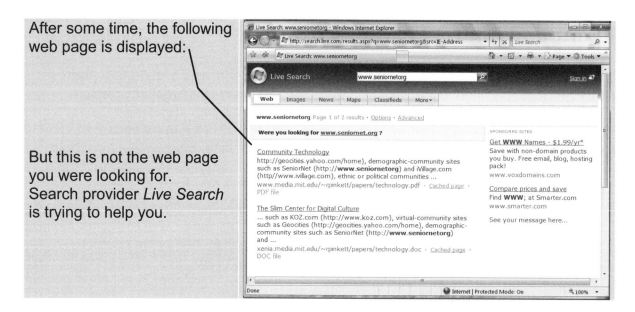

But this is not the web page you were looking for.
Search provider *Live Search* is trying to help you.

Live Search asks: **Were you looking for www.seniornet.org ?** *Live Search* has made this assumption because the address you typed - **www.seniornetorg** - was wrong. The dot before **org** is missing. The correct address for the *SeniorNet* website is:

www.seniornet.org

Try the correct address:

☞ **Click in the *Address bar***

⌨ **Type:**
www.seniornet.org

⌨ **Press** Enter ↵

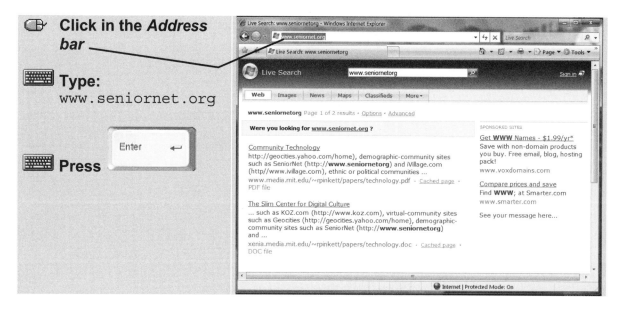

In a little while, the homepage for *SeniorNet* is displayed:

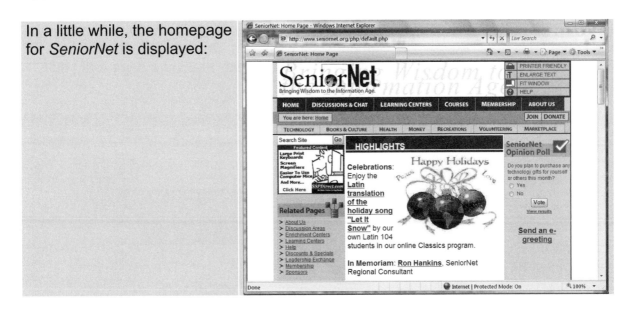

Remember, if you forget just one dot the program may not be able to find the website you want.

 Please note:

The website shown above may look different now. The Internet changes all the time.

8.7 Refreshing a Page

Sometimes a page is not displayed on your screen as it should be. When that happens, you can tell *Internet Explorer* to reload the page again: to *refresh* it. Just watch what happens:

Click

You will see that the window will be refreshed and the information is collected once again.

Everything that is shown on your screen must be sent in through the telephone line or the cable. This may take awhile. Sometimes it will seem like nothing is happening. But there is a way to check if *Internet Explorer* is still busy loading a page that you have requested:

At the bottom of the screen, the green bar indicates that information is being received:

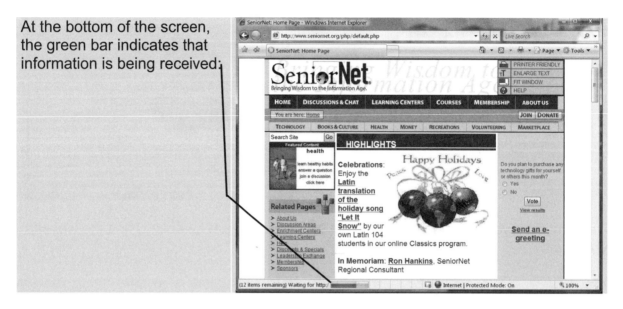

Not all information appears immediately on your screen; it may take time to *draw* (load) the entire page, especially if you are using dial-up networking to connect to the Internet.

8.8 Forward and Backward

You do not need to retype the web address of a website if you want to revisit it. *Internet Explorer* has a number of buttons that help you *navigate* the Internet.

At the top left of the window, click

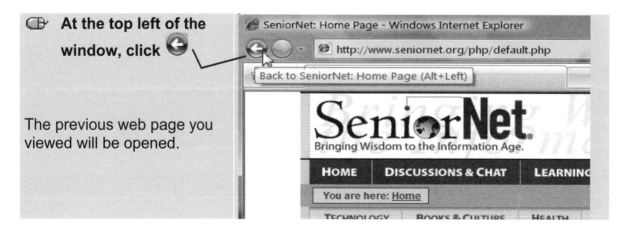

The previous web page you viewed will be opened.

What you see now is the website where search provider *Live Search* was helping you:

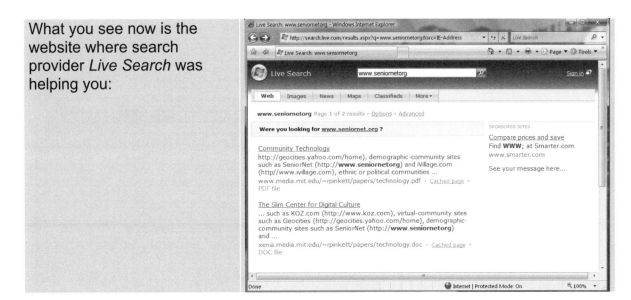

Perhaps you noticed how quickly this is done. *Internet Explorer* retains the websites you recently visited in its memory so that you can quickly look at them again without needing all of the information sent over the telephone line or cable.

Click ⬅ two more times

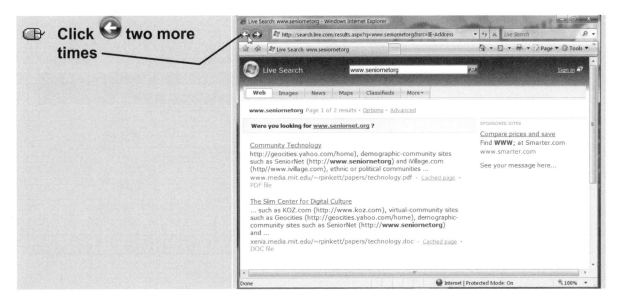

Now the website you first visited will be displayed.

Once again, the start page is displayed:

Now you can no longer browse back. That is because this was the first website you opened.

The button 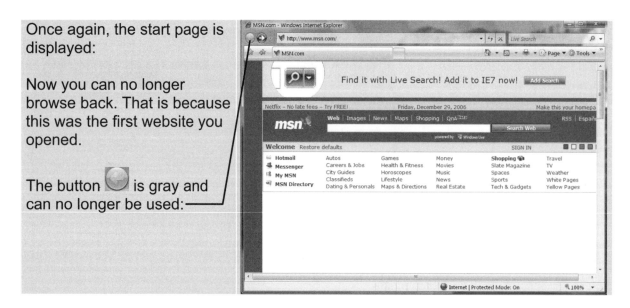 is gray and can no longer be used:

You can, however, browse the other way. There is a special button for this as well.

Click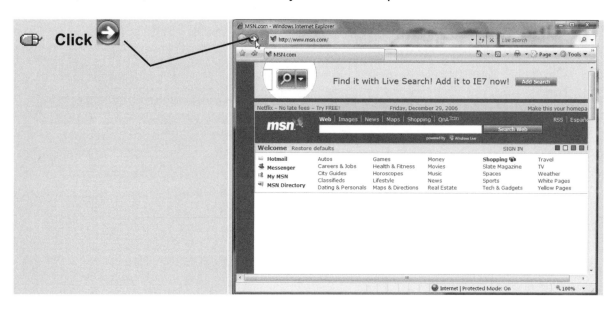

Now you see the same Visual Steps website on the screen as you did before:

As you have seen, the buttons can easily be used to switch back and forth between the websites you have viewed. This is called "surfing" the Internet. However, these websites will not remain in memory forever. When you close *Internet Explorer,* the websites will be removed from the browser's memory.

8.9 Clicking to Browse

Most websites are organized and designed to enable you to navigate through the site with relative ease. There is usually a list of topics, in the form of buttons or text that indicate what you can find on the website. You can see that the Visual Steps website has a list of topics on the left. By clicking a topic, you go to another page.

Place the mouse arrow on FAQ's

You see the mouse arrow change into a hand.

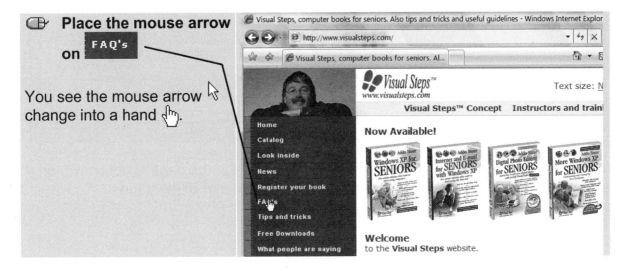

Whenever the mouse arrow changes into a hand, you can click. It may change on a button, but it can also change somewhere in the text or over a picture.

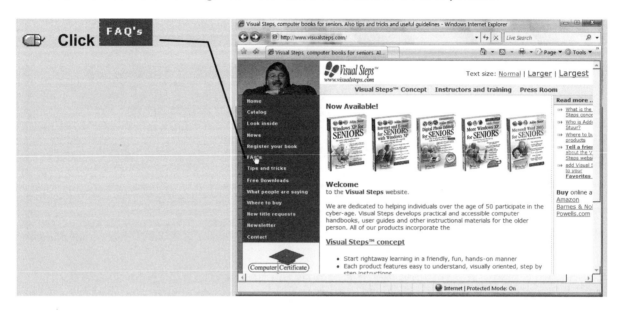

A word, button or picture on which you can click is called a **link**. A link is also called a **hyperlink**.

What you see now is a page with questions and problems:

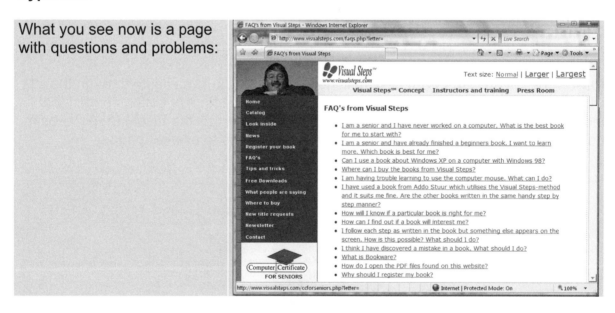

In the example above, you can see that the bottom part of the page is not shown on your screen. You need to use the scroll bar to read that part of the page.

8.10 Using the Scroll Bars

When you view pages on the Internet, you may need to use the scroll bar. Even if you maximize the browser window, it might not be large enough to hold all of the information. In order to see the rest of the page, you must use the vertical scroll bar.

 Drag the scroll bar downward

Now you can read the bottom part of the text:

 Drag the scroll bar upward

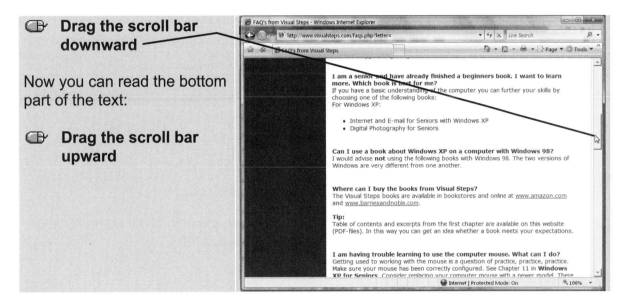

💡 Tip

The mouse wheel
The rapidly growing popularity of the Internet has resulted in various new additions to the mouse, including one called the mouse wheel. By turning the wheel with your finger, the contents of the window will scroll. This is the same thing that happens when you use the scroll bar, but it is much easier and quicker.

Once you have gotten used to a mouse wheel, you will never want to do without!
To scroll down, roll the wheel backward (toward you).
To scroll up, roll the wheel forward (away from you).
If your mouse has a scroll wheel:
☞ **Roll the wheel backward and forward with your index finger**
☞ **End the rolling when the scroll bar is upward**

A good website is made in such a way that you can easily move from one page to the next without getting lost. Most websites, for example, have a button marked *Home* or *Start* that when clicked will return you to the website's home page.

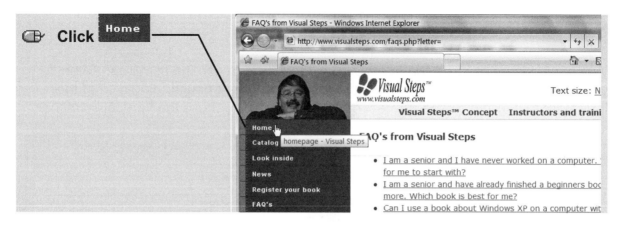

Click Home

Once again, the homepage is displayed.

8.11 Printing a Web Page

It is not always easy to read a web page on your screen, especially if it contains a lot of text. You can always choose to print the page and read it later.

No printer?

If you do not have a printer, you can skip this section.

This is how to print a page:

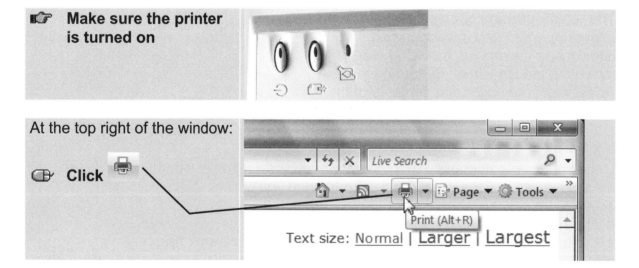

☞ **Make sure the printer is turned on**

At the top right of the window:

☞ **Click** 🖨

Shortly thereafter, the page will be printed.

8.12 Saving a Web Address

If you find an interesting website, you can save its address. Then you will always be able to quickly open the site without having to type the address.
Websites for which you have saved the address are called *Favorites* in *Internet Explorer.*
You can only save an address of a website while it is being displayed. In this example, this is the Visual Steps website.

At the top left of the window:

☞ **Click**

A menu appears:

☞ **Click** Add to Favorites...

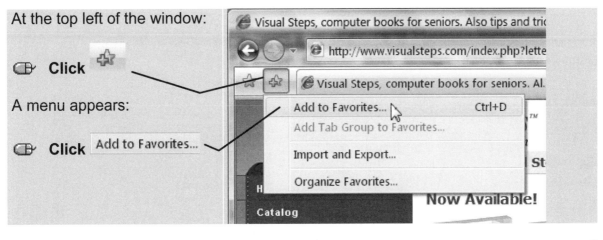

Now you see a small window on top of the web page in which the name has already been inserted:

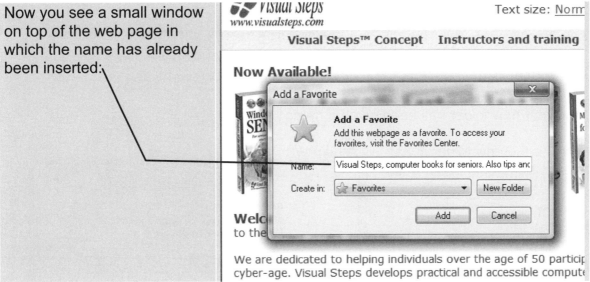

You can put all of your favorite websites in one long list, but you can also save them in separate folders. To practice, you can make a new folder for the websites that go with this book.

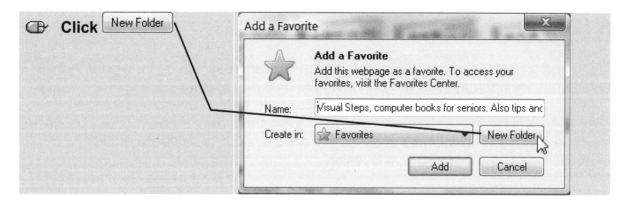

Click New Folder

A new window appears on top of the others. Now you can type in the name you want to give the new folder.

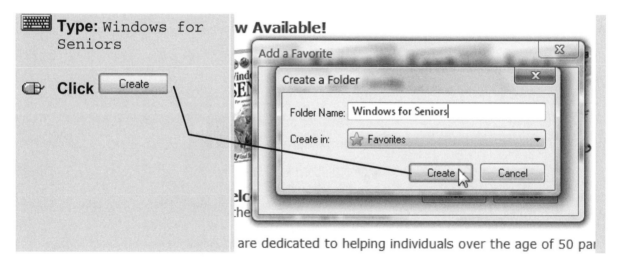

Type: Windows for Seniors

Click Create

Now your new folder has been given a name.

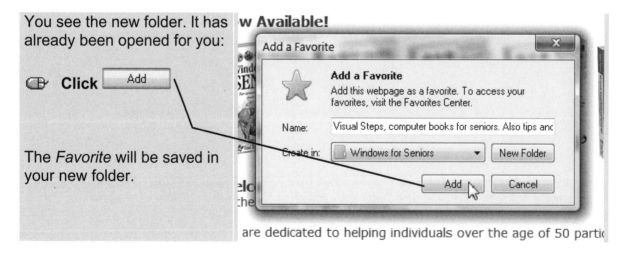

You see the new folder. It has already been opened for you:

Click Add

The *Favorite* will be saved in your new folder.

Now you can check to make sure that you can quickly open this favorite website.

8.13 The Home Button

To see how a *Favorite* works, start by going to a different website. You can go to your homepage, for example. This is the page that automatically opens when you start *Internet Explorer*. There is a special *Home* button for this.

In the top right area of the window:

☞ **Click**

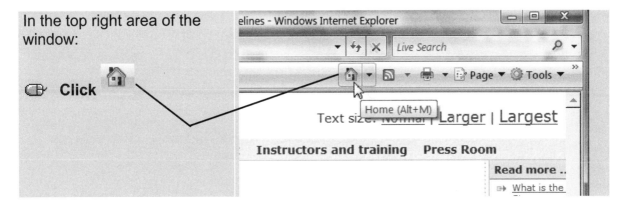

Your homepage is displayed. Now you can open your *Favorite*.

8.14 Opening a Favorite

This is how to quickly open one of your favorite websites:

At the top left of the window:

☞ **Click**

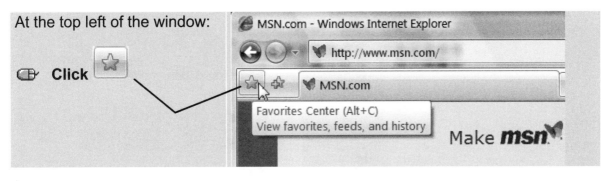

On the left side of the window a white pane is opened:

☞ **Click** ⭐ Favorites

You see the list of favorite folders:

👆 **Click**
   📁 Windows for Seniors

The folder
📁 Windows for Seniors is opened:

👆 **Click**
   🌐 Visual Steps, computer books fo

The saved favorite website appears:

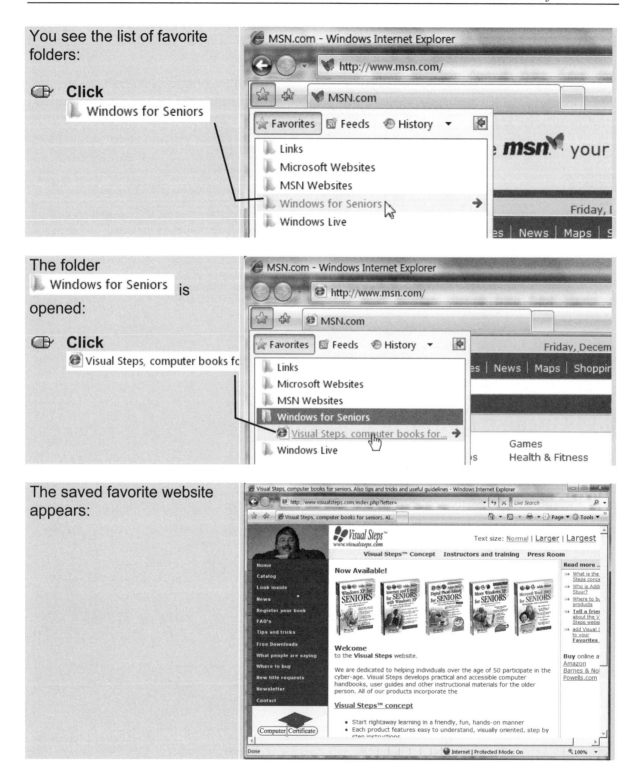

Internet Explorer remembers your *Favorites*, even after you have closed the program. Without having to remember complicated web addresses, these references to your favorite websites make it possible to quickly return to them at any given time.

8.15 Disconnecting from the Internet

If you have a common analog dial-up connection to the Internet, you have to disconnect each time you stop using the Internet. No other calls can come through to you as long as you are connected to the Internet.
If you have a broadband connection like DSL or cable, you are always connected to the Internet, whether you are using the web or not. You do not have to disconnect.

You can close the *Internet Explorer* window and disconnect in this way:

If you have a dial-up connection to the Internet, when you see this window you can disconnect:

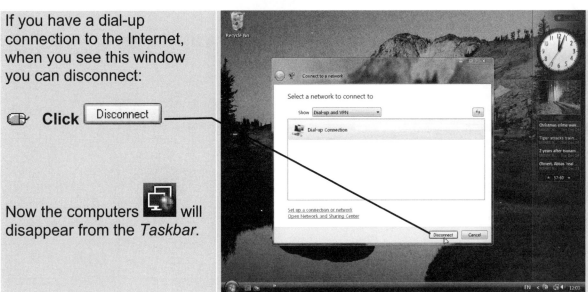

Now the computers 🖥 will disappear from the *Taskbar*.

The connection has been broken.

If you have a broadband connection such as DSL or cable you will not see a window like above. You will still see the computers 🖥 in the notification area on the far right side of the taskbar because you are continuously online.

HELP! The connection is not broken.

Do you have a dial-up connection to the Internet and you do not see the disconnection window?

Do you still see the computers 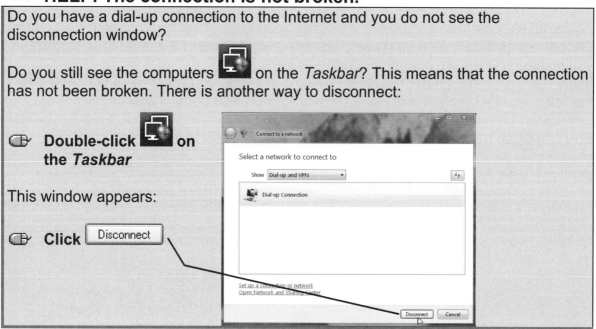 on the *Taskbar*? This means that the connection has not been broken. There is another way to disconnect:

☞ **Double-click** ▧ **on the *Taskbar***

This window appears:

☞ **Click** | Disconnect |

 Tip

Do you want to end the connection but keep viewing the *Internet Explorer* window?
Use this same way to disconnect:

☞ **Double-click** ▧ **on the *Taskbar***

☞ **Click** | Disconnect |

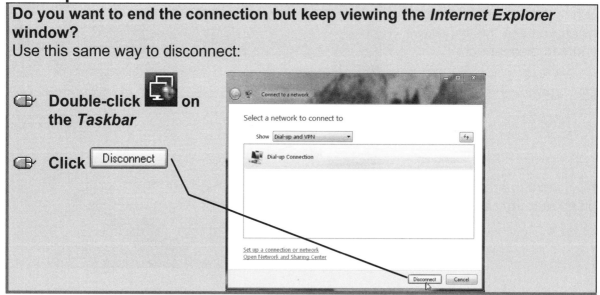

In this chapter you learned how to surf the internet and add websites to your *Favorites*. With the following exercises you can practice what you have learned.

8.16 Exercises

The following exercises will help you master what you have just learned. Have you forgotten how to do something? Use the number beside the footsteps to look it up in the appendix *How Do I Do That Again?*

Exercise: SeniorNet Favorite

In this exercise, you will open the *SeniorNet* website and add it to your *Favorites*.

☑ Open *Internet Explorer*. 𝄃𝄃**64**

☑ If necessary: connect to the Internet. 𝄃𝄃**66**

☑ Type the Internet address: www.seniornet.org 𝄃𝄃**67**

☑ Browse through the *SeniorNet* website.

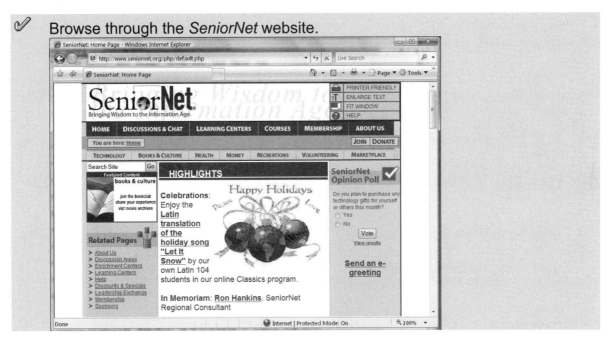

☑ Save the address for *SeniorNet* as a *Favorite*. 𝄃𝄃**68**

☑ Close the *Internet Explorer* window. 𝄃𝄃**65**

☑ If necessary: disconnect from the Internet. 𝄃𝄃**69**

Exercise: Surfing

Going from one website to another is also called surfing. In this exercise you will surf among the sites you visited earlier.

✔ Open *Internet Explorer.* $\ell\ell$64

✔ If necessary: connect to the Internet. $\ell\ell$66

✔ Using *Favorites,* open the website *www.visualsteps.com* $\ell\ell$70

✔ Using *Favorites,* open the website *www.seniornet.org.* $\ell\ell$70

✔ Type the address for the Public Broadcasting Service website: *www.pbs.org* $\ell\ell$67

✔ Now go back to *www.seniornet.org.* $\ell\ell$71

✔ Go back to the website *www.visualsteps.com* $\ell\ell$71

✔ Now go back to *www.seniornet.org.* $\ell\ell$72

✔ Go back to the Public Broadcasting Service website. $\ell\ell$72

✔ Now go back to the homepage. $\ell\ell$73

✔ Close *Internet Explorer.* $\ell\ell$65

✔ If necessary: disconnect from the Internet. $\ell\ell$69

8.17 Background Information

Dictionary	
ActiveX	Technology for creating interactive web content such as animation sequences or credit card transactions.
Broadband connection	A high-speed Internet connection. Broadband connections are typically 256 kilobytes per second (KBps) or faster. Broadband includes DSL and cable modem service.
Browser	A program used to display web pages and to navigate the Internet. *Internet Explorer* is a web browser.
Cable internet	Cable Internet access is a broadband connection that uses the same wiring as cable TV. To use cable, you need an account with a cable *Internet Service Provider* in your area. The ISP usually provides any necessary equipment, and often sends a technician to set it up for you.
Dial-up connection	Connecting to the Internet by using a modem and a telephone line. Usually a low speed analog connection.
Download	Copying a file from one computer to another using a modem or network. For example, copying software from a website.
DSL	Digital Subscriber Line - a type of high-speed Internet connection using standard telephone wires. This is also referred to as a broadband connection. The ISP is usually a phone company.
Homepage	The first or opening page of a website.
Hyperlink, Link	A hyperlink is a navigation element in a webpage that automatically brings the referred information to the user when the user clicks on the hyperlink. A hyperlink can be text or images like buttons, icons or pictures. You can recognize a hyperlink when the mouse pointer turns into a hand.
Internet	A network of computer networks which operates world-wide using a common set of communications protocols. The part of the Internet that most people are familiar with is the World Wide Web (WWW).

ISP	An *Internet Service Provider* (ISP) is a company that provides you with access to the Internet, usually for a fee. The most common ways to connect to an ISP are by using a phone line (dial-up) or broadband connection (cable or DSL). Many ISPs provide additional services such as e-mail accounts, virtual hosting, and space for you to create a website.
Log-in name	Username
Malware	Malicious software - software designed to deliberately harm your computer. Trojan horses, viruses and worms are examples of malware.
Password	A string of characters that a user must enter to gain access to a resource that is password-protected. Passwords help ensure that unauthorized users do not access your internet connection or your computer.
Security setting	Options that can help protect your computer from potentially harmful or malicious online content.
Spyware	Software that can display advertisements (such as pop-up ads), collect information about you, or change settings on your computer, generally without obtaining your consent.
Web address	The web address of a website uniquely identifies a location on the internet. An example of a web address is: www.visualsteps.com. A web address is also called an URL (Uniform Resource Locator). People use URLs to find websites, but computers use IP addresses to find websites. An IP address usually consists of four groups of numbers separated by periods, such as 192.200.44.69. Special computers on the internet translate URLs into IP addresses (and vice versa).
Web server	A computer that stores information (such as webpages or files) and makes that information available over the Internet.
Webpage	A webpage or web page is a resource of information that is suitable for the World Wide Web and can be accessed through a browser.
Website	A website is a collection of interconnected webpages, typically common to a particular domain name on the World Wide Web on the Internet.
WWW	World Wide Web - web of computers, connected to each other - containing an infinite amount of webpages.

Source: Windows Help and Support

Why do I have to wait so long sometimes?
Sometimes it takes quite a long time before a page you want loads into your browser. This depends on a number of things:

- Modems can have various speeds. The faster the speed of the modem, the faster text and pictures are transmitted. The speed of the connection type also plays an important part.
  To date, a modem connected with the normal analog telephone line is the slowest type. Other types of connections, such as ISDN, cable and DSL, are significantly faster.
  New developments will present a range of fast transmission possibilities through the regular analog telephone line.

- Some websites have more pictures and illustrations than others. Some pages have numerous pictures or various graphic effects. All those dancing figures, revolving text, pop-up assistants and other graphic effects require information to be sent to your computer, and it all has to be sent via the telephone line if that is how you are connected.
  Receiving pictures takes a particularly long time. The more efficient the web page is designed, the faster it will appear on your screen.

- Sometimes it is very busy on the Internet. So many people are surfing at the same time that traffic jams occur. When that happens, you will have to wait longer than usual.

What can be done about this?
- You do not always have to wait until all the pictures have been received. Sometimes you immediately see the topic you are looking for.

   If this is the case, click ✕ **next to the *Address bar***
  No more information is sent and you can click to go to a different page.

- Sometimes a website's opening page will have a button that says:
  Text only.
  If you click on that button, only the text will be sent, not the illustrations. That takes much less time.

Domain names

A web address is also referred to as a domain name. Every web address has an extension, such as **.com**

For example: *www.visualsteps.**com***

There are various extensions that can be used. In Europe, for example, the extension is usually an abbreviation for the country:

For example: *www.google.**nl***

This site is in the Netherlands. Other country extensions include **.be** for Belgium and **.uk** for the United Kingdom.

In the United States, however, a different system is used. Here, the extension can indicate the type of organization:

.com .... commercial business
.edu .... educational institution
.org .... non-commercial organization

Searching on the Internet

When you want to find information on the Internet, you can use a program called a *search engine*.

This is a program that tries to keep track of the contents of millions of web pages on the Internet. You can ask the search engine to find something for you based on a certain key word or phrase. The engine then uses that word or phrase to find the web addresses of web pages that include this word or phrase.

Well-known search engines are:
www.google.com
www.altavista.com
www.yahoo.com

You will discover that one search engine will render entirely different results than the other. This is why it is worth the effort to have more than one search engine perform the search.

You can visit the search engines by typing their web addresses in the *Address bar* of *Internet Explorer*.

Searching with *Live Search*
Internet Explorer has been preprogrammed to use *Live Search* as the default search engine.

In the top right corner of the *Internet Explorer* window, you will see this box:
In this box you can type one or more words that you want to base your search on and then click
🔍 .

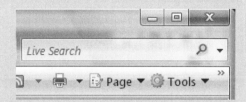

If you type more than one word, you will get a list of web pages that contain at least one of the words. However, if you put the words between quotation marks, the list will show only those pages that contain that specific combination.

8.18 Tips

 Tip

Your History
Internet Explorer also keeps track of all the websites that you have visited. It is easy to display this list:

👉 **Click** ☆

👉 **Click** 🕘 History

👉 **Click** 📅 Today

On the left side of the window, you see your history in a separate pane:

If you did not save a website as a *Favorite* but want to revisit it, you will probably be able to find it again in this list. You can click a hyperlink to visit the web page.

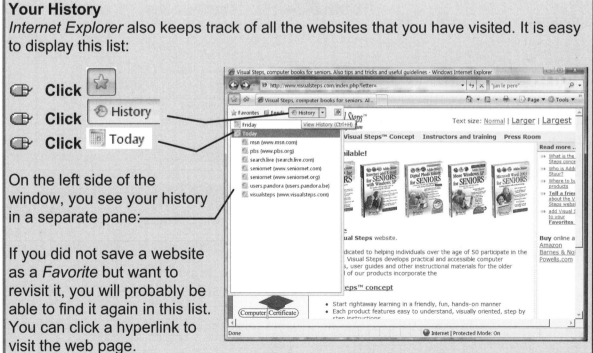

Tip

Information bar

Sometimes when you are surfing the Internet, an *Information bar* in *Internet Explorer* is shown. The *Information bar* appears below the *Address bar* and displays information about downloads, blocked pop-up windows, and other activities.

> This website wants to install the following add-on: 'Windows Genuine Advantage' from 'Microsoft Corporation'. If you trust the website and the   X
> add-on and want to install it, click here...

If *Internet Explorer* is still using its original settings, you will see the *Information bar* in the following circumstances:

- If a website tries to install an *ActiveX control* on your computer or run an *ActiveX* control in an unsafe manner. *ActiveX* is technology for creating interactive web content such as animation sequences or credit card transactions.
- If a website tries to open a pop-up window.
- If a website tries to download a file to your computer.
- If your security settings are below recommended levels.

When you see a message in the *Information bar*, click the message to see more information or to take some action.

Here you see an example of the *Information bar*:

Also a small window appeared:

When you see a window like this:

Click [Close]

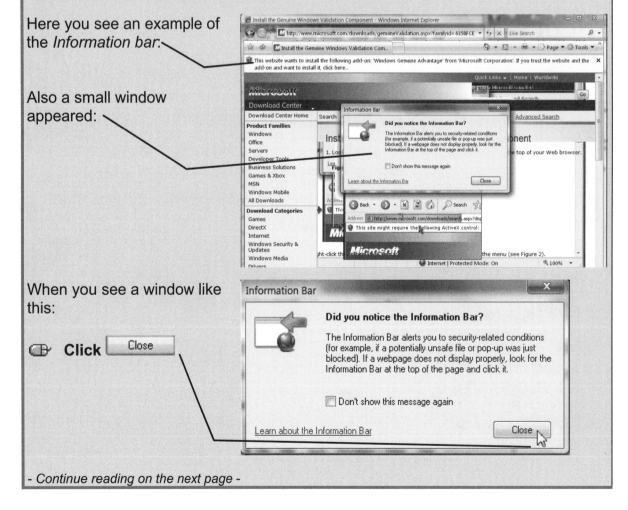

- *Continue reading on the next page -*

To get more information:

👆 **Click the *Information bar***

A small menu appears:

👆 **Click** More information

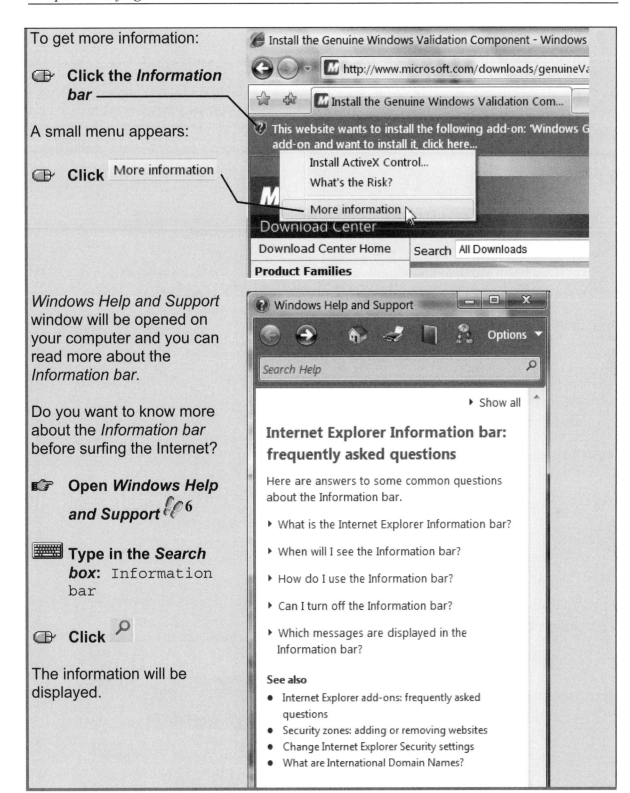

Windows Help and Support window will be opened on your computer and you can read more about the *Information bar*.

Do you want to know more about the *Information bar* before surfing the Internet?

👉 **Open *Windows Help and Support*** ✎6

⌨ **Type in the *Search box*:** Information bar

👆 **Click** 🔍

The information will be displayed.

Tip

Tabbed browsing
Tabbed browsing lets you load web pages in separate tabs of a single browser window, so you can switch between them quickly. Here you see the two tabs:

. The right tab in this example is empty.

☞ **Surf to www.visualsteps.com**

👆 **Point to** ▢ **next to**

The tab changes in ▢:

👆 **Click** ▢

You will see a webpage with information about tabs:

👆 **Click in the *Address bar***

⌨ **Type:**
www.seniornet.org

👆 **Click** →
or

⌨ **Press** [Enter ↵]

The SeniorNet website appears on this tab:

You can open several tabs if you want.
To go to another webpage, that is listed on a tab, just click that tab.

To close a tab:

👆 **Click** ✕ **on the tab**

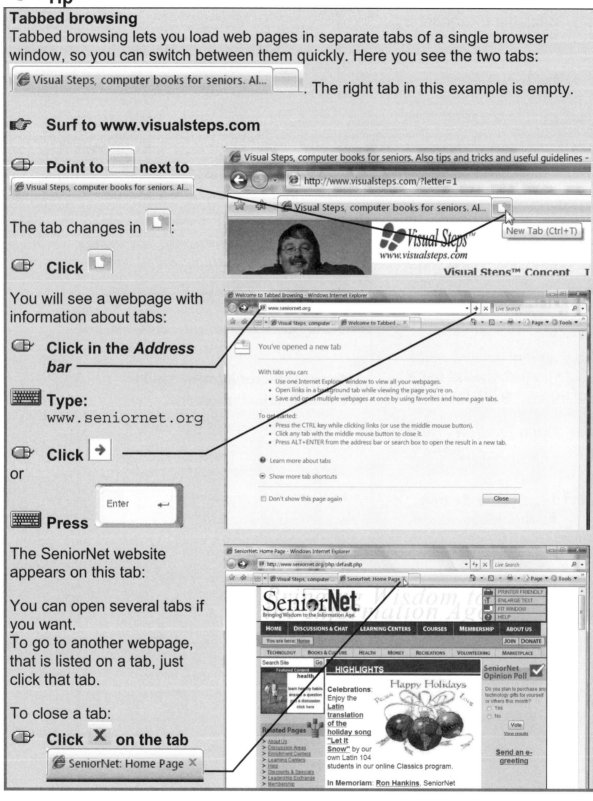

Tip

Large icons
If you think the icons in the toolbar of *Internet Explorer* are too small, you can use larger ones:

☞ **Right-click an empty area of the toolbar**

A menu appears:

☞ **Check mark**
Use Large Icons

Now you see large icons:

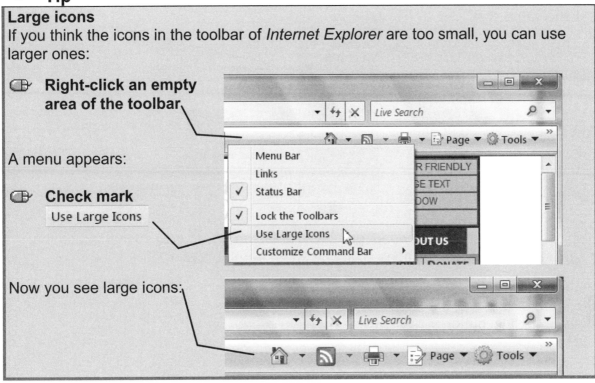

 Tip

Enlarge the font size and/or zoom in on a webpage
Some websites offer the ability to enlarge the font size of the text on the webpage. For example the Visual Steps website **www.visualsteps.com**.

There are three text sizes available: Text size: Normal | Larger | Largest

☞ **Surf to www.visualsteps.com**

In the top right corner of the window:

☞ **Click** Largest

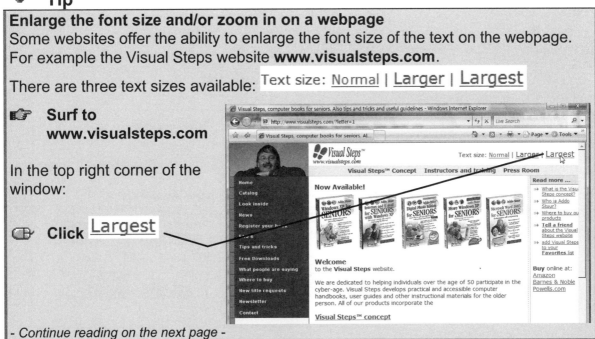

- Continue reading on the next page -

The text size is now enlarged. The images and buttons are still the same size.

☞ **Click** Normal

The text size will be normal again.

You can also *zoom in* on a webpage. *Zoom* enlarges or reduces everything on the page, including text and images. You can zoom from 10% to 1000%.

In the bottom right corner of the *Internet Explorer* window, there is a zoom button 🔍 100% ▼ :

☞ **Click** ▼ **next to** 🔍 100% ▼

A menu appears:

☞ **Click** 200%

The entire page is enlarged, including pictures, buttons and scroll bar:

Try another zoom factor:
☞ **Click** ▼ **next to** 🔍 200%

In the menu:
☞ **Click** 125%

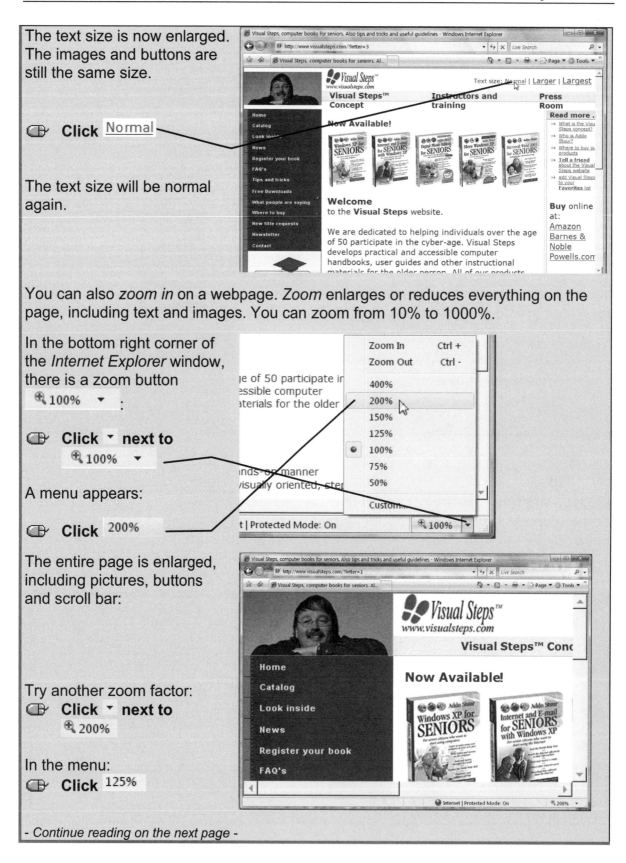

- Continue reading on the next page -

This size is better because you can read the information without too much scrolling.

Tip:
If you have a mouse with a wheel, hold down the Ctrl key, and then scroll the wheel to zoom in or out.

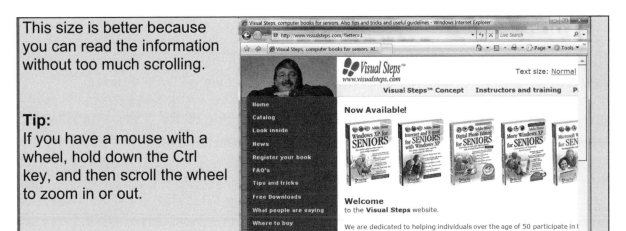

 Tip

Windows Vista Demos: Using the web
Windows Vista Demos are narrated video demonstrations, designed to introduce you to personal computing. Watch as tasks are performed on screen. This is how you start the demo *Using the web*:

🖱 **Click**

In the *Start menu*:

🖱 **Click** Help and Support

At the top of the window:

⌨ **Type:** demo

🖱 **Click** 🔍

In the search results:

🖱 **Click**
　　8.　Demo: Using the web

In the next window:

🖱 **Click** → Watch the demo

The program *Windows Media Player* opens and the demo starts playing:

☞ **Watch the demo**

To close *Windows Media Player*:

🖱 **Click** X

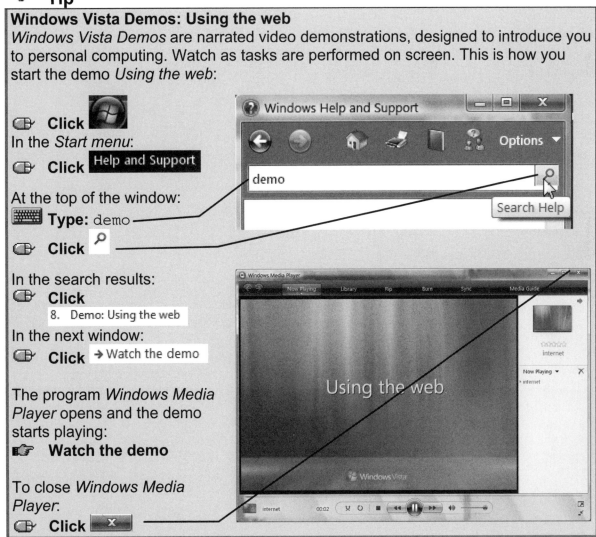

Tip

Register Your Book
You can register your book. Visual Steps will keep you aware of any important changes that are necessary to you as a user of the book and you will take advantage of our periodic newsletter (e-mail) informing you of our product releases, company news, tips & tricks, special offers, etc.

☞ **Open *Internet Explorer*** $\mathscr{U}$64

☞ **If necessary: connect to the Internet** $\mathscr{U}$66

⌨ **Type in the *Address bar*:** www.visualsteps.com/vista

⌨ **Press** Enter ↵

The web page of the book appears. At the left side you see this list:

- Home
- The book
- News
- Purchase this book
- Register your book
- **Free** Downloads
- The Visual Steps catalog
- To **Visual Steps** website

🖱 **Click**
  Register your book

You will see a window like this:

⌨ **Type your name and e-mail address**

🖱 **Click** Submit

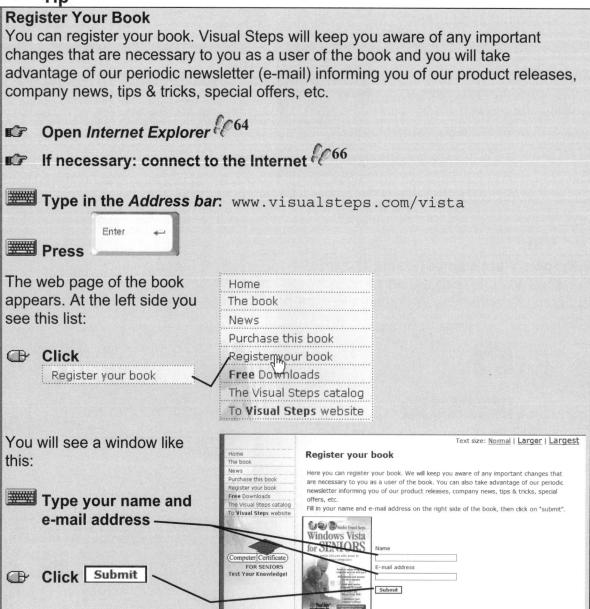

9. E-mail, Your Electronic Mailbox

One of the most widely-used applications on the Internet is electronic mail: e-mail. E-mail uses no pen, paper, envelope or stamp. You type your message into the computer and it is sent via the Internet.

If you have an Internet service subscription, you will automatically be assigned an *e-mail address*. This e-mail address can be used to send and receive mail. Your *Internet Service Provider* (ISP) has a kind of post office, also called a *mail server*. Like with regular mail, this post office handles all of the daily mail traffic.

In order to send an e-mail to someone, the addressee must also have an e-mail address, of course. But it does not matter where that person lives. Sending an e-mail to someone in Australia takes the same amount of time and money as sending an e-mail to your next-door neighbor. Unlike stamps on regular mail, there are no direct costs involved per e-mail, except for your Internet subscription. There is no limit to the number of messages that you can send or receive.

Another significant advantage is that you can send all kinds of things with your e-mail, such as a picture that you have made with a digital camera. E-mail has an extensive effect on communication at work. As the use of e-mail increases, the use of the fax and regular telephone decreases.

Windows Vista has a simple program, *Windows Mail*, with which you can quickly and easily send and receive electronic "letters". You will be using this program in this chapter. You will discover how easy e-mail is: no more stamps to buy and no more trips to the mailbox.

In this chapter, you will learn how to:
- open *Windows Mail*
- create, send, receive and read an e-mail message
- include an attachment

 Please note:

In order to work through this chapter, you need to have an e-mail address and your e-mail program must be properly installed. If this is not the case, you should contact your ISP (*Internet Service Provider*). You also need the user name and password provided by your ISP.

9.1 Opening Windows Mail

Windows Vista has a program that you can use to send and receive electronic mail. It is called *Windows Mail.* In this chapter you will learn how use this program to receive and send e-mail. This is how to open the program *Windows Mail:*

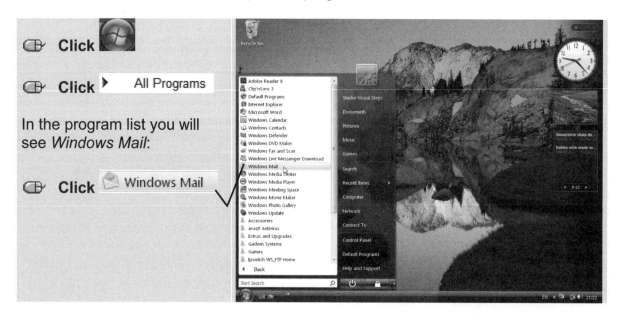

Click [Windows logo]

Click ▶ All Programs

In the program list you will see *Windows Mail*:

Click ✉ Windows Mail

Windows Mail will immediately determine whether you are connected to the Internet (online). If you are **offline**, you see a small window like below. You might want to work offline if you want to reduce the amount of time you spend online, either because your *Internet Service Provider* (ISP) charges you by the hour, or because you have only one phone line and you are not using a broadband connection.

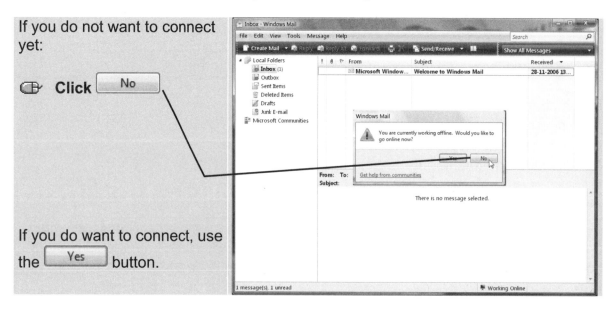

If you do not want to connect yet:

Click [No]

If you do want to connect, use the [Yes] button.

If you are using *Windows Mail* for the first time and you are **online**, you will see a window like this:

Enter your user name

Enter your password

The user name and password are provided by your ISP (*Internet Service Provider*).

 Click OK

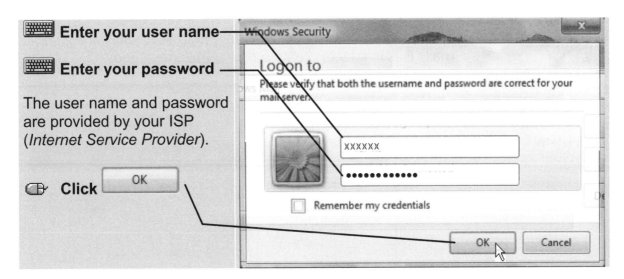

Next you will see the *Windows Mail* start-up window.

On the left there is a folder list:

On the right you see a message list with headers:

Here is the preview pane:

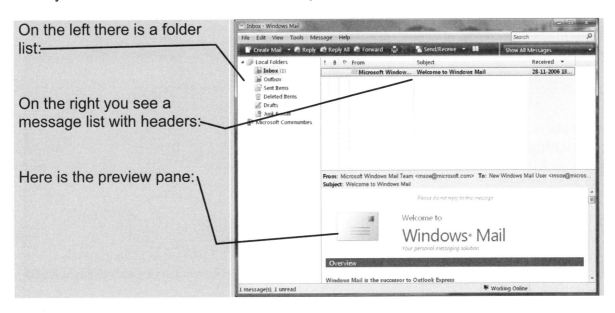

If you are the first user of *Windows Mail,* you will see a *Welcome to Windows Mail* message in the message list and preview pane.

HELP! My window looks entirely different.

When someone else already used the program, the window may look different. This does not matter. Just continue reading.

9.2 The E-mail Address

To practice, you will be sending a message to yourself. This is an excellent way to learn how to send e-mail. Since the message is sent straight to you, you will also learn how to receive e-mail. This is how to create a new e-mail message:

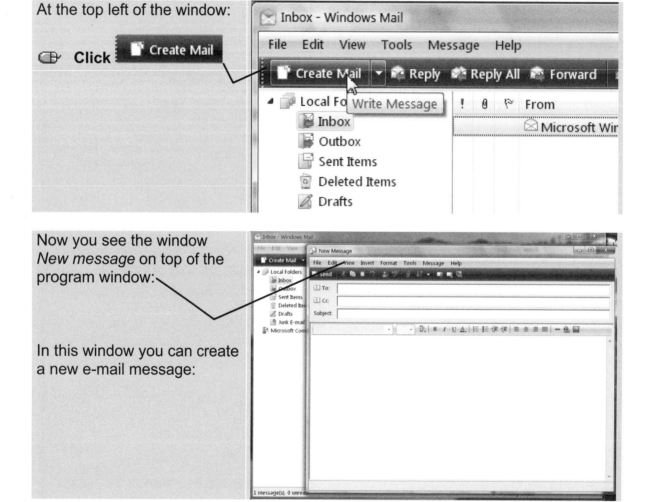

The first thing to do is to address your message using an e-mail address. Every e-mail address consists of a number of words, with the familiar symbol @ somewhere in the middle. For example:

name@provider.com

The name of the addressee is located in front of the @. Behind it, the address usually contains the name of the *Internet Service Provider* from which you received the e-mail address.

Please note:

E-mail addresses may not contain spaces.

This is why names or words are sometimes separated by a dot (**.**). These dots are extremely important. If you forget one in the address, your message will never arrive. Your mailman may understand what the sender means if the address is not completely correct. But a computer does not.

9.3 Sending an E-mail

The best way to test that your electronic mailbox works as it should is to send an e-mail message to yourself.

In the line marked To: **type your own e-mail address**

Every e-mail message is also given a subject.

☞ **Click in the box next to** Subject:

Type: test

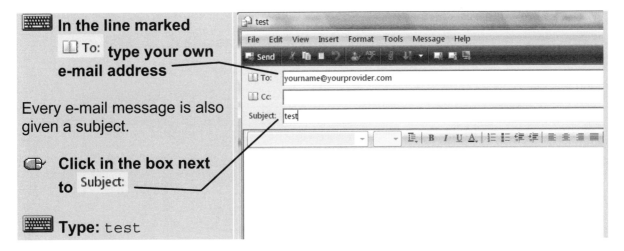

Now you can start typing the actual text of the message.

☞ **Click in the main message window**

You can type the message here.

Type:
This is a first
e-mail as a test.

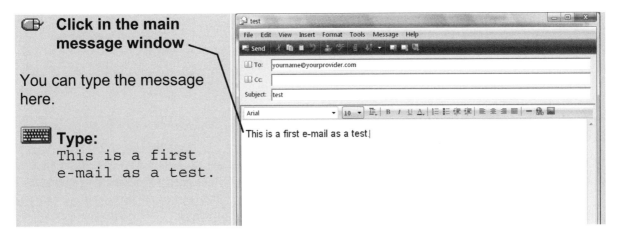

To change font type, size, style, and effects such as color, use the formatting bar
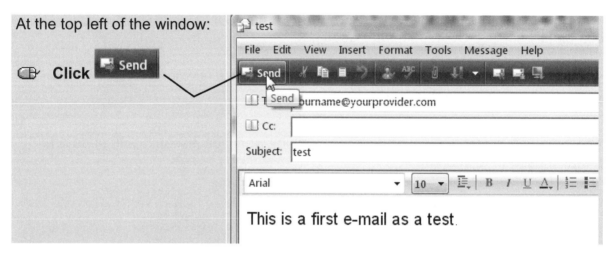 just like you did in *WordPad*.

When you have finished the e-mail, you can send it.

At the top left of the window:

☞ **Click** 🖳 Send

When you work **offline**, the program reminds you that the message is placed in the *Outbox* first:

☞ **Click** ⬜ OK

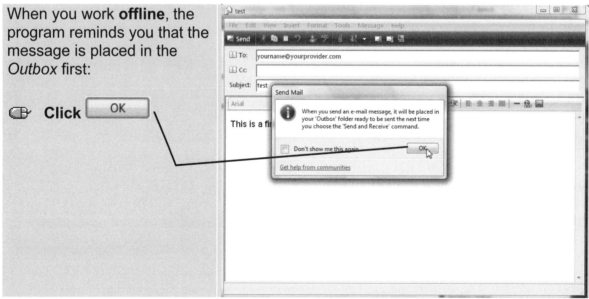

 HELP! No reminder.

Is the reminder about the *Outbox* not shown on your screen? Then you are probably using a broadband connection, for example a DSL line. This means that *Windows Mail* has a different setting, and your e-mail is immediately mailed. If this is the case, skip the following section and continue at **Reading a Message**.

9.4 The Outbox

When you work offline, all of the e-mails you make are collected in the *Outbox* first. Your message will not be sent until you connect to the Internet. This means that you can write all of the e-mails you want, and then send them all at once.

Now you see the *Windows Mail* window again.
There is one message in the *Outbox*:

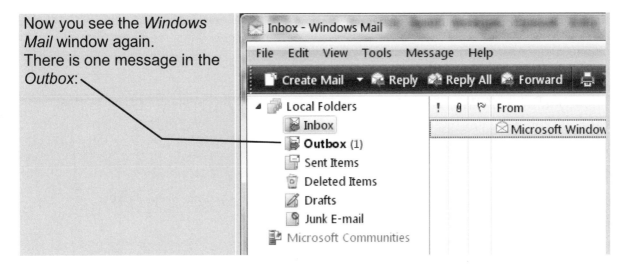

9.5 Sending and Receiving

Now you can manually send your message. The program will connect with the Internet to send it.
Sending and receiving manually is useful if you are using dial-up networking to connect to the Internet. In that case, be sure to check if your modem is ready before you try to connect.

☞ **Make sure your modem is connected to the telephone line**

Do you have an external modem?
☞ **If so, turn the modem on**

Do you have an internal modem?
☞ **Then you do not need to do anything**

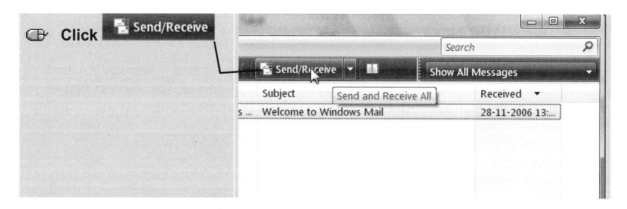

Click Send/Receive

When you work **offline**, *Windows Mail* will tell you that you are still offline and ask whether you want to go online.

You need to go online to send a message, so:

Click Yes

If you are using dial-up networking to connect to the Internet, you will see a *Dial-up Connection* window. It probably looks like this one:

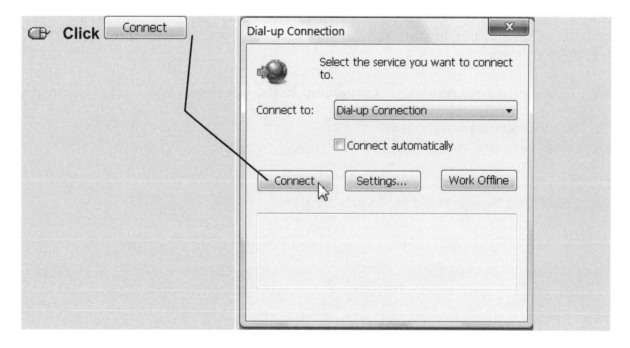

Click Connect

If your username and password are **not** displayed:

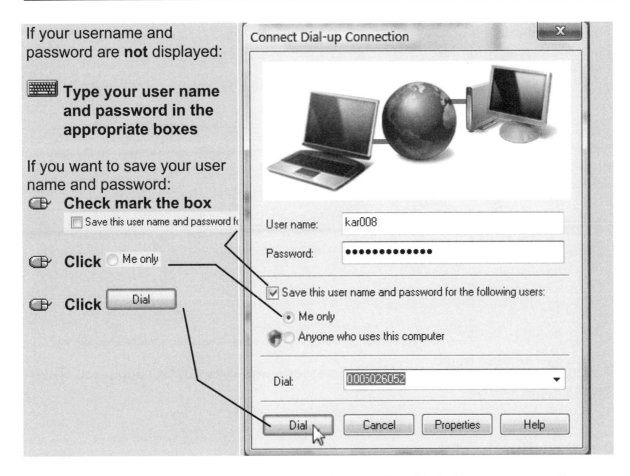

Connect Dial-up Connection

User name: kar008

Password: ●●●●●●●●●●●●●●

☑ Save this user name and password for the following users:

⦿ Me only

○ Anyone who uses this computer

Dial: 0005026052 ▼

[Dial] [Cancel] [Properties] [Help]

⌨ **Type your user name and password in the appropriate boxes**

If you want to save your user name and password:

☞ **Check mark the box**

☐ Save this user name and password for

☞ **Click** ○ Me only

☞ **Click** [Dial]

A connection is made to your ISP (*Internet Service Provider*). Next your e-mail message is sent. The program also automatically checks to see if you have any new e-mail messages.

 HELP! There are no windows like these.

Are these windows not shown on your screen?
This means that *Windows Mail* has different settings on your computer. Your program automatically connects when you click the button 📧 Send/Receive .

☞ **Just continue to read**

You can follow this process as it proceeds in a window like this:

If everything went as it should, your text message was immediately sent to you. Then it is put in the *Inbox*.

9.6 Reading a Message

All e-mail messages you receive are placed in a separate folder that is called the *Inbox*.

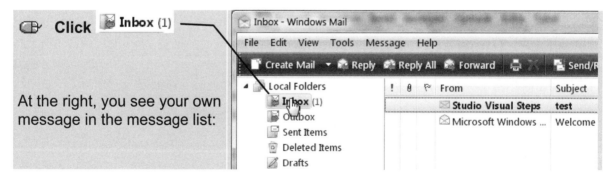

At the right, you see your own message in the message list:

HELP! I do not have any mail.

Is there no message in your *Inbox*?
Perhaps it has not yet been received. Try again later to receive the message:

 Click ![Send/Receive]

You can open the message in a larger window so that you can read it:

In the message list you see the header of your message:

☞ **Double-click your message**

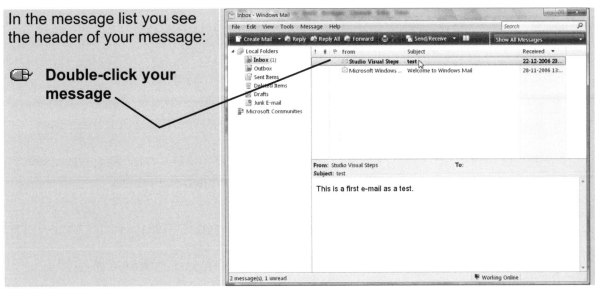

The e-mail message is easy to read in the separate window.

This window has a bar with several handy buttons for replying to e-mail messages:

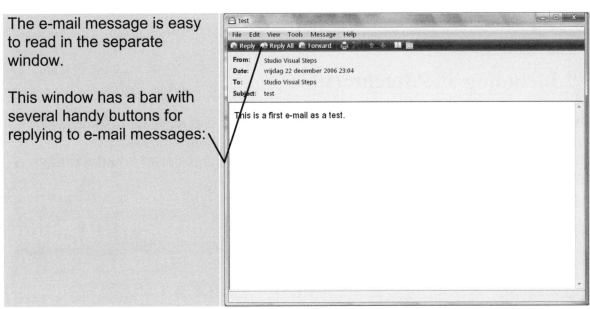

These buttons have the following functions:

Reply	**Reply** Reply to sender, the "to" portion already contains the correct e-mail address. The original e-mail message is included.
Reply All	**Reply All** An e-mail message can be sent to more than one person. This button is used to send a reply to everyone to whom the original e-mail was addressed. The original e-mail message is included.
Forward	**Forward** A new e-mail is made from the original message that can be sent to someone else. The original e-mail message is included.

☞ **Close the e-mail message window** 𝒞𝒞⁴

9.7 Including an Attachment

The nice thing about e-mail messages is that you can send all kinds of things with them. You can add a photo, a drawing, or another document, for example. Something that you want to send with an e-mail message is called an **attachment**. This is how to add an attachment to a message:

☞ Click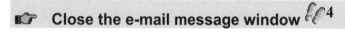

Now you see this *New Message* window, where you can type a new e-mail message:

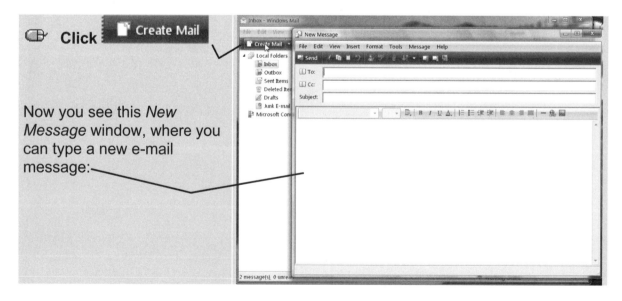

In the box next to
To: **type your own**
e-mail address

Every e-mail message should
contain a subject.

Click in the box next
to Subject:

Type:
test with
attachment

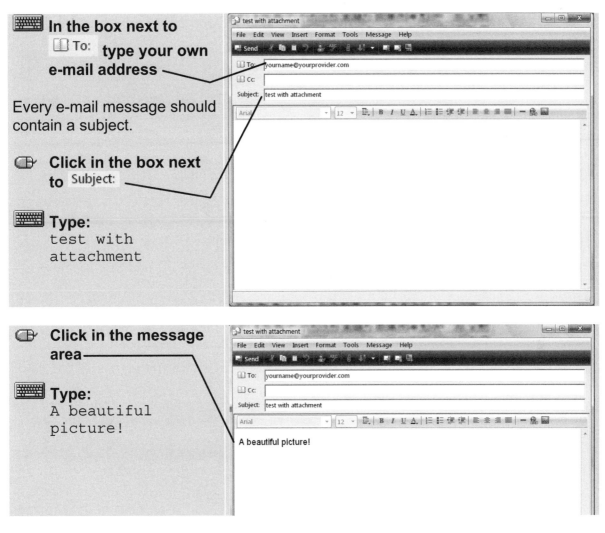

Click in the message
area

Type:
A beautiful
picture!

To attach a picture to your message, you click the "paper clip" button:

Click

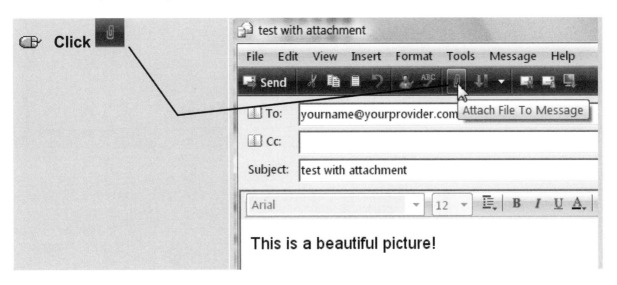

Now you see this folder window. By default, the folder *Documents* will be opened:

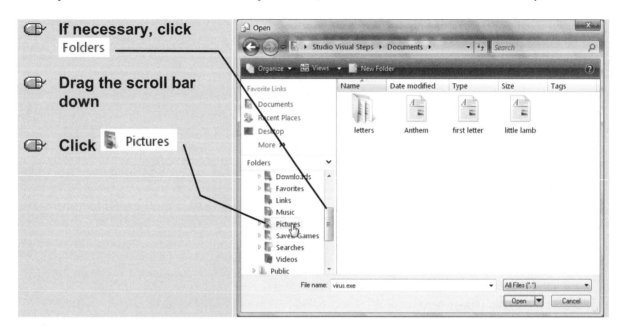

If necessary, click Folders

Drag the scroll bar down

Click Pictures

The content of the folder *Pictures* appears:

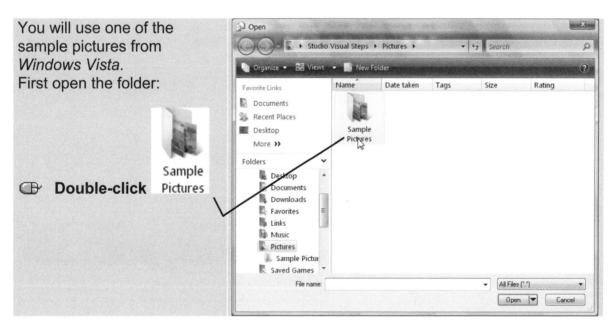

You will use one of the sample pictures from *Windows Vista*.
First open the folder:

Double-click Sample Pictures

The sample pictures appear in the file list:

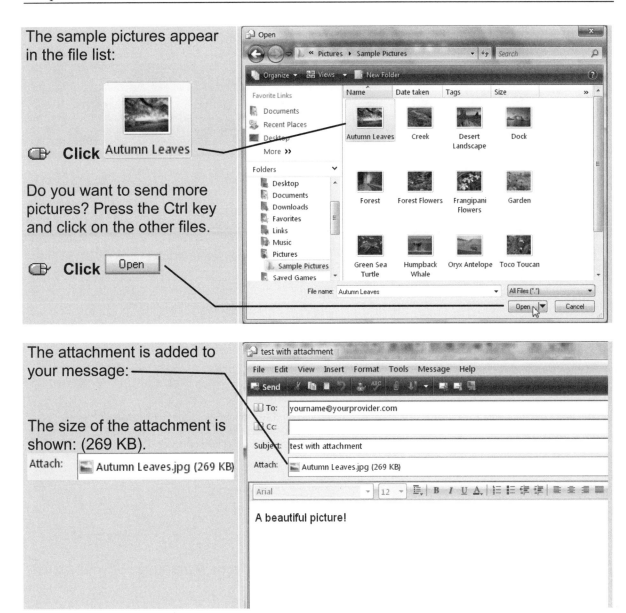

Click **Autumn Leaves**

Do you want to send more pictures? Press the Ctrl key and click on the other files.

Click **Open**

The attachment is added to your message:

The size of the attachment is shown: (269 KB).

Attach: ☐ Autumn Leaves.jpg (269 KB)

➡ **Please note:**

Sending and receiving an e-mail with an attachment takes more time than sending and receiving a "bare" e-mail message, especially if you or the addressee are using dial-up networking to connect to the Internet. Sending pictures takes a particularly long time. You may decide for yourself whether or not you really want to send this message.
If you do not want to send:
☞ **Close the message window**
The program will ask whether you want to save the changes.
Click **No**

If you really want to send the e-mail message, do the following:

At the top left of the window:

☞ **Click**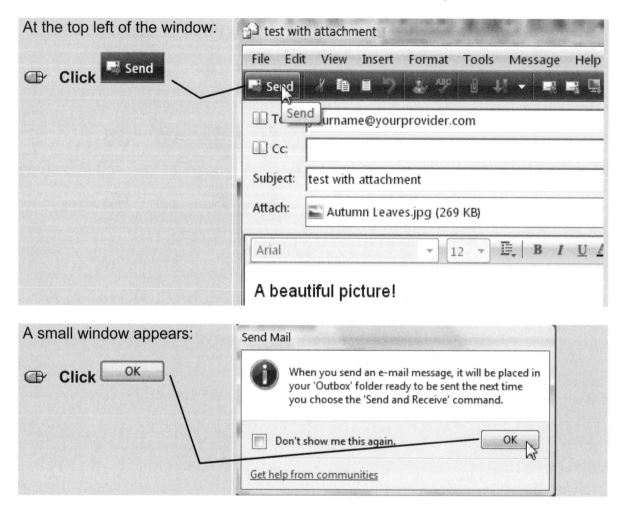

A small window appears:

☞ **Click** OK

If your message is placed in the *Outbox*, you can send it now manually. If your mail is sent immediately, you do not have to send it manually.

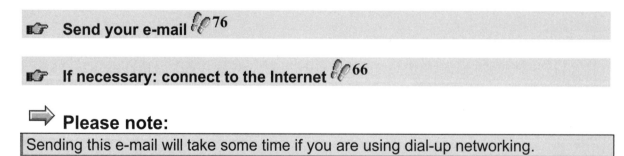

☞ **Send your e-mail** 🦶76

☞ **If necessary: connect to the Internet** 🦶66

⇨ **Please note:**

Sending this e-mail will take some time if you are using dial-up networking.

9.8 Opening and Saving an Attachment

Once your e-mail is sent, it should arrive very quickly. You can see this in the *Inbox:*

 Click Inbox

Here you see the preview of your own message:

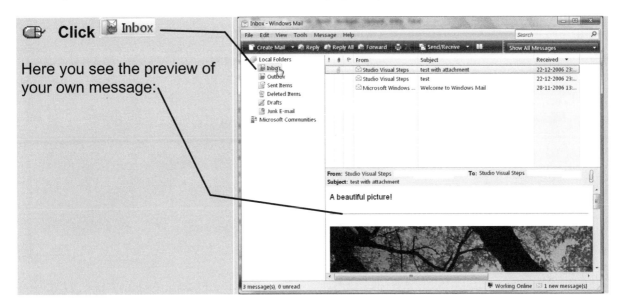

HELP! I do not have any mail.

Is there no message in your *Inbox*?
Perhaps it has not yet been received. Try again later:

Click Send/Receive

In one of the first columns in this message list, a small paper clip indicates that an attachment has been included:

 **Double-click your new message**

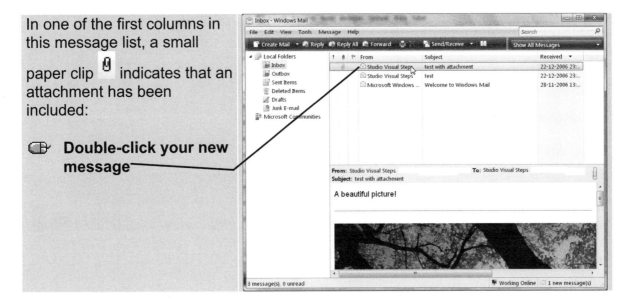

You see your message in a separate window:

The window is too small to show the whole picture. Using the scroll bar you can see the picture:

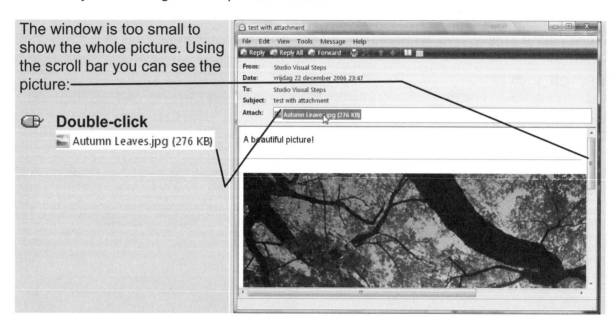

☞ **Double-click**

Autumn Leaves.jpg (276 KB)

The default program to view the picture is called *Windows Photo Gallery*. *Windows Photo Gallery* is a tool included with *Windows Vista* that you can use to view, organize, edit, share, and print your digital pictures (and videos too). On your computer the picture may be shown in another program.

After you have seen the picture, you can close the program window:

☞ **Click** [X]

You see the test message again.

9.9 Saving an Attachment

You can save an attachment from an e-mail on your computer. This is how:

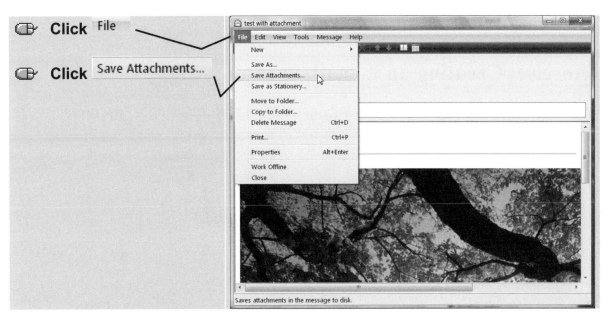

👆 **Click** File

👆 **Click** Save Attachments...

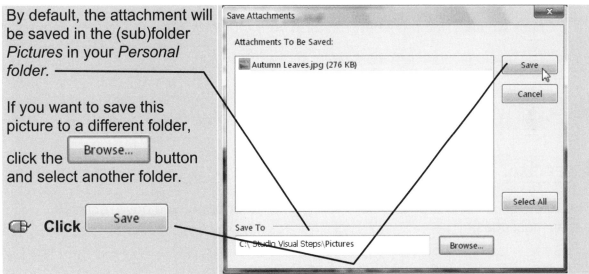

By default, the attachment will be saved in the (sub)folder *Pictures* in your *Personal folder.*

If you want to save this picture to a different folder, click the Browse... button and select another folder.

👆 **Click** Save

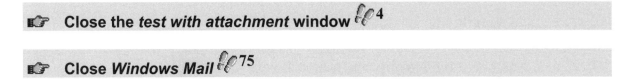

☞ **Close the *test with attachment* window** 🦶4

☞ **Close *Windows Mail*** 🦶75

Now you have learned how to send and receive e-mail messages. You can practice what you have learned by doing the exercises in this chapter.

9.10 Exercises

The following exercises will help you master what you have just learned. Have you forgotten how to do something? Use the number beside the footsteps to look it up in the appendix *How Do I Do That Again?*

Exercise: Creating an E-mail

With this exercise, you can practice writing, sending and receiving a new e-mail message.

☑ Open *Windows Mail.* 🦶74

☑ Create a new e-mail message addressed to yourself. 🦶77

☑ Send the e-mail message to yourself. 🦶78

☑ Send and receive your e-mail. 🦶76 If necessary, connect to the Internet. 🦶66

☑ Check whether you have new e-mail in your *Inbox.* 🦶80

☑ Read your e-mail message. 🦶81

☑ Close *Windows Mail.* 🦶75

Exercise: Receiving E-mail

This exercise is used to practice determining whether or not you have received e-mail messages.

☑ Open *Windows Mail.* 🦶74

☑ Send and receive your e-mail. 🦶76 If necessary, connect to the Internet. 🦶66

☑ Check whether you have any new e-mail in your *Inbox.* 🦶80

☑ Close *Windows Mail.* 🦶75

Exercise: Sending an E-mail with Attachment

With this exercise, you can send another e-mail, this time including the text file *Anthem* as an attachment.

 Please note:

You typed and saved the *Anthem* text in Chapter 5. If you did not, simply attach a different text.

☑ Start *Windows Mail*. *℮℮* 74

☑ Create a new e-mail message addressed to yourself. *℮℮* 77

☑ Add the text file *Anthem* in the folder *Documents* as an attachment. *℮℮* 82

☑ Send the e-mail message to yourself. *℮℮* 78

☑ Send and receive your e-mail. *℮℮* 76 If necessary, connect to the Internet. *℮℮* 66

☑ Check whether you have e-mail in your *Inbox*. *℮℮* 80

☑ Read your e-mail message. *℮℮* 81

☑ Open the attachment (*WordPad* or *MS Word* will be opened to show the text). *℮℮* 83

☑ Close *WordPad / MS Word*. *℮℮* 4

☑ Close *Windows Mail*. *℮℮* 75

9.11 Background Information

Dictionary	
Attachment	Documents, images, and other files sent as attachments to an e-mail message. Messages that contain attachments are indicated by a paper clip icon in the attachment column of the message list. For security reasons many e-mail programs (including *Windows Mail*) prevent recipients from opening executable file attachments, such as those with .exe, .bat and .inf file name extensions.
Deleted Items	Deleted e-mails are moved to the *Deleted Items* folder. To permanently remove deleted items from your computer: delete the message in the *Deleted Items* folder.
DSL	A type of high-speed Internet connection using existing copper telephone wires. Also referred to as a broadband connection.
E-mail	Short for electronic mail. Messages sent via the Internet.
E-mail account	The server name, user name, password, and e-mail address used by *Windows Mail* to connect to an e-mail service. You create the e-mail account in *Windows Vista* by using information provided by your *Internet Service Provider* (ISP).
E-mail header	Information included at the top of an e-mail message: name of the sender and recipient, subject, date, and other information.
Inbox	The *Inbox* is where all of the e-mail messages that you receive are placed.
ISP	*Internet Service Provider* - A company that provides Internet access. An ISP provides a telephone number, a user name, a password, and other connection information so that users can access the Internet through the ISP's computers.
Message list	List of messages in various folders in *Windows Mail*.
Outbox	When you manually send e-mail and you finish writing a message and click on the *Send* button, the message will be placed in your *Outbox* folder. Messages in the *Outbox* folder will be sent when you click the *Send/Receive* button.

- Continue reading on the next page -

Preview pane	Here you can view the message's contents without opening the message in a separate window. To view an e-mail message in the *Preview* pane, click the message in the message list.
Sent Items	A copy of every message you send is saved in the *Sent Items* folder, just in case you need it later.
Virus	A piece of code or program designed to cause damage to a computer system (by erasing or corrupting data) or annoying users (by printing messages or altering what is displayed on the screen).

Source: Windows Help and Support

The smaller, the faster

On the Internet, there is one golden rule: the smaller the message, the faster it is sent. The same applies to attachments. If you send a small attachment, such as a small photograph, the transmission will only take a few seconds. If you send a larger drawing, it will take more time and the telephone line will be used longer.

Along with the name of an attachment, such as a text or a picture, its size is always shown, expressed in MB or KB: Attach: 🖼 Autumn Leaves.jpg (269 KB)

The size of a file is always indicated in KB or MB. These are measurements for sizes, just like inches and ounces.

A **Kilobyte** is (about) one thousand bytes.
This means that: 20 Kilobytes is 20,000 bytes. The abbreviation of kilobyte is **KB**.

A **Megabyte** is (about) one thousand kilobytes.
This means that one Megabyte is (about) one million (one thousand times one thousand) bytes. The abbreviation of megabyte is **MB**.

How long does it take to send or receive something?

The speed at which something can be sent or received depends on a number of things, including the speed of your modem, the type of connection and how busy it is on the Internet.
If for example, you are using dial-up networking to connect to the Internet, you can receive **6 KB** per second with a regular modem. This translates into 360 KB or 0.36 MB per minute.

- Continue reading on the next page -

A message that consists of 16 KB therefore takes about three seconds.
The size of the picture attachment you used in this chapter, is 269 KB. It takes about 45 seconds to send or receive. The directions text as shown in our illustrations measures 1.73 MB and will take about three minutes. As you see, this is quite a long time.

You can send different types of files with an e-mail message. You can even send sounds or video clips! But be careful: sound and video files are usually quite large. It may take a long time to send or receive files of this type. However, when you are using a broadband connection, for example a DSL line, this will not be a problem. This type of service offers high speed connection to the Internet.

How much fits?

Now you now what a kilobyte and a megabyte are. You can read here how much data fits on various types of data storage devices:

A diskette (floppy): 1.44 MB.
A CD-ROM (CD-R) / CD-Rewritable (CD-RW): 640 MB.

A larger size is used these days for different kinds of data storage: the Gigabyte.
A Gigabyte is (about) one thousand Megabytes, or one billion bytes.
The abbreviation of Gigabyte is **GB.**

A USB stick: 16 MB to 4 GB or even more.
A DVD-ROM (DVD-R) / DVD-Rewritable (DVD-RW): 4,7 GB or more (double layer).
Hard disks on today's computers have a capacity of at least 80 GB or 120 GB.
More powerful computers may have hard disks with 200 GB or even more!

Busy?

Do you connect to the Internet via the telephone line (dial-up networking)? If you are connected to the Internet and someone tries to call you, the caller will get a busy signal. So if you are expecting a call, do not connect to the Internet.
Do you connect by using an ISDN or DSL line? Then you can receive calls while you are connected to the Internet.
Do you have a cable connection? In that case, you can continue regular telephone service because your Internet connection does not interfere with your telephone.

Attachment blocked

Windows Mail blocks certain types of file attachments that are commonly used to spread e-mail viruses. A *virus* is a piece of code or program designed to cause damage to a computer system (by erasing or corrupting data) or annoying users (by printing messages or altering what is displayed on the screen).

When an e-mail message contains a blocked picture or other content, a red "X" will appear in place of the blocked content.

If *Windows Mail* blocks an e-mail or an attachment, the *Information bar* will display a message letting you know that it has done so.

Although it is not recommended, you can enable access to blocked attachments. This should only be done by advanced users, and only with an up-to-date virus checker running.

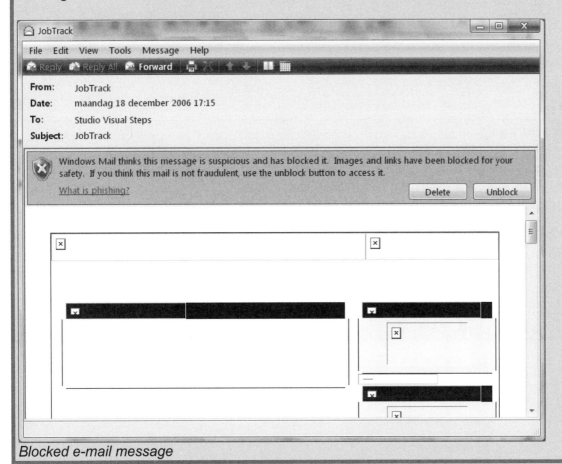

Blocked e-mail message

9.12 Tips

 Tip

Enter username and password again every time?
Do you have to enter your password every time in this window?
You can change the settings in this window.

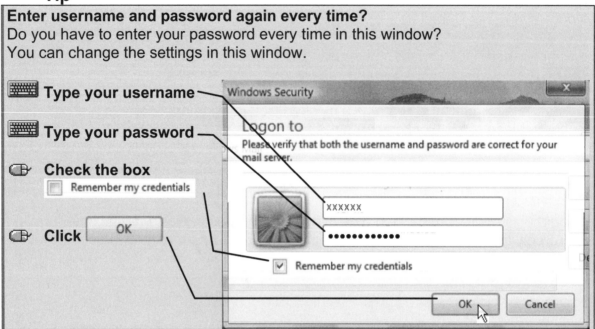

⌨ **Type your username**

⌨ **Type your password**

☞ **Check the box**
　　☐ Remember my credentials

☞ **Click** [OK]

 Tip

Wrong address?
If you make a mistake in the address to which the message is to be sent, it will be returned to you by the *Internet post office*. This post office will return your message as an attachment to a message explaining why it is being returned.
This message will be sent to your *Inbox:*

!	0	⚑	From	Subject
	0		✉ Mail Delivery Subsystem	Returned mail: see transcript for details

Open the folder 📁 Sent Items to see whether you made a typing error in the address.
You can create a new message with the correct address.

Tip

Keeping a list of addresses

Generally, you will have to keep track of the e-mail addresses you want to use yourself. There is no book of reference that lists everyone's e-mail address (like a telephone directory for telephone numbers). You can find lists of e-mail addresses on the Internet, but it is unlikely that you will find all the addresses you want.

Windows Mail can help you to keep track of e-mail addresses that you have used, which can be saved in the folder *Contacts*:

⊙➥ **Click an e-mail you received**

⊙➥ **Click** Tools

A menu appears:

⊙➥ **Click** Add Sender to Contacts

Once an address has been saved, you can enter it in a *New message* without typing the address. This is how:

⊙➥ **Click** To:

- Continue reading on the next page -

Now you can select the address you want from the list.

 Click the name

 Click To: ->

 Click OK

The e-mail address will appear in the "to" box of the new message.

To: Yvette <y.huijsman@XXXX.XX>

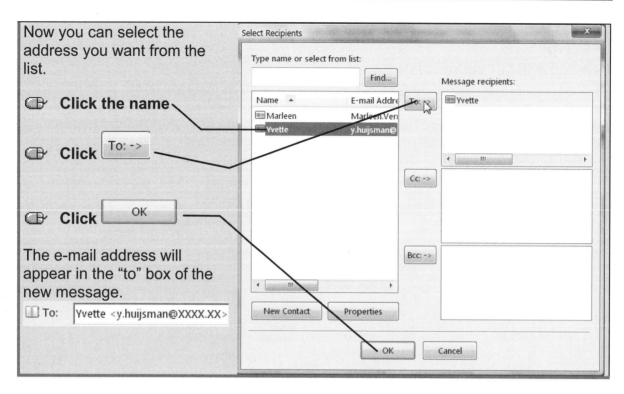

 Tip

Printing an e-mail

Use this button on the toolbar if you want to print an e-mail message.

 Tip

Deleting an e-mail

Use this button on the toolbar if you want to delete an e-mail message. First click the message you want to delete in the message list.

Then click this button .

The message will be stored in the folder 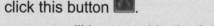 Deleted Items .

Open the folder Deleted Items and delete the message once more. Now it is permanently removed from your computer.

 Tip

If you want to send your e-mail to more than one address, you must type a semi-colon (;) or comma between the addresses.
If you select more than one address from your list of addresses, *Windows Mail* will automatically enter these for you.

Tip

Security settings in Windows Mail
Take a look at security settings in *Windows Mail:*

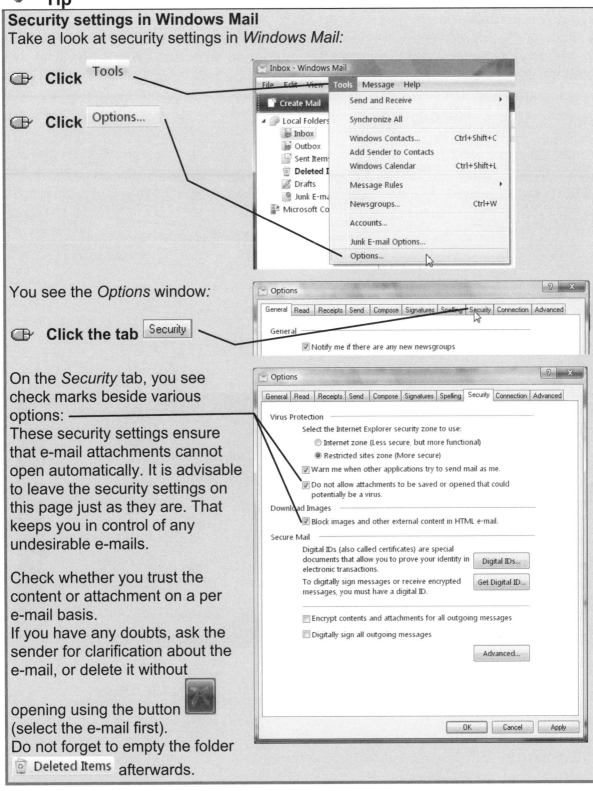

☞ **Click** Tools

☞ **Click** Options...

You see the *Options* window:

☞ **Click the tab** Security

On the *Security* tab, you see check marks beside various options:
These security settings ensure that e-mail attachments cannot open automatically. It is advisable to leave the security settings on this page just as they are. That keeps you in control of any undesirable e-mails.

Check whether you trust the content or attachment on a per e-mail basis.
If you have any doubts, ask the sender for clarification about the e-mail, or delete it without opening using the button (select the e-mail first).
Do not forget to empty the folder Deleted Items afterwards.

Tip

Windows Vista Demos
Windows Vista Demos are narrated video demonstrations, designed to introduce you to personal computing. Watch as tasks are performed on screen. This is how you start the demo *Using Windows Mail*:

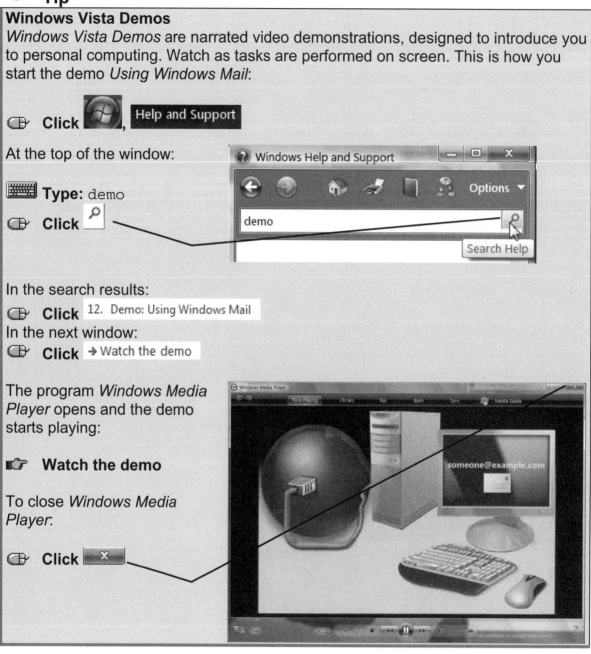

☞ **Click** ⊞, Help and Support

At the top of the window:

⌨ **Type:** demo

☞ **Click** 🔍

In the search results:
☞ **Click** 12. Demo: Using Windows Mail
In the next window:
☞ **Click** → Watch the demo

The program *Windows Media Player* opens and the demo starts playing:

☞ **Watch the demo**

To close *Windows Media Player*:

☞ **Click** ✕

10. How to Make Working with Your Computer More Pleasant

You now have some experience and feel more confident working with your computer. Did you know that nearly every part of your computer can be customized to make it even more pleasant?

It is like taking a new car for a drive: First you adjust the seat for the length of your legs and you make sure that all of the mirrors are in the right position.

Customizing your computer is worth the effort not only because this avoids frustration, but also because it prevents negative consequences in the longer term.

It is rather easy, for example, to adjust the mouse settings so that you can work more easily with it and prevent your hand or wrist from becoming strained.

This chapter explains which parts of the computer you can change. Particular attention is devoted to aspects that can be important for seniors, requiring you to use your motor skills, your eyesight and your hearing.

Feel free to experiment to determine whether these changes make it more pleasant for you to work with the computer. Remember that any change you make can just as easily be turned back to its original value.

In this chapter you will find answers and solutions to the following questions and problems:

- the mouse pointer moves too fast
- I can not double-click with the mouse
- I am left-handed
- I keep losing the mouse pointer on the screen
- my mouse does not move smoothly; it jerks
- I often type double letters
- I can not type apostrophes or accents
- everything on the screen is too small
- the letters on the screen are too small
- *Windows Vista* is much too busy and confusing for me
- the sound on my PC is too loud or too soft
- how can I connect a headset or extra speakers to my PC?
- I want to hear sound signals

10.1 The Control Panel

Many of the settings on your computer can be adjusted in a special window: the *Control Panel.* This is how to open it:

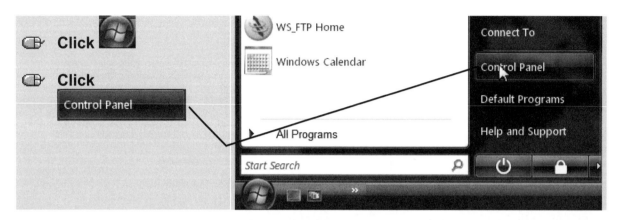

Now you see this window containing icons for the various parts of your computer, divided into categories.

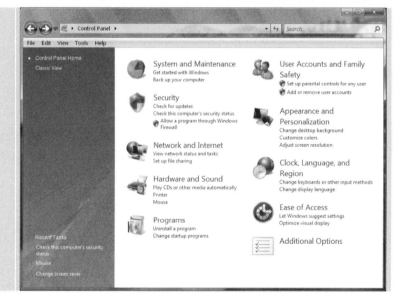

You can adjust one of the parts by clicking the icon or category title.

 HELP! I can not see the Control Panel with categories.

Do you see a lot of icons? This means your *Control Panel* is displayed in the *Classic View* . At the lop left of the window:

> Control Panel Home
> • Classic View

⊞ **Click**

Now you can see the icons in the *Category View*.

10.2 Customizing the Mouse

There are various ways to adjust the settings for your mouse. If you still are not working comfortably with the mouse despite sufficient practice, you can try changing the settings. You can set:

- the speed
- the double-click speed
- the buttons for left-handed users
- the mouse pointer

All of these settings can be adjusted in the following window.

The mouse is located in the category
Hardware and Sound :

Click Mouse

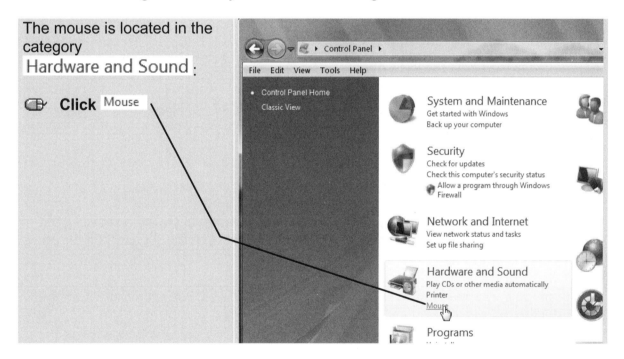

You now see the window *Mouse Properties*:

Please note:
This window may have a different appearance on your screen. Mouse manufacturers sometimes make a modified version of this window for their products.

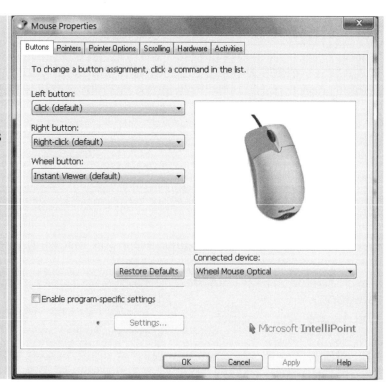

10.3 The Pointer Speed

The speed of the mouse pointer determines the relationship between a movement made with the mouse over the tabletop and the movement of the mouse pointer on the screen.

> If the pointer speed is **too fast**, when you move the mouse only slightly on the tabletop the **movement on the screen is too large**.
>
> If the pointer speed is **too slow**, when you move the mouse a long way on the tabletop the **movement on the screen is only slight**.

For most people, the pointer speed is correct if a movement with the mouse on the tabletop surface or mousepad within the surface of a CD box (this is approximately a 5 inch square) moves the mouse pointer from one corner of the screen to another corner.

If you still think your mouse pointer is too slow or too fast after practicing, you can try adjusting the speed. This is how:

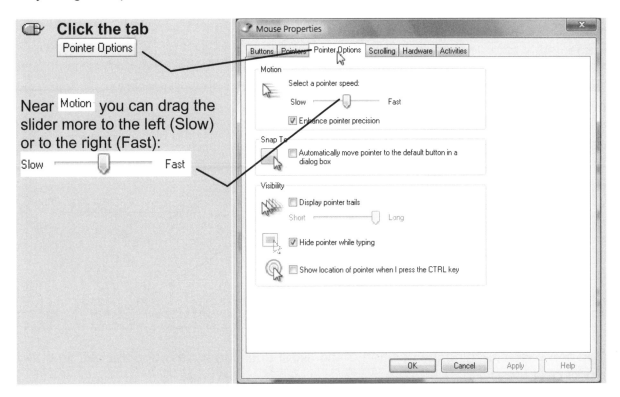

☞ **Click the tab**

Pointer Options

Near Motion you can drag the slider more to the left (Slow) or to the right (Fast):

Slow ——————◻—————— Fast

⦿ Make the setting **faster** if you have to move the mouse over too long a distance on the tabletop.

⦿ Make the setting **slower** if the mouse pointer moves too quickly over the screen.

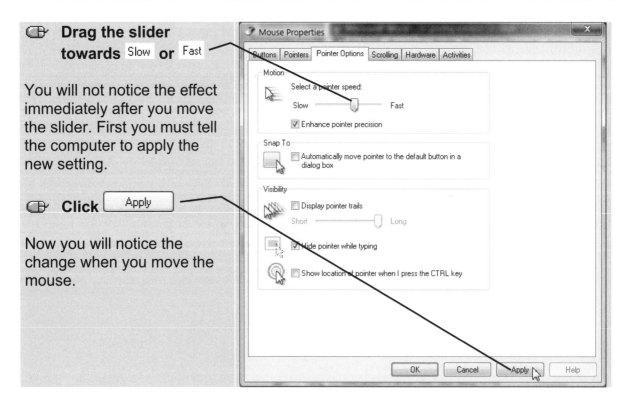

Drag the slider towards Slow **or** Fast

You will not notice the effect immediately after you move the slider. First you must tell the computer to apply the new setting.

Click Apply

Now you will notice the change when you move the mouse.

You can keep changing the position of the slider until you have found the setting that works best for you.

Do not forget to click Apply to apply the new setting.

10.4 The Mouse Pointer Visibility

Many computer beginners complain that they regularly lose track of the mouse pointer on the screen. It is very easy to add an effect to the mouse pointer to make it more visible. One of the things you can do is to give the mouse pointer a *tail* or a *pointer trail*. Try it:

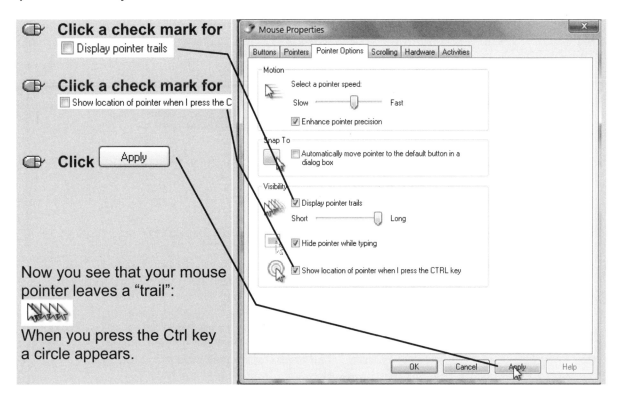

Click a check mark for
☐ Display pointer trails

Click a check mark for
☐ Show location of pointer when I press the C

Click Apply

Now you see that your mouse pointer leaves a "trail":

When you press the Ctrl key a circle appears.

With most mice, you can also adjust the length of the trail.
If you do not like these effects, simply click the boxes again to remove the check marks and do not forget to click Apply to apply the new setting.

10.5 The Size of the Mouse Pointer

You can also make the mouse pointer more visible by making it larger. This is done with a different tab:

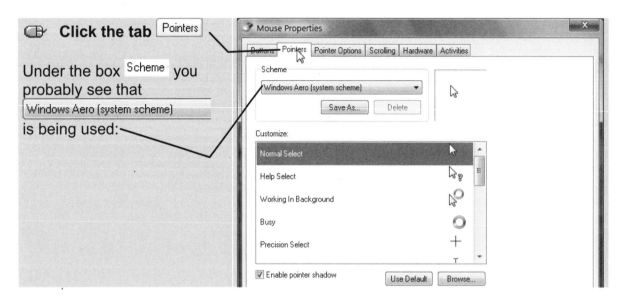

Click the tab Pointers

Under the box Scheme you probably see that
Windows Aero (system scheme)
is being used:

You can choose a larger mouse pointer. It might be easier for you to see. This is how:

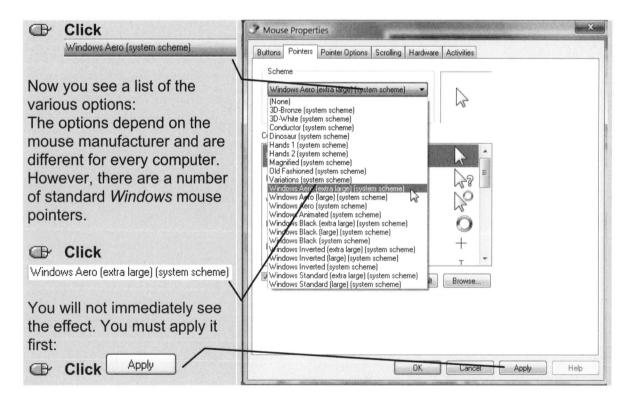

Click
Windows Aero (system scheme)

Now you see a list of the various options:
The options depend on the mouse manufacturer and are different for every computer. However, there are a number of standard *Windows* mouse pointers.

Click
Windows Aero (extra large) (system scheme)

You will not immediately see the effect. You must apply it first:

Click Apply

Now you see that you have a very large mouse pointer:
If you like it, you can leave the setting as it is. If not, you can select the regular
scheme Windows Aero (system scheme) ▼ or you can try one of the other options.

 HELP! Nothing changes.

When you select a different setting, you must always first tell the computer to apply it:

⬤➔ **Click** Apply

10.6 A Black Mouse Pointer

You will also a see a number of options in the list to make the **mouse pointer
colored black**:

For some people, the black version is easier to follow on the screen. Try one of these
Windows Black (extra large) (system scheme)
Windows Black (large) (system scheme)
this settings Windows Black (system scheme) to see if you like it.

 HELP! Nothing changes.

When you select a different setting, you must always first tell the computer to apply it:

⬤➔ **Click** Apply

10.7 The Double-Click Speed

The double-click speed can also be adjusted. If you do not double-click fast enough, *Windows Vista* does not recognize your two clicks as a double-click. Perhaps changing the setting will make it easier for you to double-click.

☞ **Click the tab** [Activities]

Under the section Double-click speed you see another slider that you can drag to change the speed:

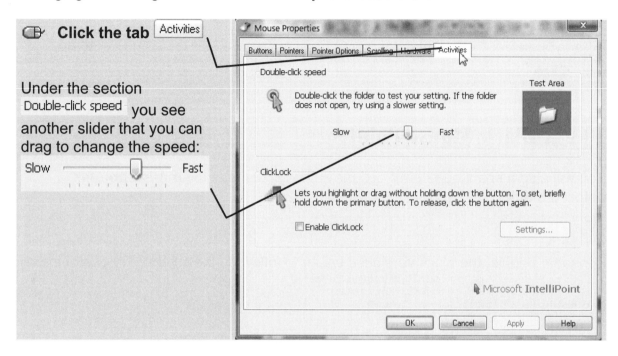

Make the setting **slower** if you have trouble double-clicking.

You can make the double-click speed **faster** once you have mastered the technique of clicking in rapid succession.

HELP! I am having trouble with double-clicking.

You can use the following trick:

☞ **Click the icon just once**

The icon will turn blue to show that it has been clicked.

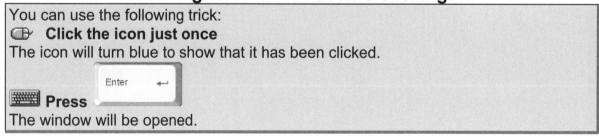

⌨ **Press** [Enter ↵]

The window will be opened.

Drag the slider towards Slow

You can use the test area and make sure that *Windows Vista* recognizes your double-click:

Click Apply

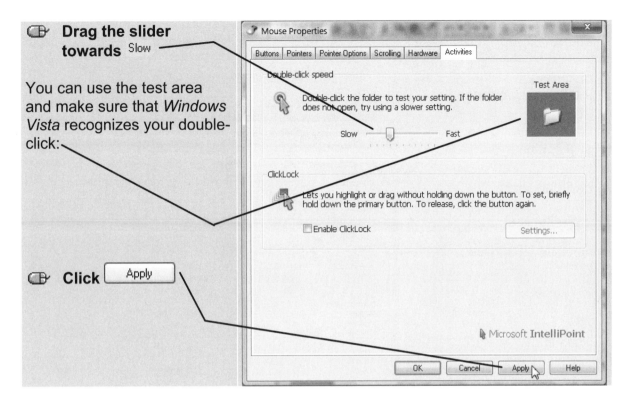

If you are left-handed, you may be interested in the following. If not, you can skip the following section and continue with *Has the Mouse Been Customized?*

10.8 Left-Handed Users

If you are left-handed, you should also customize the mouse so that you can use it in your left hand.
Naturally, you will place the mouse to the left of your keyboard. But you can also switch the mouse buttons so that you can click with the pointing finger of your left hand:

Click the tab Buttons

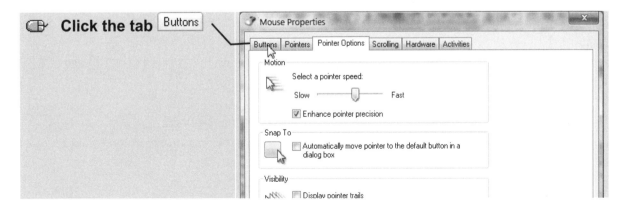

The original setting for the left button is: <u>Click (default)</u>.

You can easily change this setting:

☞ **Click** Click (default)

A menu appears:

☞ **Click** Right-click

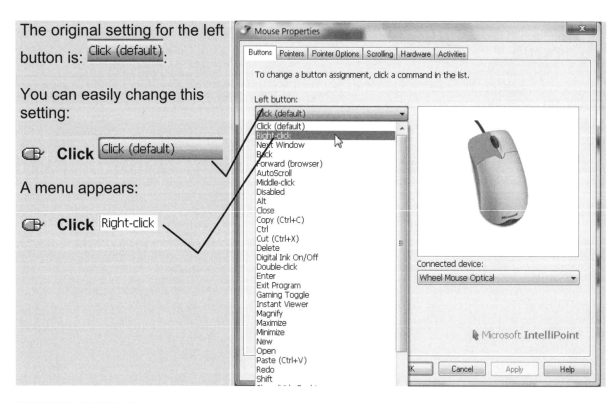

To change the setting for the right mouse button:

☞ **Click** Right-click (default)

A menu appears:

☞ **Click** Click

Now the functions of the mouse buttons have been switched.

☞ **Click** Apply

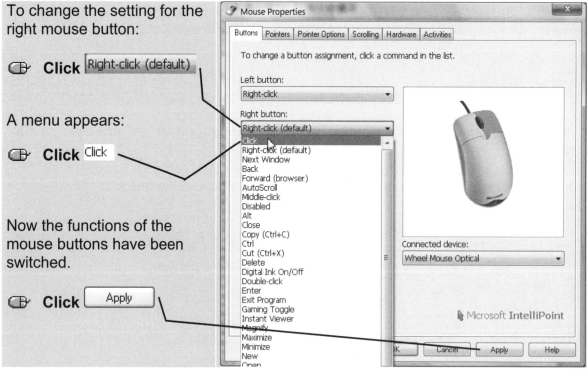

Tip

Ergonomic mice?
Many mice are shaped to ergonomically fit into the hand. However, these are often only suitable for users who are right-handed. Other mice are universal and can be used in either hand.

ergonomic right-handed   *universal*

The mouse is the part of the computer that gets the most intensive use. Make sure you use a suitable mouse. Some manufacturers also have ergonomically-shaped mice for users who are left-handed.

10.9 Has the Mouse Been Customized?

Once you have customized the mouse to suit your preferences, you can close the window *Mouse Properties*.

Click `Apply`

Click `OK`

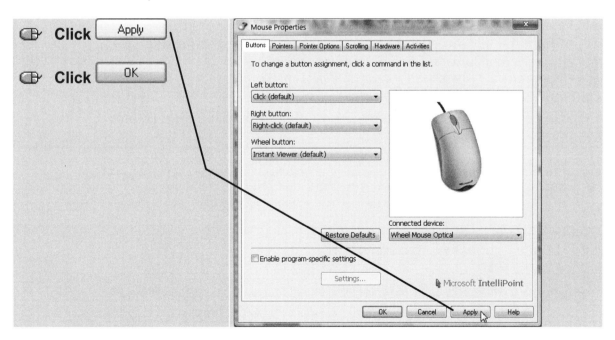

All of the changes that you have made to the settings will be saved and you will return to the *Control Panel*.

10.10 Tips for Using a Mouse

 Tip

Prevent RSI
People who use a mouse often run the risk of getting RSI (Repetitive Strain Injury). This can be prevented with the proper posture. Make sure that your lower arm, wrist and hand are in a horizontal position. Your wrist and hand should rest lightly on the tabletop. It is also important to regularly take a break and change your position.

 Tip

Cleaning your mouse
Because of the way they are constructed, sooner or later every mouse will become dirty and not work properly. The surface underneath the mouse gets dirty after a while, and the ball inside of the mouse also collects dirt. This dirt prevents the mouse from working precisely. It is as if the mouse jerks. You should therefore regularly clean the mouse with a cloth, cotton swabs and a de-greasing cleaning agent, such as *Windex*. This is how:

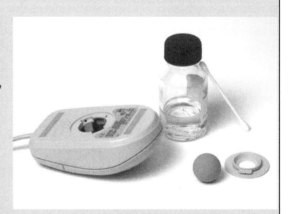

☞ **Clean the sliding surfaces on the underside of the mouse**
If you have a mouse with a ball on the underside:
☞ **Twist the round ring to release the ball**
☞ **Take out the ball and clean it thoroughly**
☞ **On the inside, use cotton swabs to clean the three little rollers**
☞ **Put the mouse back together**

 Tip

A mouse pad
A mouse will only work properly on a flat, hard surface. Is your mouse clean but it still seems to jerk?
You might consider using a mouse pad. These are available from your local computer retailer or discount store.

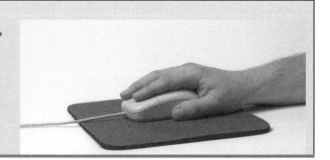

Tip

The trackball

If you are still having trouble using the mouse, you might consider using what is known as a *trackball*.

A trackball is actually kind of like an upside-down mouse. The trackball remains on a single spot on the tabletop. You use your thumb to turn the ball in order to move the mouse pointer.

The trackball also has the same buttons as a regular mouse.

The newest trackballs may have additional options for Internet use.

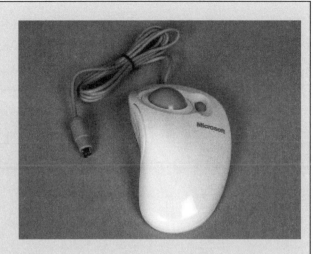

Some computer users like using a trackball because they like the relief they get from not having to grip a mouse. The trackball is also often used by people who have difficulty with their motor skills.

 Tip

Double-clicking with a special mouse button

Mice with multiple buttons may feature the ability to "program" the extra buttons. You can assign the function of "double-clicking" to one of these buttons. You can do this in the window *Mouse properties*. Once you have done this, you only have to press this button once in order to double-click.

10.11 Customizing the Keyboard

Your keyboard can also be changed in various ways. This is also done with the *Control Panel*.

☞ **Open the *Control Panel*** ℰ℮25

☞ **Click**
Hardware and Sound

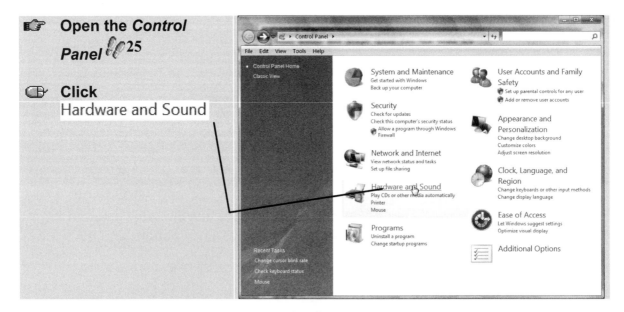

☞ **Drag the scroll bar down - if necessary**

☞ **Click** Keyboard

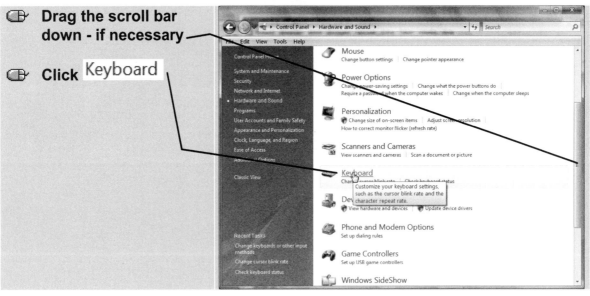

Now you see the window for customizing the keyboard:

👆 **Click the tab** Speed

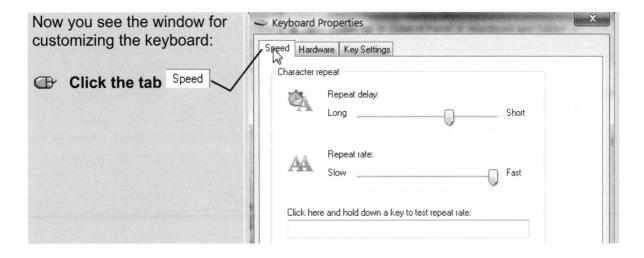

10.12 Your Keystroke

Do you often type double letters by accident? This happens when you press a key for too long. You can adjust the keyboard to reduce the chance of a repeated keystroke.

In the Character repeat section you see a slider that you can drag towards Long or Short:

If you want a longer delay before *Windows Vista* repeats the letter:

👆 **Drag the slider to the left**

👆 **Click** Apply

👆 **Click** OK

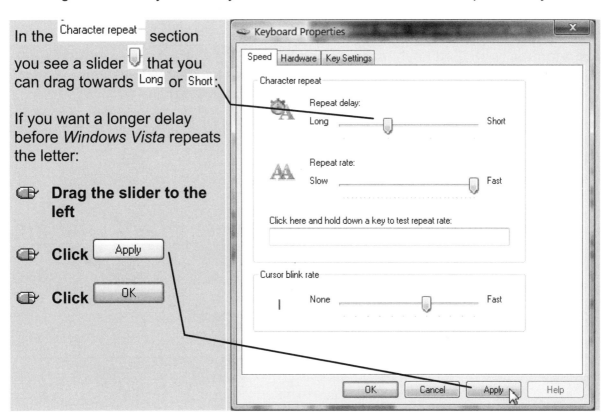

Now you will not type double letters by accident as often as before.

Tip

Slanting the keyboard

Nearly every keyboard has two supports on the bottom with which the keyboard can be slanted.

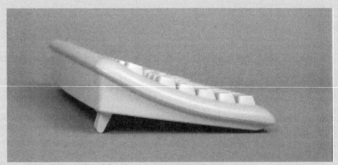

Support   *Keyboard with the supports in use*

You can flip the supports up or out and try the slanted position. You will immediately notice whether this makes your wrists feel more relaxed.

 Tip

Ergonomically-shaped keyboards

In recent years a wide variety of ergonomically-shaped keyboards have been introduced. The positions of the keys on these keyboards are adjusted to fit the natural position of the hands and wrists

The rows of keys on these keyboards have been moved to suit the natural hand position, so that the wrists are not forced as closely together.
These keyboards take some getting used to. But if you have learned how to type properly, they can be very pleasant to use.

10.13 Customizing the Display

Many older users complain about the poor legibility of their computer screen. For example the standard size of the text used for menus and buttons in *Windows Vista* is too small for them. Fortunately, this can be changed. Experiment a little to see what is best for you.

You can change the following display settings to make things easier to see:

- the size of the text and icons
- the background used with *Windows Vista*

☞ **Open the *Control Panel*** 𝄞25

🖱 **Click** Ease of Access

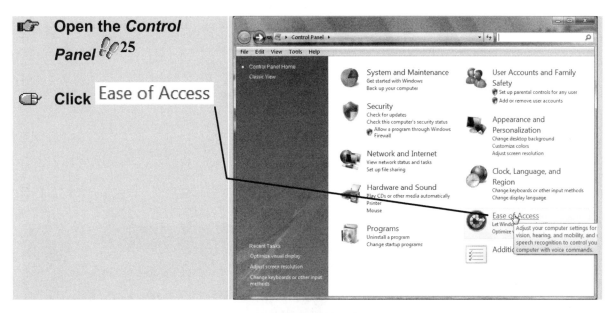

🖱 **Click** Optimize visual display

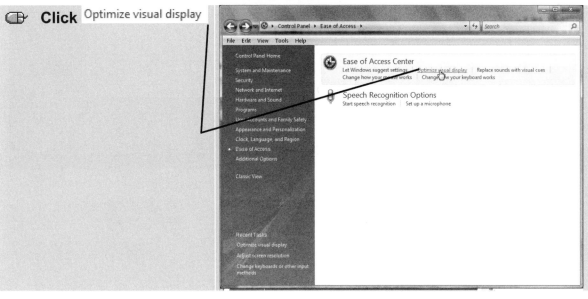

10.14 Changing the Size of Text and Icons

You can change the size of the text and the icons. This is how:

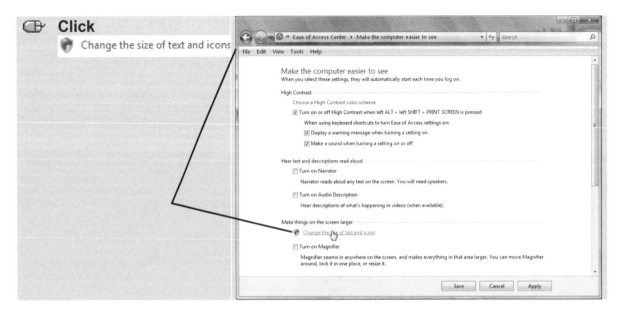

The monitor turns dark. A window like this appears:

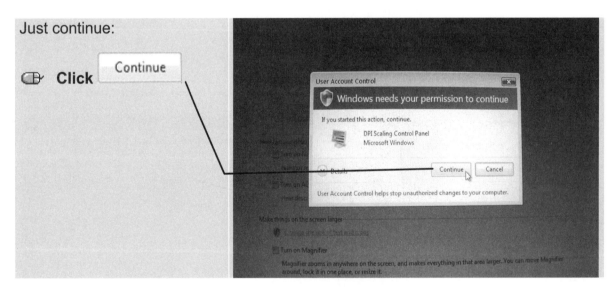

The default scale is 96 DPI (dots per inch):

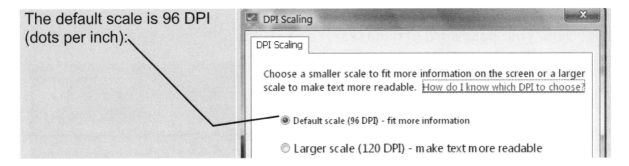

You can change the setting to a larger scale:

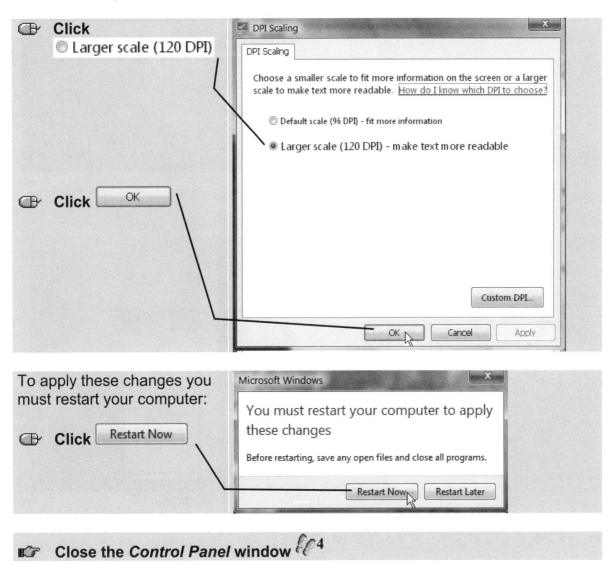

To apply these changes you must restart your computer:

Your computer will restart now. After a short time, you will see the *Welcome Screen*.

☞ **Type your password (if necessary) and click**

The *Desktop* appears:

☞ **Click**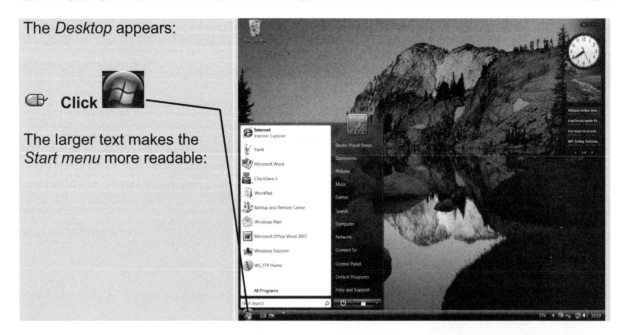

The larger text makes the
Start menu more readable:

Comparing the different sizes
of the *Start menus:*
on the left side you see the
Start menu in the 120 DPI
setting and on the right side
in 96 DPI setting:

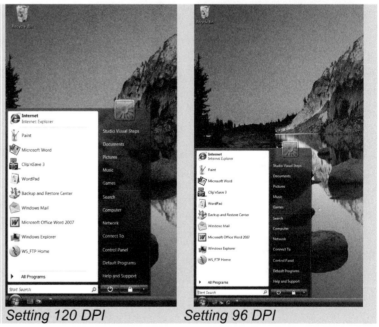

Setting 120 DPI   *Setting 96 DPI*

Would you like to go back to the original setting?

☞ **Start the section *Change the Size of Text and Icons* from the beginning
and change back to the default settings - 96 DPI.**

HELP! Part of the image is missing.

Nine out of every ten programs will work with the larger scale 120 DPI setting. However it is possible some programs do not, and then parts of the program are not displayed on your screen. When this happens, you must close the program and select the original 96 DPI setting.

Is it not possible for you to close a program because the "close" button is not displayed on your screen?
You can always close a program using the **Alt** and **F4** keys on your keyboard.

Press and at the same time

The program will stop and you can then change the settings in the *Control Panel*.

10.15 A Different Background

For many people, working on a computer is more enjoyable with a tranquil or neutral background on the *Desktop*. But perhaps you think your background is too boring, you would prefer something more vivid, or maybe you just want to try something new. It is very easy to select a different background.

☞ **Open the *Control Panel*** 25

Look for the category
Appearance and
Personalization :

⊞ **Click**
Change desktop background

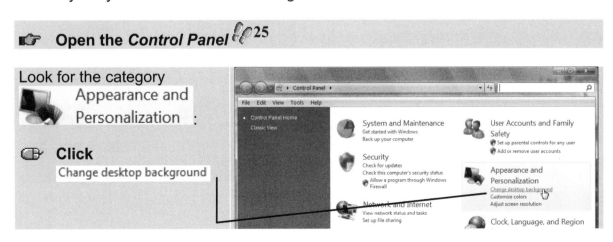

The *Choose a desktop background* window appears:

☞ **Drag the scroll bar up and down** ⎯

You will see many beautiful pictures.

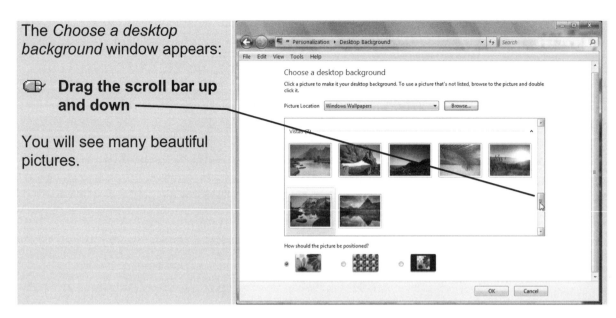

At the top of the list you see some black and white pictures:

Try one:

☞ **Click**

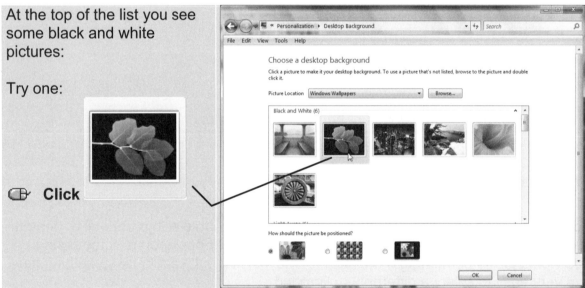

☞ **Minimize the *Control Panel* window** 🦶1

Next to the *Start button* is a special icon to show the *Desktop*:

☞ **Click**

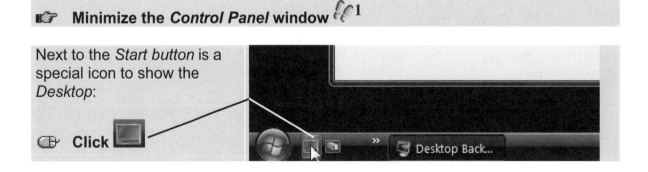

You see the new *Desktop* background:

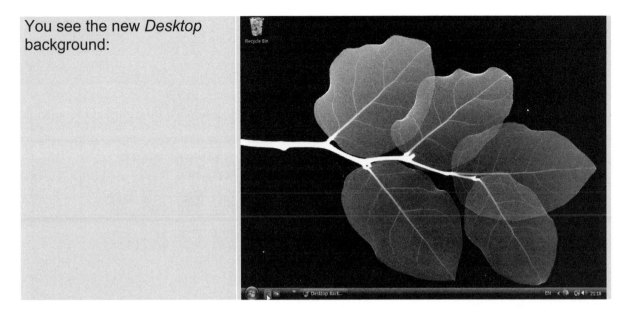

☞　**Open the *Choose a background* window using the *Taskbar button* ℓℓ26**

It is also possible to choose a solid color for your background:

Click [Windows Wallpapers]

A menu appears:

Click [Solid Colors]

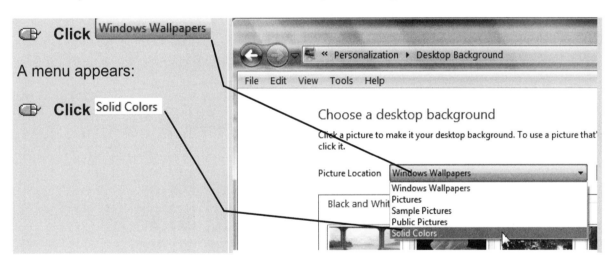

Click one of your
favorite colors.

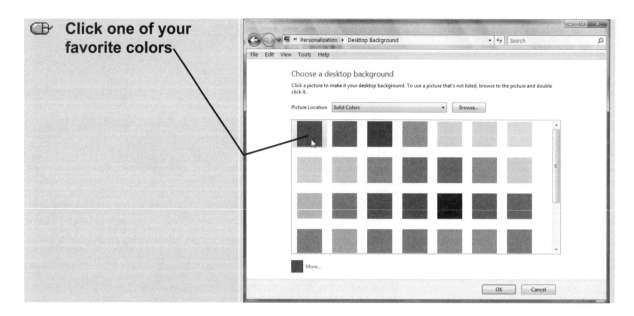

☞ Use the icon ▢ on the *Taskbar* to view the color, try other colors, too

☞ Open the *Choose a background* window using the *Taskbar button* 🐾²⁶

Do you like this background?
Click [OK]

Would you prefer a picture as
background?
Click [Solid Colors]

Click [Windows Wallpapers]

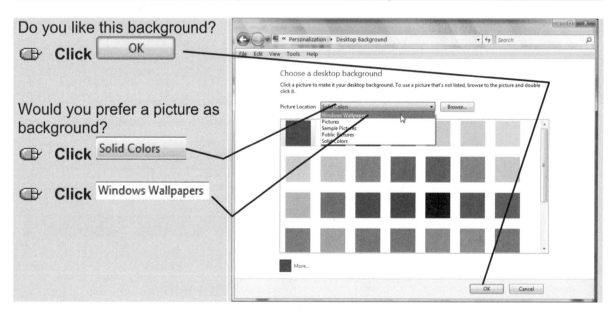

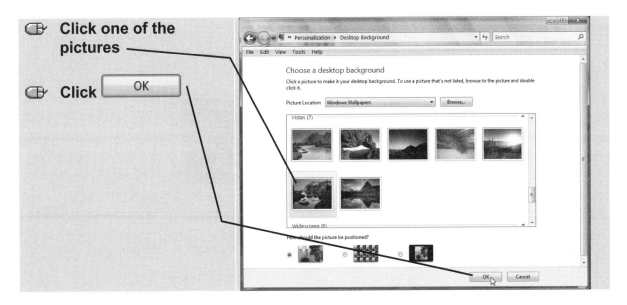

Click one of the pictures

Click OK

The background has changed. The *Control Panel* window appears.

10.16 The Screen Saver

Do you notice that a moving pattern appears on your screen when you stop using the mouse or keyboard for a while? This is a *screen saver*. The screen saver prevents your screen from "burn-in". Burn-in happens if the same motionless image remains on the screen for a long period of time. You can set the screen saver yourself in *Windows Vista*. The screen saver is not only functional: it can be fun to watch. Some of the options are very surprising.

In the *Control Panel* window:

Click
Appearance and
Personalization

Click Change screen saver

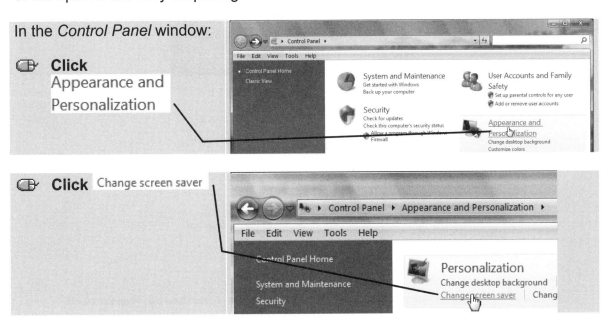

☞ **Remove your hands from the mouse and keyboard for a moment**

In a short while, you will see an example of a screen saver in this little box:

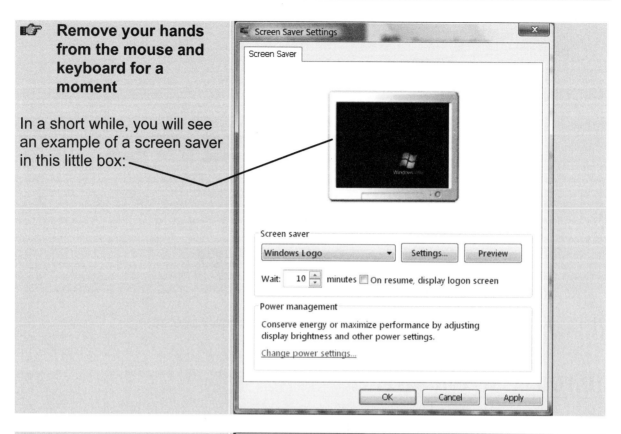

Try another screen saver:

🖰 **Click** Windows Logo

🖰 **Click** Bubbles

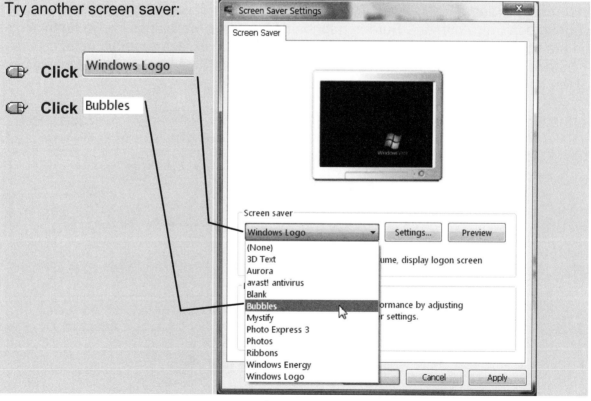

☞ **Remove your hands from the mouse and keyboard once more**

Now you see an example of the bubbles screen saver:

Do you like this choice?

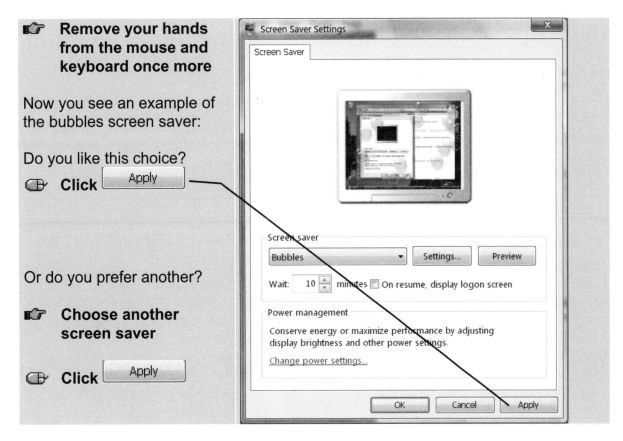

☞ **Click** Apply

Or do you prefer another?

☞ **Choose another screen saver**

☞ **Click** Apply

 Tip

Once you have selected a screen saver, there is another setting that can be changed.

The time allotted before the screen saver is activated: Wait: 10 minutes

You can change the time by clicking the arrow buttons.

When you are ready:

☞ **Click** OK

You will see the *Control Panel* window.

☞ **Close the *Control Panel* window**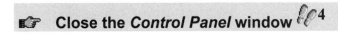

10.17 Tips for the Display

 Tip

The position of the monitor
According to OSHA guidelines, you should place your monitor directly in front of you, about 20 to 40 inches from your face. The top of the screen should be level with your eyes. However, if you have half-shaped reading glasses or multi-focus lenses, the monitor may be lower.

 Tip

Your reading glasses and the screen
The distance from your face to the screen is a bit longer than the distance for which your reading glasses were made. Reading glasses are made for a reading distance of 15 - 20 inches. In theory, you should be able to easily read the letters on your screen with the distance viewing section of the bifocal glasses.
However, if you can only read the letters with the reading section of the lenses, you can move the monitor a bit closer. You can also position the monitor as low as possible so that you do not have to strain to look through the reading part of the lenses, with your face turned upward. This would quickly tire your neck.
If you can not read the letters on the screen easily with the distance viewing section of the glasses, please contact your optician. There are special "computer glasses available that are intended for an intermediate screen distance.

 Tip

Adjusting the screen
Like most television sets, your monitor has buttons for adjusting settings such as brightness and contrast.

It is also possible to change the position of the image on the screen. This is important, for example, if parts of any *Windows* screen are located off the *Desktop*. On some displays, these buttons are hidden behind a cover:

Take the time to optimally adjust your display. If necessary, consult the manual that came with your monitor.

10.18 Customizing Windows Sidebar

Windows Sidebar provides a way to organize the information, games, and tasks that you want to access quickly without cluttering your workspace. It is made up of *gadgets*, which are customizable mini-programs that can display continuously updated headlines, a picture slide show, contacts, and more, without having to open a new window.

Windows Sidebar is open by default.
In this example you see a clock, a picture slide show and news headlines:

The news headlines are available if you're working online.

 HELP! I do not see Windows Sidebar on my Desktop.

The *Windows Sidebar* does not appear on your screen?
Look down in the right corner of your screen.

To open *Sidebar*, right-click the *Sidebar* icon in the notification area of the taskbar:

A menu will appear: click Open in the menu.

No icon in the notification area of the *Taskbar*?

Click , All Programs , Accessories , Windows Sidebar

You can customize *Windows Sidebar* by hiding it, keeping it on top of other windows, or adding and removing gadgets from it. Here is how to do this:

Open the *Control Panel* window $\mathscr{C}^{25}$

Click

Appearance and
Personalization

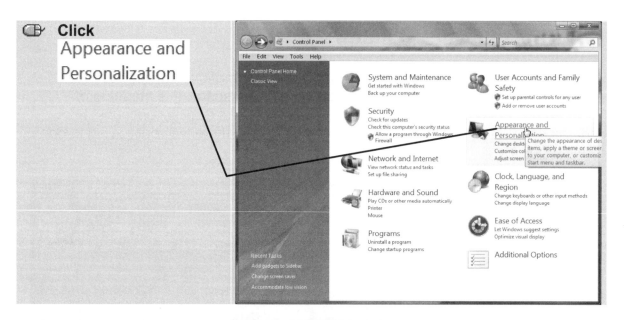

Click

Choose whether to keep Sidebar on top of oth

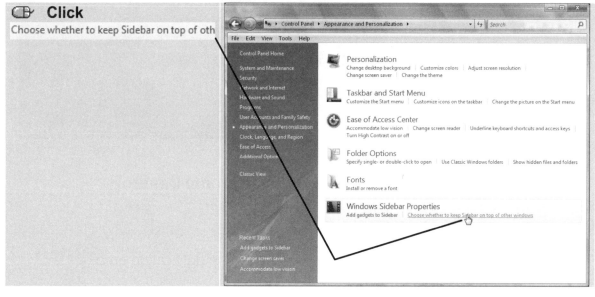

Now you can take a look at the settings of *Windows Sidebar*.

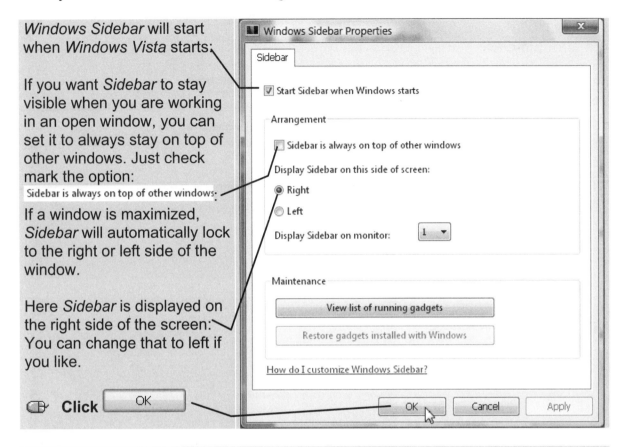

Windows Sidebar will start when *Windows Vista* starts.

If you want *Sidebar* to stay visible when you are working in an open window, you can set it to always stay on top of other windows. Just check mark the option:

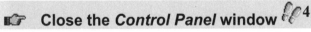

If a window is maximized, *Sidebar* will automatically lock to the right or left side of the window.

Here *Sidebar* is displayed on the right side of the screen. You can change that to left if you like.

🖱 **Click** OK

🖙 **Close the *Control Panel* window** 🦶4

To add a gadget from *Windows Sidebar*, do the following:

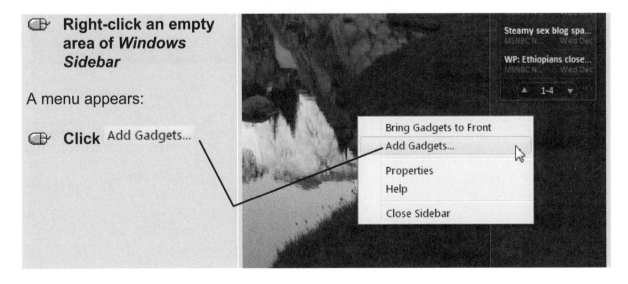

🖱 **Right-click an empty area of *Windows Sidebar***

A menu appears:

🖱 **Click** Add Gadgets...

Do you like to play games?
Try this gadget:

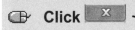 **Double-click**

Picture Puzzle

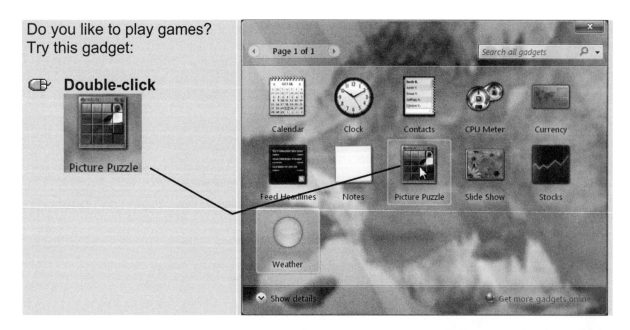

Picture Puzzle appears on
top of *Windows Sidebar*.

You can drag it to another
place in the *Sidebar* if you
like.

To close this *Gadget* window:

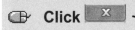 **Click** [X]

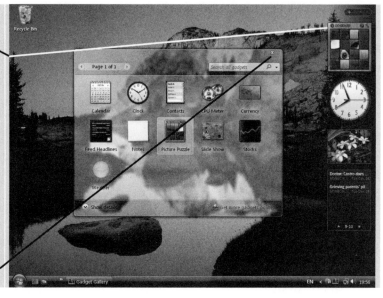

Removing a gadget is just as easy:

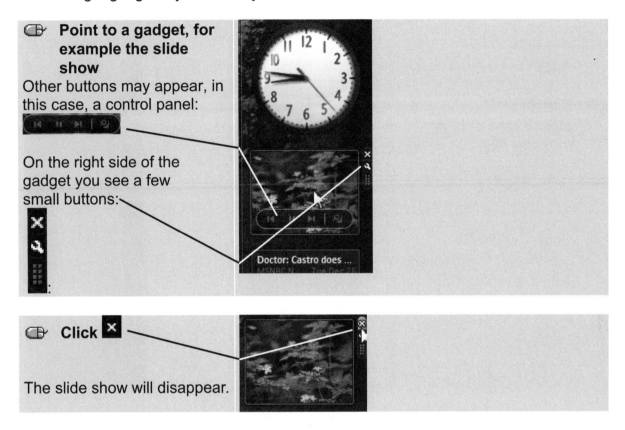

⊕ **Point to a gadget, for example the slide show**

Other buttons may appear, in this case, a control panel:

On the right side of the gadget you see a few small buttons:

⊕ **Click** ✕

The slide show will disappear.

Some of the gadgets themselves have options, for example the clock:

⊕ **Point to**

The buttons appear:

⊕ **Click** 🔧

In this window you can choose another type of clock. Eight clocks are available:

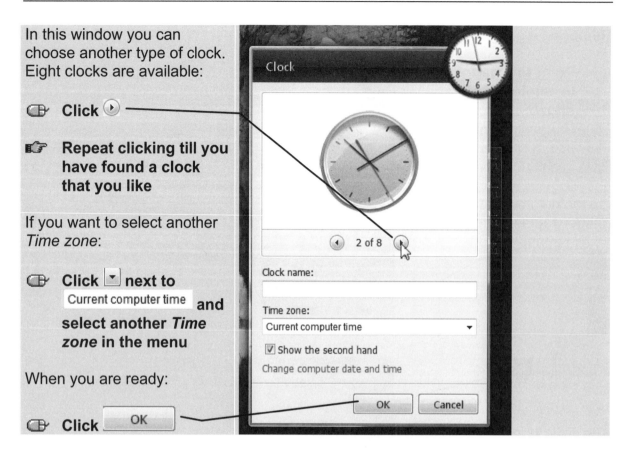

☞ **Click** ▶

☞ **Repeat clicking till you have found a clock that you like**

If you want to select another *Time zone*:

☞ **Click** ▾ **next to** Current computer time **and select another** *Time zone* **in the menu**

When you are ready:

☞ **Click** OK

Now you know how to customize some *Windows Sidebar* settings.

10.19 Customizing the Sound

The term *multimedia* refers to software in which (moving) images and sound play important parts. If you have a program that uses many voices or sounds, you must be able to hear these. You can adjust the sound level on your computer to suit your taste. There are two ways to do this:

○ in *Windows Vista* itself
○ with the volume knob on the computer, the speakers or the monitor

It is a matter of experimenting. If the sound in *Windows Vista* is very low or off, you will still hear nothing even if you set the volume knob on the computer or speakers to high. If this is the case, you will have to set the sound level in *Windows Vista* first.

Look down in the right corner of your screen. A speaker icon 🔊 is shown in the notification area of the *Taskbar*. This icon shows the current volume level of your computer.

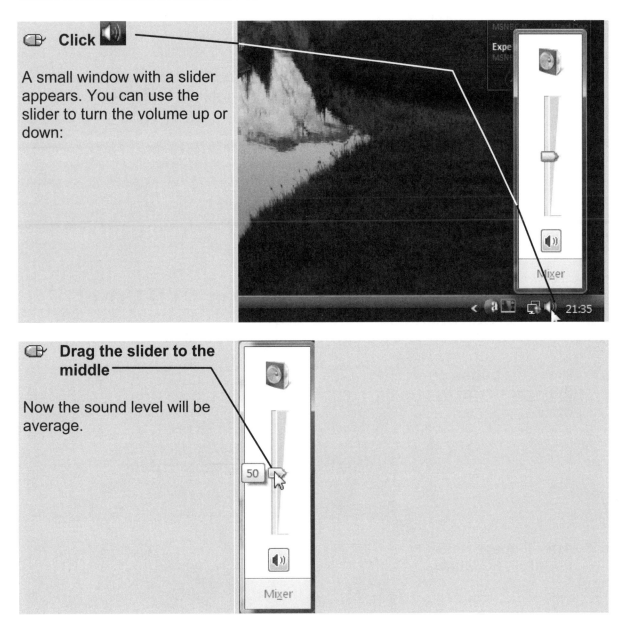

☞ **Click** 🔊

A small window with a slider appears. You can use the slider to turn the volume up or down:

☞ **Drag the slider to the middle**

Now the sound level will be average.

This is how to set the sound level in *Windows Vista*. The best way to further adjust the sound level is to play some music on your computer. You will need a music CD to do so.

10.20 Music as a Test

Your computer can play regular music CDs. This is a good way to adjust the sound level to suit your taste. It is also sometimes pleasant to listen to music while you are working.

You need a music CD for this section:	

10.21 How Do I Insert a CD in the CD or DVD Drive?

CD drives and DVD drives have a drawer into which the CD must be inserted:

☞ **Press the button <u>on</u> <u>the right</u> side of the drive**

☞ **After it opens, insert the CD in the drawer**

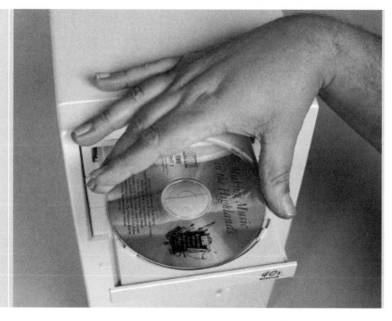

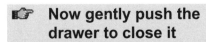 **Now gently push the drawer to close it**

Now the computer asks you what you want to do:

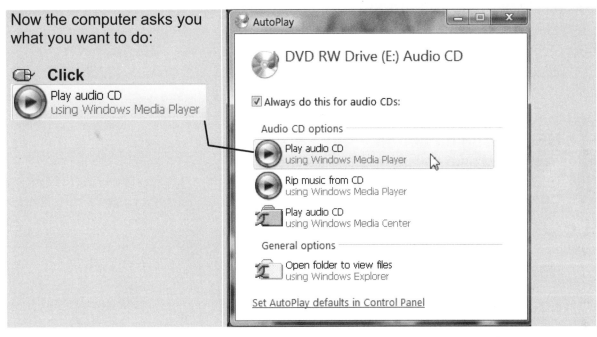

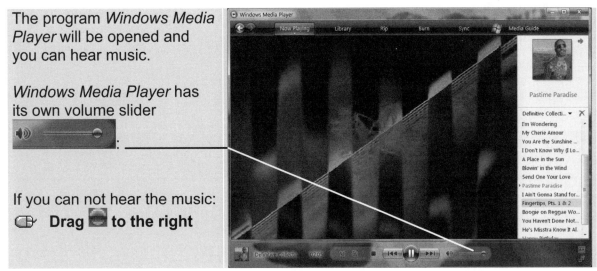 **Click**

Play audio CD
using Windows Media Player

The program *Windows Media Player* will be opened and you can hear music.

Windows Media Player has its own volume slider

If you can not hear the music:
 Drag ▇ **to the right**

Tip

Using *Windows Media Player*, you can play audio CDs or data CDs that contain music.

To skip a song, click the **Next** button  while the song is playing.

To hear the previous song, click the **Previous** button while the song is playing.

To stop playing, click the **Stop** button .

It will change into a **Play** button . You can use that button to continue the playing.

 HELP! I still do not hear any music.

Is there still no sound?

☞ **Check the *Taskbar* to make sure the speaker icon is not crossed out:** This means the sound has been turned off.

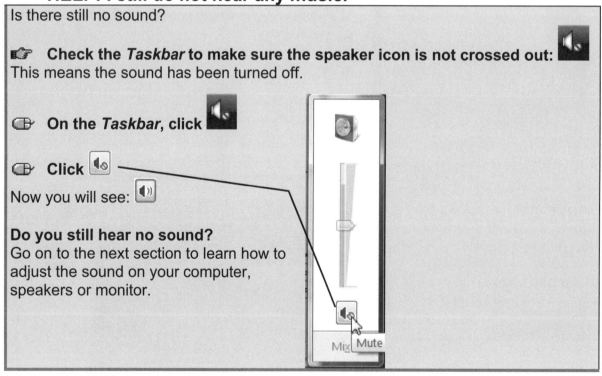

☞ **On the *Taskbar*, click**

☞ **Click**

Now you will see:

Do you still hear no sound?
Go on to the next section to learn how to adjust the sound on your computer, speakers or monitor.

10.22 Sound Knobs on Your Computer

Most computers have knobs somewhere for turning the sound up or down, on or off.

The knobs are on the computer itself sometimes, as is the case with a laptop:	

With other computers, the knobs will be on the speakers:	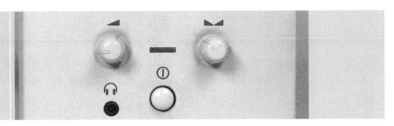

However, if the speakers are built into the display, you will find the knobs on the monitor:	

 Adjust the volume using these knobs

Now you should be able to hear the sound.

✖ HELP! I still hear no sound.

Check on the *Windows Vista* taskbar to make sure the sound has not been muted. Next check to make sure that the sound has not been switched off on the computer itself.

Some computers, displays or speakers have a knob that can be used to turn the speakers completely off:

 Turn the sound on

Do you still hear no sound?

 Make sure the speakers have been properly connected to your computer or consult your computer supplier

When you are finished, you can stop *Windows Media Player* and take out the CD:

To close the program
Windows Media Player:

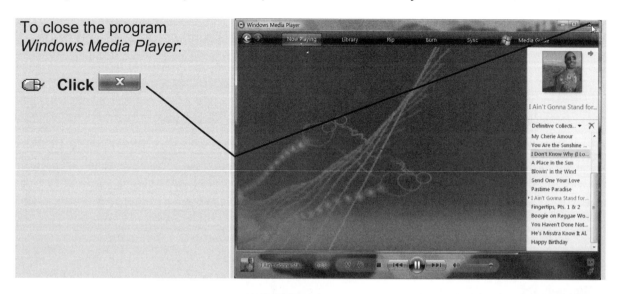

To take out the CD:

☞ **Press the button <u>on the right</u> side of the drive**

☞ **After it opens, lift out the CD**

☞ **Now gently push the drawer to close it**

10.23 Customizing Sound Signals

Windows Vista has a wide variety of sounds built in that work as warning signals. In some situations, it is handy to have a sound signal warn you about something. In situations in which something may go wrong, for example. Perhaps you have already noticed that your computer makes noises, for example when *Windows Vista* is started or stopped. But there are more sound signals that you can customize.

☞ **Open the *Control Panel*** 𝒢25

👆 **Click**
Hardware and Sound

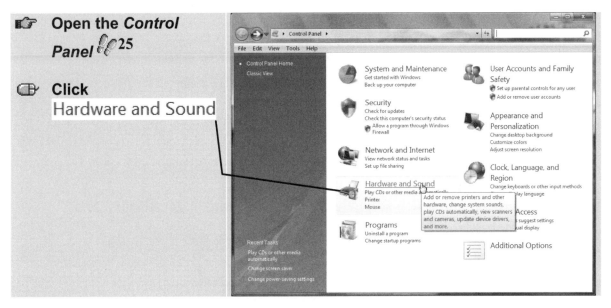

👆 **Click** Change system sounds

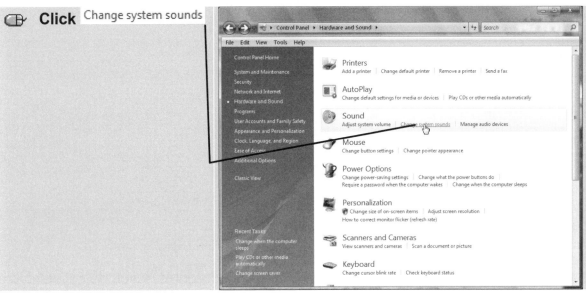

Now the *Sound* window appears in which various settings can be selected.

Under Sound Scheme: you see the current selection:

Do you see No Sounds ? If this is selected your computer will not make any sound.
To change this setting:

Click No Sounds

Click Windows Default

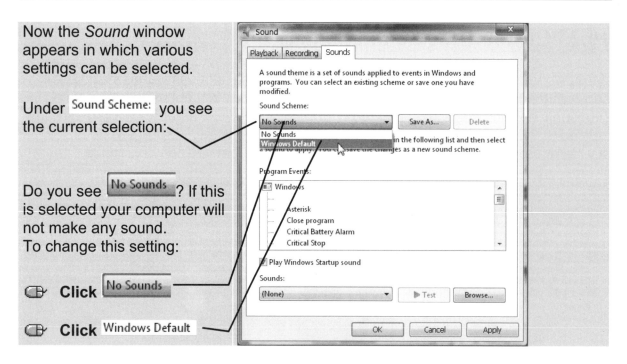

You can also determine which sound signals will be heard in which situations.

Under Program Events: you see a list of possible situations in which *Windows Vista* will give a sound signal:

Click Critical Stop

Click Test

You will hear the sound signal.

You can change this sound by selecting another one here:

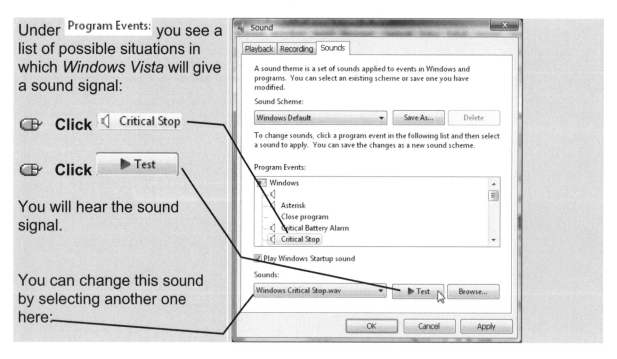

It is worth the effort to test and see if you like the sound signals. If you do not want to hear the sound signals, you can always select No Sounds in the window shown above. If you only do not want to hear the *Windows Startup sound*: remove this check mark Play Windows Startup sound .

Have you customized the sound? Now you can save the changes you made to the sound settings.

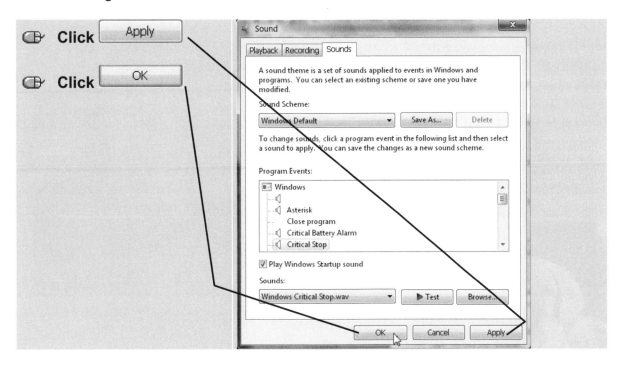

The window is closed and you will return to the *Control Panel*.

10.24 Tips for the Sound

 Tip

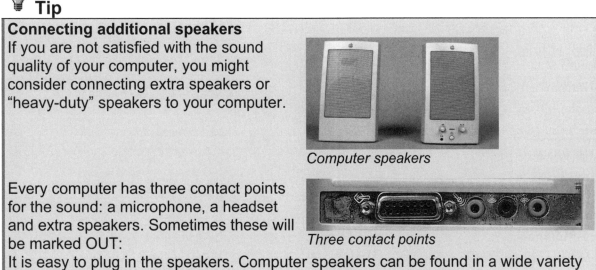

Connecting additional speakers
If you are not satisfied with the sound quality of your computer, you might consider connecting extra speakers or "heavy-duty" speakers to your computer.

Computer speakers

Every computer has three contact points for the sound: a microphone, a headset and extra speakers. Sometimes these will be marked OUT:

Three contact points

It is easy to plug in the speakers. Computer speakers can be found in a wide variety of types and sizes at your local computer retailer or discount store.

Tip

Connecting a headset

Undoubtedly, you will hear best if you use a headset. You can adjust the volume to any level you want without bothering others. Nearly every type of headset can be connected to the computer. You do not need a special computer headset.

Naturally, the plug has to fit. Some computers have a separate plug for the headset that is marked accordingly.

If your computer does not have this, you can connect the headset to one of the three contact points shown in the previous tip.

10.25 Adjusting the Power Plan

A *power plan* is a collection of hardware and system settings that manages how your computer uses power. Power plans can help you save energy, maximize system performance, or achieve a balance between the two.

You can take a look now at the power plan of your computer:

In the *Control Panel*

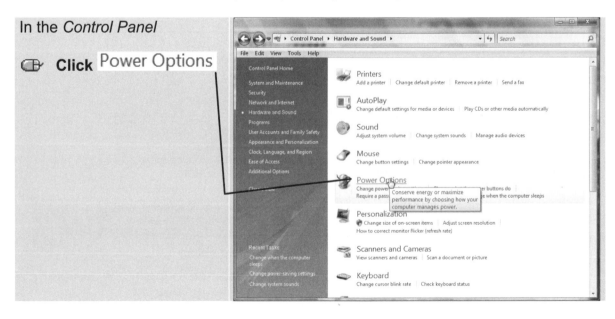

☞ **Click** Power Options

Windows Vista provides the following default plans to help you manage your computer's power:

- Balanced : The plan *Balanced* offers full performance when you need it and saves power during periods of inactivity.
- Power saver : The plan *Power saver* saves power by reducing system performance. This plan can help laptop users get the most from a single battery charge.
- High performance : The plan *High performance* maximizes system performance and responsiveness. Laptop users may notice that their battery does not last as long when using this plan.

The computer manufacturer may provide additional power plans.

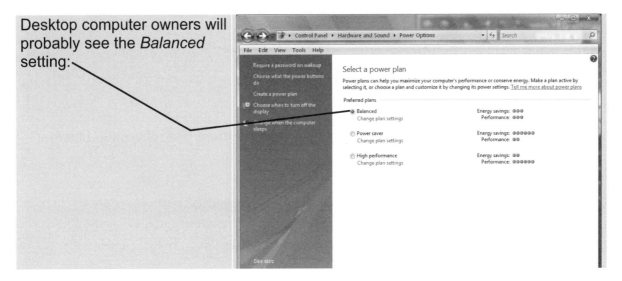

Desktop computer owners will probably see the *Balanced* setting:

Laptop owners will see this *Balanced* setting:

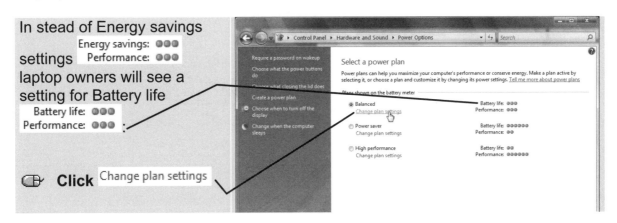

In stead of Energy savings settings
Energy savings: ●●●
Performance: ●●●
laptop owners will see a setting for Battery life
Battery life: ●●●
Performance: ●●● :

☞ **Click** Change plan settings

If your desktop computer or laptop performs as you wish, you should not need to change the default settings. If you are not satisfied, for example because your display turns black too soon, or when your laptop goes to sleep too soon, you can adjust the settings.

Desktop computer owners will now probably see this settings:

If you are not satisfied you can change these settings by selecting another time next to **Turn off the display:** and **Put the computer to sleep:** .

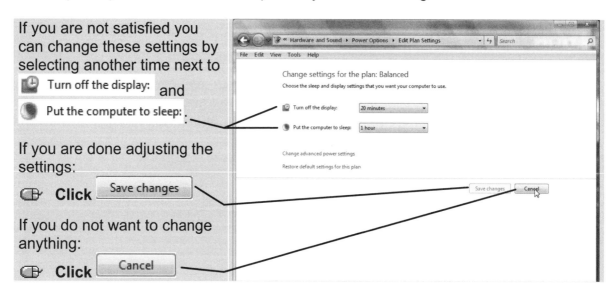

If you are done adjusting the settings:

☞ **Click** [Save changes]

If you do not want to change anything:

☞ **Click** [Cancel]

Laptop owners will probably see this settings. You see there is a difference between the settings for 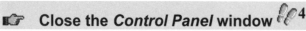 **On battery** and **Plugged in** :

You can change these settings by selecting another time next to **Turn off the display:** and **Put the computer to sleep:** .

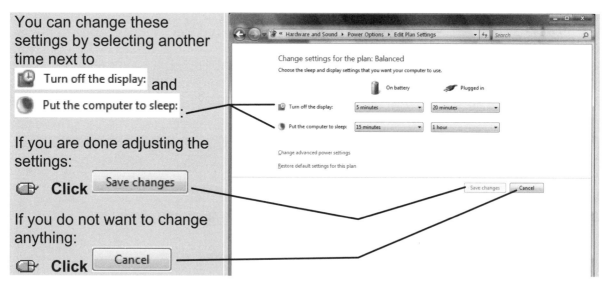

If you are done adjusting the settings:

☞ **Click** [Save changes]

If you do not want to change anything:

☞ **Click** [Cancel]

 Close the *Control Panel* window 𝓮𝓮⁴

HELP! I am not able to adjust the power plan.

If your computer is part of a network at an organization - such as a school, or business - your organization's system administrator might have disabled or even removed certain settings. In that case you will not be able to adjust the power plan.

Tip

> **How can I wake my sleeping computer?**
> Sleep is a power-saving state of your computer. Sleep saves all open documents and programs, and allows the computer to quickly resume full-power operation (typically within several seconds) when you want to start working again. Putting your computer to sleep is like pausing a DVD player: the computer immediately stops what it is doing and is ready to start again when you want to resume working.
>
> On most computers, you can resume working by pressing the power button of the computer. However, not all computers are the same. You may be able to wake your computer by pressing any key, clicking a mouse button, or opening the lid on a laptop. To learn about the different ways you can wake your computer, check the documentation that came with your computer, or go to the manufacturer's website.

In this section you have learned how to customize the settings of your computer's *Power Plan*. Not satisfied about a particular setting? You can always go back to the original settings. Just follow this section and restore the default settings.

10.26 Test Your Knowledge

You are at the end of this Visual Steps book. You learned the basics about computing and *Windows Vista*. Now you can test your knowledge about the computer, *Windows Vista* and *Vista* related programs, like *Internet Explorer, WordPad* and *Windows Mail,* with our free online quizzes. Visual Steps offers a series of multiple-choice quizzes over a range of different topics created specifically for seniors. A special certificate is available to all individuals who can successfully answer the questions.

If a sufficient score is achieved you will be able to receive your Computer Certificate by e-mail. This service is free for all participants.

The online quizzes are available at the website **www.ccforseniors.com**

☞ **Open *Internet Explorer*** 64

☞ **If necessary: connect to the Internet** 66

☞ **Type the Internet address: www.ccforseniors.com** 67

You will see this website:

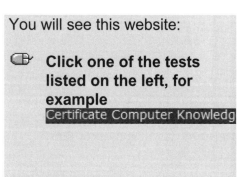 **Click one of the tests listed on the left, for example**
Certificate Computer Knowledg

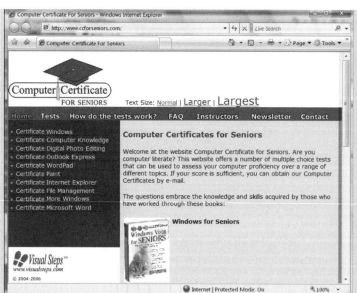

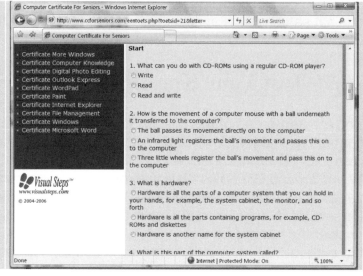 **Read the question and click the right answer**

☞ **Repeat this for all questions**

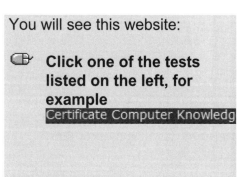 **Drag the scroll bar to see the other questions**

Type your name and e-mail address

Click Score test

Your Computer Certificate will now be sent to you for free by e-mail.

You will see your result:

If it is sufficient, you will automatically receive the Certificate by e-mail.

Drag the scroll bar to see the form

☞ **Open *Windows Mail* 74 and click** Send/Receive

☞ **Open the e-mail message that you have received from ccforseniors.com**

You did not receive it yet? Wait a few minutes and try again.

The Certificate is attached to this e-mail:

☞ **Open the attachment**
   🐾83

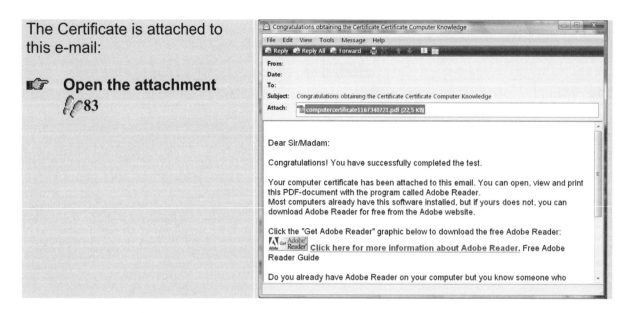

The Certificate is a PDF-file. It will be opened in the program *Adobe Reader*. On most computers this free program is already installed. If it is not on your computer, read the information in the e-mail about this subject.

You will see your own Certificate:

Now you can print it:

☞ **Make sure the printer is turned on**

👆 **Click** 🖨 ─────

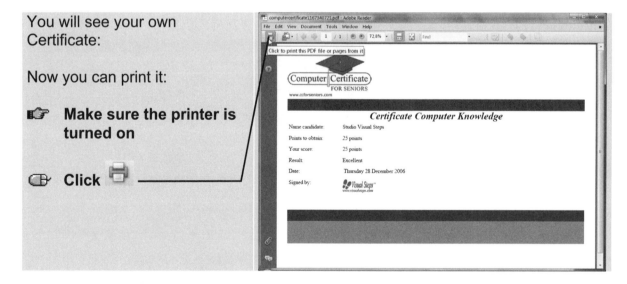

Your Certificate will be printed.

☞ **Close all windows** 🐾4

10.27 More about Windows Vista

The book **Windows Vista for SENIORS** has taken you through the basics of computing and *Windows Vista*. Now you can write a letter, surf the internet, send an e-mail and personalize *Windows Vista*. Interested in gaining more skills? If you would like to know more about our other books in the Vista for SENIORS series, please visit our website www.visualsteps.com.

 Tip

Security and privacy

In this book you learned the basics of surfing the Internet. But there is much more to know, for example about security.

Internet Explorer offers a number of features to help protect your security and privacy when you browse the web. By default, *Internet Explorer* is set to provide a level of security that protects you against common threats like spyware or other types of malware and against known security threats like websites installing add-ons or other programs without your knowledge.

Do you want to know more about protecting your computer from potentially harmful or malicious online content?
This Visual Steps book will be an excellent choice:

Internet and E-mail for SENIORS with Windows Vista
ISBN 978 90 5905 284 0

Like all Visual Steps books it is a learn-as-you-go-book:
• easy step-by-step approach
• screen shots illustrate every step

You will learn how to:
• search the Internet effectively to find information
• download free software from the internet
• play games on the internet
• prevent virus attacks, spyware, pop-ups, phishing websites and spam
• personalize your e-mail
• send, receive, open and save attachments
• save e-mail addresses in the *Contacts* folder

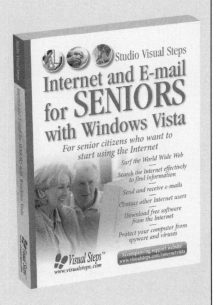

Tip

The Visual Steps Newsletter
Do you want to be informed about the release date of our new books? You can subscribe to the free Visual Steps Newsletter. We will send out periodic e-mails to inform you of our product releases, tips & tricks, special offers, free guides, etc.

☞ **Open *Internet Explorer*** 𝄞64

☞ **Surf to the website www.visualsteps.com** 𝄞67

🖝 **Click** `Newsletter`

On the right side of the page you will find the newsletter subscription form:

☞ **Fill in your name and e-mail address in the box to the right side**

🖝 **Click** `Submit`

This is an example of the Visual Steps Newsletter:

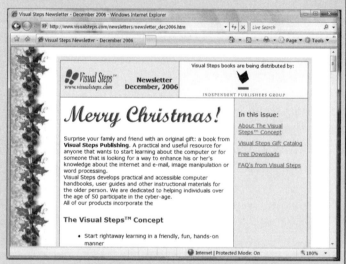

Note: You will automatically receive our newsletter if you have registered your book.
Privacy: Please be sure that we will not use your e-mail address for any purpose except to send you the information you have requested and we will not share this address with any third-party.
Each newsletter contains a clickable link to unsubscribe from our Newsletter.

10.28 Background Information

Dictionary	
Background Desktop	One of the easiest ways to personalize your computer is to change the *Desktop* background, also called the *wallpaper*. You can choose one of the backgrounds provided with Windows, or use a solid background color.
Control Panel	You can use *Control Panel* to change settings for *Windows*. These settings control nearly everything about how *Windows* looks and works and they allow you to set up *Windows* so that it is just right for you.
DPI	Dots per inch - number of dots per inch. The standard used to measure screen and printer resolution, expressed as the number of dots that a device can display or print per linear inch.
Power plan	A power plan is a collection of hardware and system settings that manages how your computer uses power. Power plans can help you save energy, maximize system performance, or achieve a balance between the two.
Screen saver	A moving picture or pattern that appears on a computer screen when the mouse or keyboard has not been used for a specified period of time. *Windows Vista* comes with several screen savers. You can choose the one you like most.
Sleep	Sleep is a power-saving state of your computer. Sleep saves all open documents and programs, and allows the computer to quickly resume full-power operation (typically within several seconds) when you want to start working again. Putting your computer to sleep is like pausing a DVD player: the computer immediately stops what it is doing and is ready to start again when you want to resume working. On most computers, you can resume working by pressing the hardware power button. However, not all computers are the same. You may be able to wake your computer by pressing any key, clicking a mouse button, or opening the lid on a laptop. To learn about the different ways you can wake your computer, check the documentation that came with your computer, or go to the manufacturer's website.

Source: Windows Help and Support

Appendices

A. Clicking, Dragging and Double-Clicking in Solitaire

The card game *Solitaire* is not only very popular among computer users, but also an extremely pleasant way to practice working with the mouse. The game requires a lot of clicking and dragging. This section describes how to play the game.

Starting Solitaire

Click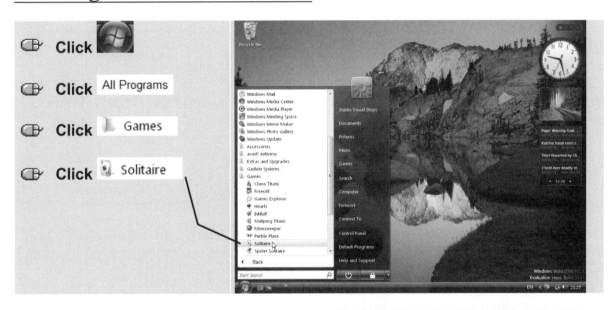

Click All Programs

Click Games

Click Solitaire

You now see this window with seven piles of cards:

This is how to play the game: At the top left there is a pile of cards that are face down, called the *deck*. You can turn over the cards in this pile by clicking the deck.

Click the deck

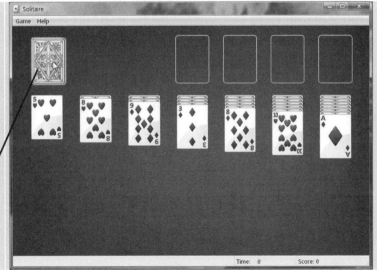

The top three cards are turned over:

You can place a card in the correct spot by dragging it with the mouse.

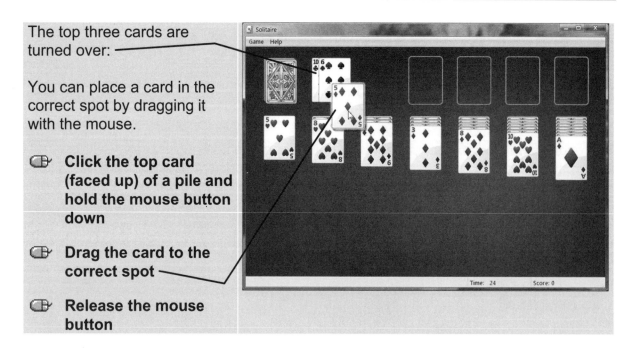

- Click the top card (faced up) of a pile and hold the mouse button down

- Drag the card to the correct spot

- Release the mouse button

You can move the card to one of the seven lower piles, called "row stacks". There you release the mouse button.

- If the card can be played here, it will remain there.
- If the card cannot be played here, it will remain face up and returns automatically to the pile.

Do you already know how to play this version of the card game *Solitaire*?
Then you really already know how to play: try to play all of the cards and get them all up to the suit stacks.

Do you not know how to play this version of the card game *Solitaire*?
Then you can read the objective of the game and the rules below.

The Rules for Solitaire

The Objective

The objective of this game is to play all of the cards in proper order (from aces to kings) on the suit stacks at the top right. Next to the deck, you see the empty spaces for the four suit stacks:

The first card that you can play on these piles is the ace; then you must play the two, three, four, and so on, up to the king.

Spades, clubs, diamonds and hearts each have their own pile.

Some of the cards are divided over seven stacks:

The rest of the cards are in the deck at the top left.

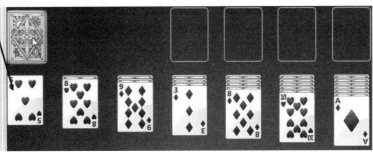

The Beginning

You must try first to play cards on the seven playing stacks.

You can take a card from these stacks by *dragging* it with your mouse:

⇨ **Please note:**

A card can only be played on these seven stacks if it is the next descending card of the opposite color: red eight on black nine, black jack on red queen, and so on.
In *Solitaire*, the **king** is the **highest** card and the **ace** is the **lowest**.

The Seven Stacks

You can play a card from one of the playing stacks to a different playing stack:
This can only be done if the card fits.

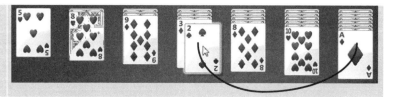

In this way you must try to turn over all of the cards and play them on one of the row or suit stacks.
But there are a few more things you need to know:

If there is a stack of cards that fits onto a different stack, you can move the entire stack by dragging the first card in the stack:

In this case the stack with the 7 of diamonds underneath is being dragged:

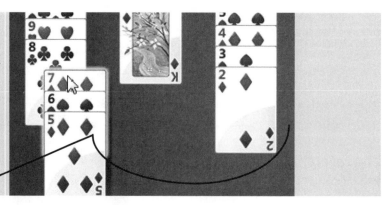

If one of the seven playing stacks at the bottom is emptied, you can only start it again by placing a **king** there:

Once your entire deck has been turned over, you will see a circle in the empty space. You can turn back the pile of cards from the deck that could not yet be played by clicking the circle:

Playing Suits

You can also play cards by suit. There is a space for each of the four suits at the top right of the screen.

If an **ace** has turned up, you should start the suit stacks by moving it to one of the four spaces, as illustrated here with the ace of spades. You can move cards to a suit stack not only by dragging them, but also by double-clicking with the left mouse button:

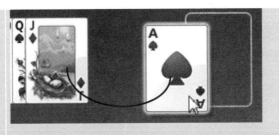

If a two of spades turns up later, you can play it on top of the ace of spades:

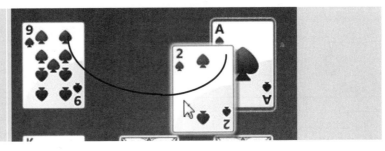

End of the Game

You have **won the game** if you succeed in completing all of the four suit stacks, one for clubs, one for diamonds, one for hearts and one for spades.

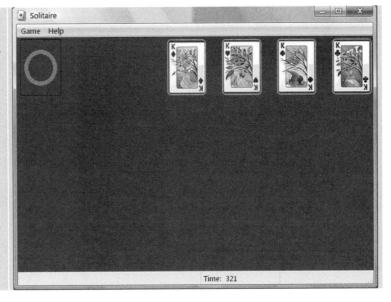

A New Game

You are "stuck" if you can no longer turn over cards from the deck or move any of the cards in the stacks. The best thing to do when this happens is to start a **new game**. This is how to start a new game:

 Click Game

 Click New Game

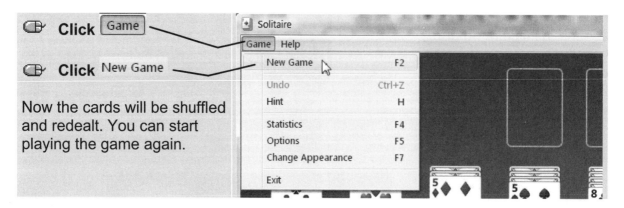

Now the cards will be shuffled and redealt. You can start playing the game again.

Tips

💡 **Tip**

Paying attention and a bit of luck!
Solitaire is a game in which you must pay attention. You have to continually look carefully to see if a card can be played somewhere. But you also need a bit of luck. Even the very best players can not win every game.

💡 **Tip**

Always pay attention to the following:
- Look to see if a card can be played on one of the seven row stacks.
- Check to see if you can play a card on one of the four suit stacks.
- Do not turn cards over from the deck until you have played all of the cards that you can.

Tip

Do you want a different deck of cards?
You can change the deck as follows:

Click `Game`

Click `Change Appearance`

Click the deck that you want to use

Then click `OK`

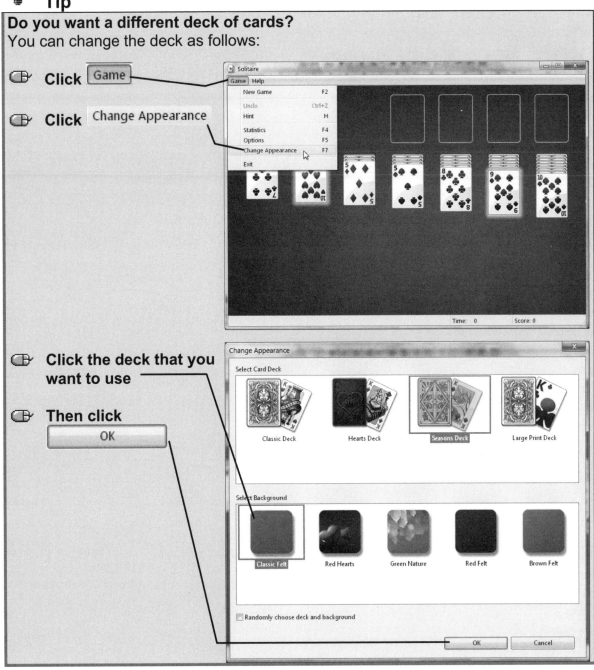

B. How Do I Do That Again?

In this book you will find many exercises that are marked with footsteps. 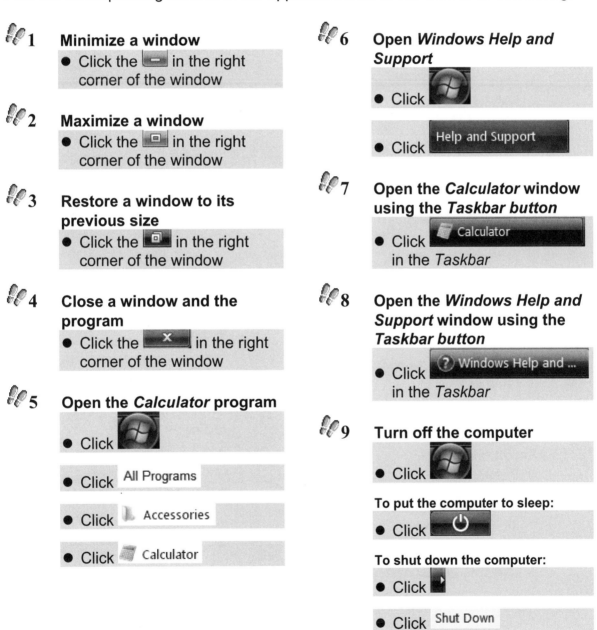 x
Find the corresponding number in the appendix below to see how to do something.

1 Minimize a window
- Click the ⬜ in the right corner of the window

2 Maximize a window
- Click the ⬜ in the right corner of the window

3 Restore a window to its previous size
- Click the ⬜ in the right corner of the window

4 Close a window and the program
- Click the ⬜✕ in the right corner of the window

5 Open the *Calculator* program
- Click ⬜
- Click All Programs
- Click 📁 Accessories
- Click 🗔 Calculator

6 Open *Windows Help and Support*
- Click ⬜
- Click Help and Support

7 Open the *Calculator* window using the *Taskbar button*
- Click 🗔 Calculator in the *Taskbar*

8 Open the *Windows Help and Support* window using the *Taskbar button*
- Click (?) Windows Help and ... in the *Taskbar*

9 Turn off the computer
- Click ⬜

To put the computer to sleep:
- Click ⏻

To shut down the computer:
- Click ▶

- Click Shut Down

10   Open the *Recycle Bin*

- Double-click

11   Drag a window
- Point to the *Title bar* at the top of the window

- Press the left mouse button and hold it down

- Slide the mouse over the table top

- Release the mouse button

12   Change the size of a window
- Point to an edge of the window. The pointer

  changes to ⬅➡ or ↕

- Press the left mouse button and hold it down

- Slide the mouse over the table top

- Release the mouse button

13   Scroll text
- Point to the scroll bar

- Press the left mouse button and hold it down

- Slide the mouse slowly - upwards or downwards

- Release the mouse button

or:
- Click in the window

- Roll the scroll wheel of the mouse forward to scroll up or backward to scroll down

14   Open the program *WordPad*
- Click

- Click   All Programs

- Click   Accessories

- Click   WordPad

15   Close the program *WordPad*
- Click   File

- Click   Exit
or:
- Click   X

16   Start a new file
- Click   File

- Click   New...

17   Start a new file - save changes
- Click   File

- Click   New...

In the window *New:*
- Click   OK

Question: Save Changes?
- Click   Save

18 Start a new file - <u>do not</u> save changes
- Click │ File
- Click New...

In the window *New:*
- Click │ OK │

Question: Save Changes?
- Click │ Don't Save │

19 Print a document
- Click │ File
- Click Print...
- Click │ Print │

20 View the contents of *Windows Help and Support*
- Click

21 View the topics in *Windows Basics*
- Click Windows Basics

22 Copy a selection
- Click Edit
- Click Copy

23 Paste a selection
- Click Edit
- Click Paste

24 Cut a selection
- Click Edit
- Click Cut

25 Open the *Control Panel*
- Click
- Click Control Panel

26 Open a window using the *Taskbar button*

On the taskbar:
- Click the *Taskbar button* for the program

27 Save a new file
- Click │ File
- Click Save
- At File name: , type the name of your file: File name: test2
- Click │ Save │

28 Save an existing file
- Click │ File
- Click Save

29 Save a new file in the folder *Documents*
- Click │ File
- Click Save
- At File name: , type the name of your file: File name: test2

- Check in the *Address bar* if the folder ▸ Documents is opened

If you see another folder at the Address bar:
- Click 🗀 Documents on the left side in the *Navigation pane*

- Click Save

30 Save to a USB stick
- Click File

- Click Save

- At File name: , type the name of your file: File name: test2

- Click 💾 Removable Disk (E:) on the left side in the *Navigation pane*

- Click Save

31 Save with a different name
- Click File

- Click Save As...

- At File name: , type the new name of your file:
  File name: new test

- If applicable, click the folder name where you want to save the new file on the left side in the *Navigation pane*

- Click Save

32 Save in a different folder
- Click File

- Click Save As...

- Click the folder in which you want to save the new file on the left side in the *Navigation pane*

- Click Save

33 Start a new file - save changes
- Click File

- Click New...

- Click OK

Question: Save Changes?
- Click Save

34 Start a new file - <u>do not</u> save changes
- Click File

- Click New...

- Click OK

Question: Save Changes?
- Click Don't Save

35 Open a file
- Click File

- Click Open...

- Click the name of the file

- Click Open

36   Open a file in the folder *Documents*

- Click on File
- Click on Open...
- Click Documents on the left side in the *Navigation pane*
- Click on the name of the file
- Click on Open

37   Open a file from USB stick

- Click on File
- Click on Open...
- Click Removable Disk (E:) on the left side in the *Navigation pane*
- Click the name of the file
- Click on Open

38   Open a file in a different folder

- Click on File
- Click on Open...
- Click the relevant folder on the left side in the *Navigation pane*
- Click the name of the file
- Click on Open

39   Move the cursor

- Use the cursor keys

40   Move cursor to the beginning of the line

- Press Home

41   Move cursor to the end of the line

- Press End

42   Start a new paragraph / line

- Press Enter

43   Erase letters or a selection (word, sentence or paragraph / line)

- Press Backspace

44   Erase letters or a selection

- Press Delete

45   Selecting a word

- Double-click on the word

To select several words:

- Click in front of the first word
- Drag the mouse pointer over the words

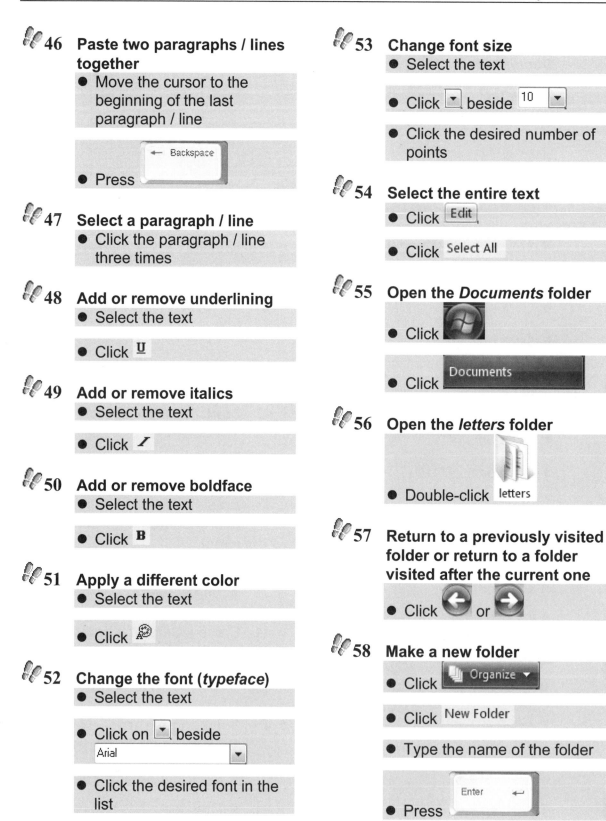

46 Paste two paragraphs / lines together
- Move the cursor to the beginning of the last paragraph / line
- Press ← Backspace

47 Select a paragraph / line
- Click the paragraph / line three times

48 Add or remove underlining
- Select the text
- Click **U**

49 Add or remove italics
- Select the text
- Click *I*

50 Add or remove boldface
- Select the text
- Click **B**

51 Apply a different color
- Select the text
- Click

52 Change the font (*typeface*)
- Select the text
- Click on ▼ beside Arial ▼
- Click the desired font in the list

53 Change font size
- Select the text
- Click ▼ beside 10 ▼
- Click the desired number of points

54 Select the entire text
- Click Edit
- Click Select All

55 Open the *Documents* folder
- Click
- Click Documents

56 Open the *letters* folder
- Double-click letters

57 Return to a previously visited folder or return to a folder visited after the current one
- Click ← or →

58 Make a new folder
- Click Organize ▼
- Click New Folder
- Type the name of the folder
- Press Enter ←

59 Open a folder
In the *File list*:

● Double-click the folder

or:
● Click the relevant folder name on the left side in the *Navigation pane*

60 Copy a file to a folder
● Select a file by clicking it

● Click Organize ▼

● Click Copy

● Open the correct folder

● Click Organize ▼

● Click Paste

or:
● While holding the mouse button down, drag the file to the correct folder

● Release the mouse button

A menu appears:
● Click Copy Here

61 Rename a file or folder
● Right-click the file or folder name

● Click Rename

● Type the new name

● Press

62 Delete a file
● Select a file by clicking it

● Click Organize ▼

● Click ✗ Delete

● Click Yes

63 Copy a file to USB stick
● Open the folder that contains the file

● Insert the USB stick - the folder window will be opened

● Reduce the size of both windows so you can see them next to each other

● Drag the file (hold left mouse button down) from the folder window to the window of the USB stick

● Release the mouse button

64 Open *Internet Explorer*

● Click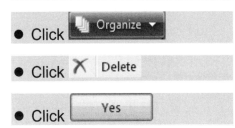

● Click **Internet** Internet Explorer

65 Close *Internet Explorer*
● Click

66 Connect using the *Dial-up Connection* window
- Type your user name and password if necessary
- Click [Connect]

67 Type in a web address in *Internet Explorer*
- Click the *Address bar*

  http://www.live.com/

- Type the web address
- Press [Enter ⏎]

68 Add a website to *Favorites*
- Click [⭐]
- Click [Add to Favorites...]
- Click [Add]

69 Disconnect from the Internet
In the *Disconnect* window:
- Click [Disconnect]

70 Open a *Favorites* website
- Click [☆]
- Click [☆ Favorites]
- Click the website name

71 View a previously visited website
- Click [⬅]

72 View a website visited after the current one
- Click [➡]

73 Go back to the homepage
- Click [🏠]

74 Open *Windows Mail*
- Click [Windows logo]
- Click All Programs
- Click [✉ Windows Mail]

75 Close *Windows Mail*
- Click on [X]

76 Send and receive e-mail
In the *Windows Mail* window:
- Click on [Send/Receive]
- Click [Connect] (if necessary)

77 Create an e-mail message
In the *Windows Mail* window:
- Click [Create Mail]

78 Send an e-mail message
In the *New Message* window:
- Click [Send]

79 View the message list in the *Outbox*
In the *Windows Mail* window:
- Click [Outbox]

80 View the message list in the *Inbox*
In the *Windows Mail* window:
- Click 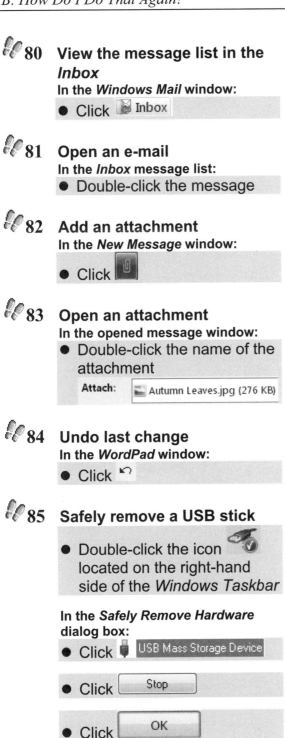 Inbox

81 Open an e-mail
In the *Inbox* message list:
- Double-click the message

82 Add an attachment
In the *New Message* window:
- Click

83 Open an attachment
In the opened message window:
- Double-click the name of the attachment

  Attach: Autumn Leaves.jpg (276 KB)

84 Undo last change
In the *WordPad* window:
- Click ↰

85 Safely remove a USB stick
- Double-click the icon located on the right-hand side of the *Windows Taskbar*

In the *Safely Remove Hardware* dialog box:
- Click USB Mass Storage Device
- Click Stop
- Click OK
- Remove the USB stick from the computer

86 Open your *Personal Folder*
- Click

In the *Start menu*:
- Click your name on the top right of the *Start menu*, for instance Studio Visual Steps

C. Changing Your Keyboard Settings

In order to type foreign language characters and symbols such as ñ, á, ö, and ç, you may need to change your keyboard settings. You can do this with the *Control Panel*.

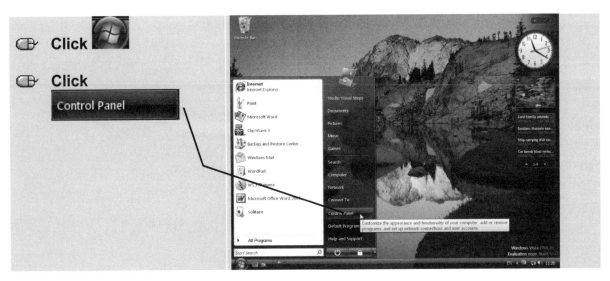

👆 **Click**

👆 **Click**

    Control Panel

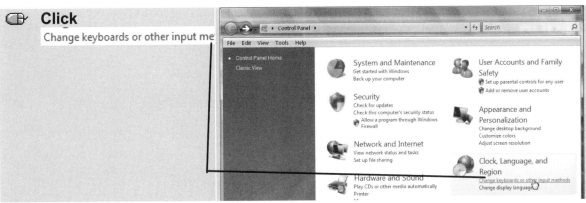

👆 **Click**

    Change keyboards or other input me

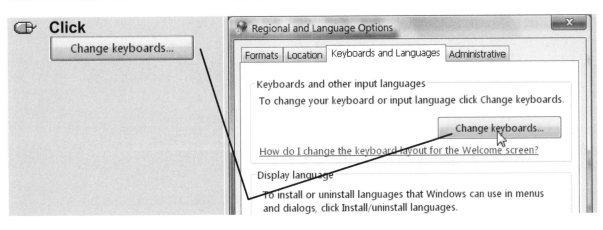

👆 **Click**

    Change keyboards...

You will see a window with several language settings.
The setting English (United States) - United States-International ▼ is the one you need
to type foreign letters on a QWERTY keyboard. If this setting does not appear in your
list, you can choose an international keyboard setting. Here is how to do that:

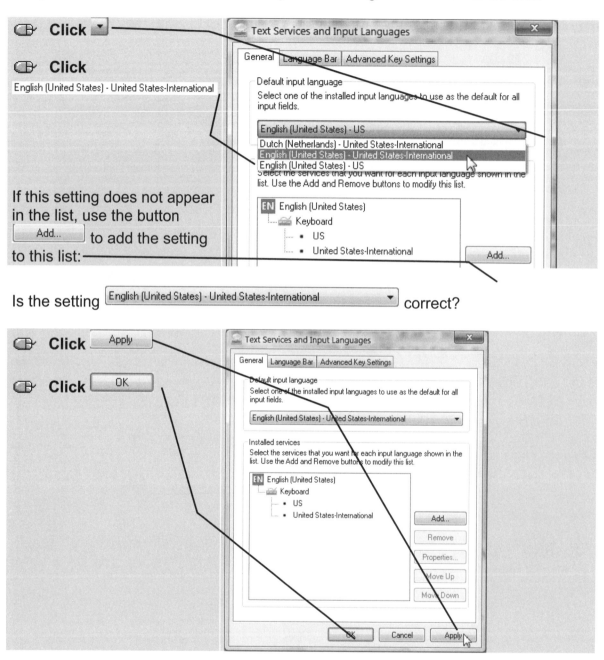

Now you can type accents and umlauts just as we have described in this book.

D. Index

A

Accents, typing 124
Activating
    Details Pane 186
    Navigation Pane 186
Adding a gadget 349
Address bar 187, 219
Adjusting
    black mouse pointer 325
    Desktop background 339
    double-click speed 326
    keystroke 333
    left-handed users 327
    mouse 319
    mouse pointer size 324
    mouse pointer speed 320
    mouse pointer visibility 323
    power plan 362
    screen 346
    screen saver 343
    sound knobs on monitor 357
    sound level 353
    sound signals 359
Apostrophes, typing 125
Applying mouse settings 329
Attachment 308
    blocked 311
    including 298
    opening 304
    saving 305

B

Back and forward buttons 96
Backspace key 113
Back to previous screen 78
Beginning a new paragraph 115
Black mouse pointer 325
Boldface 231
Broadband connection 275

Browser 249, 275
Buttons in *WordPad* 156, 179

C

Cable Internet 275
Calculator 44
    calculating 49
    closing 55
    opening 44
Caps Lock key 132
CD 154
CD-ROM 220
Changing
    Desktop background 339
    display of folders 87, 185
    double-click speed 326
    file name 204
    mouse pointer speed 320
    mouse pointer visibility 323
    power plan 362
    screen 346
    screen saver 343
    size of text and icons 336
    sound signals 359
    view 87
Characters 246
Cleaning the mouse 330
Clicking 33, 96
Close button 38, 66
Closing
    program 55
    window 38, 57
    WordPad 126, 140
Colored letters 232
Connecting
    additional speakers 361
    headset 362
    to the Internet 252
Control key 202
Control Panel 318, 371

Copying
files	195
to USB stick	210
word	169
Correcting typing errors	120
Creating an e-mail	290
Cursor keys	117, 129

Customizing
display	335
keyboard	332
mouse	319
sound	352
sound signals	359
Windows Sidebar	347
Cutting a word	171, 172

D

Date and/or time, inserting	135

Deactivating
Details Pane	186
Navigation Pane	186
Dead key	124, 129
Deleted items	308

Deleting
e-mail	314
file	206
word	160
Desktop	40, 63
background	37, 371
Desktop computer	22
Desktop keyboard	132
Details pane	187
Determining layout in advance	240
Dial-up connection	275
Disconnecting from the Internet	271
Diskette	220
Domain names	278
Double-clicking	83, 96
adjusting speed	326
with special mouse button	331
Download	275
DPI	337, 371
Dragging	71, 96
in *Solitaire*	72
paragraph	164
with scroll bar	73
word	161
Dragging and dropping files	201
DSL	275, 308
DVD	154
DVD-ROM	220

E

E-mail account	308
E-mail address	290
saving	313
E-mail header	308
Emptying the *Recycle Bin*	208
End key	121
Enlarging a window	76
Enlarging font size web page	283
Enter key	115
Ergonomically-shaped keyboard	334
External modem	250

F

Favorites	267
File	183, 219
changing name	204
copying	195
deleting	206
icons	189
moving	199
pasting	197
File list	187, 219
Finding a file	223
Floppy disk	220
Folder	183, 219
Documents	188
icons	189
opening	194
selecting	207
window	219
Font	150, 235, 245
selecting	235
Font size, selecting	238

G

Gigabyte 310

H

Hard disk 152, 219
History 279
Holding the mouse 27, 28
Home key 121
Homepage 275
Http:// 257
Hyperlink 264, 275

I

Icons 25, 63, 189
Inbox 296, 308
Including an attachment 298
Information bar 280
Inkjet printer 151
Inserting date and/or time 135
Inserting symbols 248
Internal modem 250
Internet 275
Internet Explorer, starting 251
Internet Service Provider (ISP) 249, 276
Italics 232

K

Keyboard 111, 129
    ergonomically-shaped 334
    slanting 334
Keystroke 333
Kilobyte 309

L

Laptop computer 22, 97
Laptop keyboard 132
Larger font 134
Laser printers 151
Left-handed users 327

M

Mailserver 287
Making a new folder 190
Malware 276
Maximize button 52, 66
Maximizing a window 52, 77
Megabyte 309
Menu bar 47, 63, 66
Message list 308
Minimize button 50, 66
Minimizing a window 50, 53
Modem 250
Mouse 26, 98
    actions 31, 63, 70
    buttons 33
    holding 27, 28
    left-handed users 100
    moving 28
    proper placement 99
Mouse actions 31, 63, 70
    click (single-click) 31, 33
    double-click 31, 83
    right-click 31, 90
    drag 31, 71
Mouse pad 330
Mouse pointer size 324
Mouse pointer visibility 323
Mouse wheel 265
Moving
    cursor 117, 118, 122
    file 199
    mouse 28
Moving cursor
    through text 117, 118
    to beginning of line 122
    to end of line 122
Multiple files, selecting 202

N

Navigation pane 187, 219
    folder list 222
Notebook computer 22
Numeric keypad 130

O

Online	249
Opening	
attachment	304
Calculator	44
favorite website	269
folder	194
Home page	269
Internet Explorer	251
Personal Folder	184
previous web page	260
Start menu	42
window from *Taskbar*	54
Windows Help and Support	51
Windows Mail	288
WordPad	110
Optical Character Recognition	247
Outbox	293, 308

P

Paragraph	129
dragging	164
selecting	163
Parts of folder window	187
Parts of the computer	97
computer case	97
monitor	97
Parts of *Open* window	221
Password	249
Pasting	
file	197
word	170
PC	21
Personal Computer	21
Personal Folder	184
Photo printer	151
Pointer	25
speed	320
visibility	323
Pointing	32
to an object	41
Position of monitor	346
Power button	57, 63, 67

Power button, pressing	23
Power plan	362, 371
Preventing RSI	330
Preview pane	309
Printers	151
Printing	
e-mail	314
letter	142, 145
web page	266
Print Preview	143, 150
closing	143, 144
opening	143, 144
Program	43, 63
closing	55
opening	44
Proper mouse placement	99
Proper working posture	131

R

Reading a message	296
Recycle Bin	208, 219
emptying	208
Reducing size of a window	77
Refreshing a web page	259
Registering the book	286
Removing	
empty lines	121
gadget	351
letters	113, 120
Repeat keys	129
Restore button	56, 66
Restoring window to former size	56
Right-clicking	90, 96
RSI	29
preventing	330
Rules for file names	155

S

Safely removing a USB stick	214
Saving	
attachment	305
changes	146, 147, 148
document	138

e-mail addresses 313
in a folder 191
on the computer 152
web address 267
Screen saver 68, 371, 343
Scroll bar 73, 96, 265
Scroll wheel 75, 96
Scrolling 75
Search box 219
Search engine 278
Search folder 224
Searching
files in folder 223
on the Internet 278
with *Live Search* 279
Security settings 315
Selecting
Desktop background 339
dragging 180
entire folder 207
font 235
font size 238
larger font 134
lines by clicking and dragging ... 181
multiple files 202
paragraph 163
with keys 180
word 159
Sending an e-mail 291
Sending and receiving messages ... 294
Sent Items 309
Shift key 114
Shutting down the computer 60
Size mouse pointer 324
Slider 96
Space bar 111, 129
Splitting paragraphs 168
Spyware 276
Start button 42, 57, 63
Start menu 42, 63, 65
opening 42
Starting
Internet Explorer 251
new document 122

program 51
Windows Vista 21, 24
Subfolder 183
Surfing 249
Symbols, inserting 248

T

Tabbed browsing 282
Taskbar 41, 63
Taskbar button 45, 63
Templates 157
Testing your knowledge 365
Title bar 46, 63, 66
Touchpad 22, 26
working with 103
Trackball 331
Turning off the computer 57
Turning on the computer 23
Typing
accents 124
apostrophes 125
capital letters 114
skills 130
special characters 116
web address 255

U

Underlining words 230
Undoing
command 136
effects 234
formatting 234
selection 160
USB port 210, 220
USB stick 210, 220
copying to 210
inserting 210
safely removing 214
Username 249

V

Views 87
Large Icons 88

List	88
Medium Icons	89
Tiles	186
Virus	309
Visual Steps newsletter	370

W

Waking your computer	58
Web address	276
saving	267
typing	255
Web page	276
printing	266
refreshing	259
Web server	276
Website	249, 276
Welcome Screen	24, 63
Window	38, 64
buttons	64
closing	38, 57
enlarging	76
maximizing	52, 77
minimizing	50, 53
opening from *Taskbar*	54
reducing size	77
restoring to former size	56
Windows Flip 3D	102
Windows Help and Support	51, 73, 97
opening	51
using	79
viewing topics	80
Windows Mail	287
opening	288
security settings	315
Windows Sidebar	64
adding a gadget	349
customizing	347
removing a gadget	351
Windows Vista	21, 64
starting	21, 24
Windows Vista Demos	101
Desktop basics	101
Learning to use the mouse	182

Using the web	285
Using Windows Mail	316
Working with files and folders	225
WordPad	129
buttons	156, 179
closing	126, 140
opening	110
Word	
copying	169
cutting	171, 172
deleting	160
dragging	161
pasting	170
selecting	159
Word processing programs	178
Working memory	152
Working with touchpad	103
World Wide Web	249